CHILDCARE SETTINGS

BASED ON REAL LIFE EXPERIENCE:
A SELECTION OF GUIDANCES TO
THE UK CHILDCARE NVQ LEVEL 3 DIPLOMA

AN EXPLORATION OF CHILDCARE AND PLAY: A CHILDCARE SETTING DEVELOPMENT TEXT BOOK.

by

Ibrahim Nelson Kaggwa

Childcare Settings

By

Ibrahim Nelson Kaggwa

ISBN: 978-0-9573291-3-3

This book is published by Future Reality Limited in conjunction with **WRITERSWORLD**, and is produced entirely in the UK. It is available to order from most bookshops in the United Kingdom, and is also globally available via UK based Internet book retailers.

Copy edited by Ian Large
Cover design by Jag Lall

WRITERSWORLD
2 Bear Close Flats, Bear Close, Woodstock
Oxfordshire, OX20 1JX, England
☎ 01993 812500
☎ +44 1993 812500

www.writersworld.co.uk

The text pages of this book are produced via an independent certification process that ensures the trees from which the paper is produced come from well managed sources that exclude the risk of using illegally logged timber while leaving options to use post-consumer recycled paper as well.

To

Maama and Taata, the best child carers ever.

ACKNOWLEDGEMENTS

Appreciation to the following people:

My publisher Graham Cook of Writersworld.

My copy editor Ian Large.

My cover designer Jag Lall.

My family who support me with my work.

My friends and work colleagues among childcare providers.

All Children I provide care for.

Cover photo shows Aminah, aged five, celebrating on the occasion of the Jubilee of Queen Elizabeth II, at the Kingsmead Estate in Sheffield City.

CONTENTS

CONTEXT AND PERSPECTIVE

Children brought up well are most likely to be successful as adults. This is only possible where government, parents and childcare providers work together. At one time, whole families with their children used to work long hours to earn the bare minimum to have something to eat in England. The Poor Law Amendment Act 1834 was legislated, which resulted in governments of the day setting up 'clubs of workhouses' in which the paupers were to live. In a way this was as if guaranteeing them an even more miserable time; here widows and orphans lived. The Work Reform Act decided that children under 9-years old should not work, although strangely the law makers seemed oblivious to the reality that children were not working for fun, but for survival due to poverty. Surely childcare has come a long way.

1. This book gives new ideas to the learner/practitioner of how best to present material, the implementation of good practice, sharing knowledge and experience. Therefore, this book only offers guidance, ideas and pointers of the best responses to commonly asked topical questions in the UK NVQ Level 3 Diploma in Childcare. The suggested responses are exhaustive. The selected topics are based on real units and questions or tasks.

2. I have used personal experience in 'my setting'. This experience is what has been used to address most of the topics and questions, drawing from real life situations of safeguarding and caring for children. The book is written in the first person context of 'I' or in 'my setting' so that the upgrading or aspiring practitioner can put themselves in the context of what is happening in their own setting, in order to draw parallels and learn by inclusion and participation of shared good practice towards safeguarding, playing with and the development of children.

3. The book provides a preamble in the form of a model self-evaluation of a childcare setting, to help practitioners evaluate their own provisions. There are key factors of how to deal with different situations and a summary of headings of usable policies that can be developed by a starting practitioner.

4. There is also advice for practitioners and learners to deal with various situations such as learning differences, bullying and keeping an outstanding setting.

5. In its remit the book offers learners and practitioners an adaptable handbook to be used in any setting, and gives learners and practitioners an overview of the English Early Years Framework.

PREAMBLE

Start your pursuit of an outstanding performance to achieve a UK NVQ Level 3 Diploma or to maintain an excellent childcare provision by self-assessment of where you are now. When you know where you are, i.e. your strengths and weaknesses, you will demonstrate that you know your work and you will be able to take action to correct any shortfalls. This is how you would achieve outstanding performance marks but also, in your practice, inspectors will be more than satisfied.

This is how to achieve an outstanding position in an inspection.

In my setting I work towards achieving an outstanding position when inspected. I do not leave things to chance. The preamble to this book is therefore a self-evaluation to help a practitioner adapt his/her language in order to achieve an outstanding evaluation.

Example of self-evaluation:

My Setting name:	My Setting	
Government/department setting unique reference number:	MS 888888888	
Setting address:	My Setting	
	8 Setting Street	
	London	
	Postcode	E28 7GN
Evaluation completed by (name and role):	IBRAHIM NELSON KAGGWA	
	Manager	
Date completed:	18th October 2013	

A chart may help clarify some aspects of your work

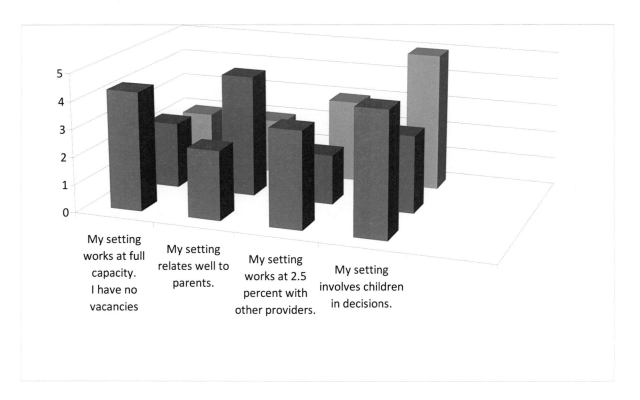

Colour Code:

COLUMN 1
Blue: Vacancies filled.
Green: Vacancies already held by waiting list.
Red: Vacancies held by siblings due in.

COLUMN 2
Blue: Parent volunteers on outings off-site.
Green: Parent volunteers in sessions of learning on-site.
Red: Parents in planning programmes.

COLUMN 3
Blue: Statutory agencies worked with.
Green: Voluntary agencies worked with.
Red: = Private agencies worked with.

COLUMN 4
Green: Children helped to make decisions in what play they want.
Blue: Children helped to make decisions in what to eat.
Red: Children make some decisions in how they are taught.

The following information is firstly to inform myself, and secondly an inspector or evaluator about those who use my setting. This demands that I have to think about the quality of my setting and the services that I offer. I therefore describe the key characteristics of my setting, highlighting the traditions and culture, environment and backgrounds of the children attending. I include key issues such as children who have special learning differences or educational needs. In my setting the new jargon, which is more user-friendly, is to talk of learning differences rather than difficulties; this enables me to capitalise on abilities rather than disabilities. In the UK, I ensure that I highlight the needs of children who have a mother tongue other than English and only speak it as an second or additional language. Therefore I would say the following:

My setting is a unique, strong and compliant environment with the requirements of childcare in the following areas:

- It is a welcoming, safe, warm, caring, and friendly environment for children when out of school. It is based in bright well-maintained premises. The culture and backgrounds of the children are local, and they are aged from 0-16 years old. My setting engages children all of the time, offering a flexible/approachable atmosphere including homework, subject support and recreation.

- Under 8s come with mothers to have cuddles and group hugs, play and learning as appropriate. Staff/volunteers talk to the children all the time. My setting allows provision for children with learning differences and/or disabilities, or speak English as an additional language. (My setting's staff speak seven main languages: English, Arabic, Swahili, French, Swedish, Luganda and Somali.)

- Staff and volunteers are professional and have safeguarding qualifications.

- The premises/building is a Community Enterprise Building with secluded fencing at the rear with car parking and high security gates, coupled with 24-hour CCTV monitoring to ensure the safety of the children. Areas/rooms used include two rooms for under 8s, one large hall for over 8s, kitchens, a baby changing room and toilets. All children are always accompanied to the toilets. Play items are checked (for damage and if necessary replaced) and sanitised everyday before opening. The premises are cleaned daily. My setting employs cleaners who also deal with emergency spillages etc. The provision is located close to four local schools. Children have access to on-site recreation, and benefit from off-site organised recreation at community centres, ball games in nearby parks and outdoor space. My setting also provides a pick up and drop off service.

- Pre-school Learning Alliance carried out a comprehensive assessment and evaluation of the work of my setting and the property management company for the local city council, to ensure that the premises are suitable.

- The provision offers guidance and information to children and parents on their safety and well-being, so that the children can be healthy. Information on communicable diseases and other matters is available on display.

- Policies of the setting are implemented and available on display for reference.

- Staff and volunteers have certification in:

  DBS (Disclosure and Barring Service, formerly CRB) checks; Safeguarding; Paediatric First Aid; Level 1 and 3 Diplomas in Childcare and Education; General First Aid; Child Psychology Degree; Nursing and Midwifery, and Registered Nursing for Learning Disabilities, Advanced Diploma; Certificate of Community Development and Health; Level 1 in Drug Awareness; Level 2 in Sport; Certificate of Health and Social Care. This enables us to ensure quality of service, and the safety and well-being of the children.

- Access to and within the building is convenient on the ground and basement floors with a lift and stairs. My setting presently operates for children on weekdays and no child stays for more than a 2 hour-long session. My setting is open between 9am and 7pm (staff are on site from 8am until 8pm).

- Risk is assessed regularly; the supervisor takes a good look round on a daily basis to ensure the provision is safe, and my setting has comprehensive insurance for £5 million minimum risk, for public, employer and children's liability.

- Whilst outstanding, my setting always looks out for areas of improvement.

When self-evaluating I talk about the views of those who use my setting and of those I work with.

To do this effectively I write about the views of the children who attend the setting, mentioning the opinions of parents or carers. Mention the views of any professionals you work with, especially the local city council/authority. If in the UK, mention your local children's centre and/or health professionals. I would also mention the details of any quality assurance scheme that my setting participates in. Some local authorities rate local provisions, which is worth mentioning to show any levels of intervention the local education authority offers. I would include some incidents of how I seek ideas, views and any actions I may have taken to bring about improvements.

I would state the following. In my setting, the views of parents/carers of children, the children themselves and other professionals who work with me are very important. Their views are gathered by five clear methods:

1. Staff spend time with the parent/carer of every child on a weekly basis to discuss issues and needs to tease out information of their dis/satisfaction and ensure to work on any areas where improvement in service is required.

2. Every quarter and when contracts end, I ask parents and carers to complete a questionnaire about how satisfied they are with the provision. Staff know the children's views and ideas through:
   - (a) talking to them to establish their dis/likes;
   - (b) ensuring that they have options in available activities or outings;
   - (c) discussing with them options for the next/following day's activities, food menu and learning (e.g. painting/drawing).

3. I listen to the views of any professionals who work with my setting, especially the local authority, local children's centre and/or any health professionals:
   - (a) My setting is a member of OSN (Out of School Network), and also a member of the Pre-school Learning Alliance. This ensures hands-on, close and independent professional regular assessment, monitoring and support. These also ensure quality and provide necessary interventions.
   - (b) My setting developed with the support from the local city council's 'Pathways'. These links are maintained.
   - (c) Details of any quality assurance scheme my setting participates in, include being a member of the 'Children's University' to uphold quality assurance for children and on-going assessments.

4. Here are some examples of action taken to change my setting as a result of users' views (not only to change, but the whole inception was from the views and ideas of children, parents and local councillors):
   - (a) Children suggested an on-site games console with a large-screen TV, which could be used for team play indoors; my setting provided them.
   - (b) Children suggested group outings, which are organised for them.
   - (c) My setting ensures different options, within reason, for activities.
   - (d) My setting developed from the parents and children in the local area seeking to find a way to:
     - support children with their homework, as many parents in BAME (Black, Asian and Minority Ethnic) groups are from migrant backgrounds and do not speak English and therefore could not participate in their children's learning;

- help local parents and local authority councillors work to take children off the street as there was no space to play for children aged over 8 who reside in the nearby sky-rise housing without gardens;
- help children that were lagging behind in attainment. My setting has developed Individual Learning Plans based on where the children themselves request specific support, e.g. Maths, English and Science subjects.

5. My setting seeks the views of local schoolteachers to gauge the impact of subject support, developing relationships, encouraging parents to be interested in their children's learning, seeking improvement in attainment and engaging in recreation.

Therefore my setting demonstrates that it is outstanding.

Ensure that when self-evaluating, you discuss the quality and standards of your provision.

I would discuss and make my own judgement about how well my setting is doing in the following areas:

How well my setting meets the needs of the range of children who attend.

In my setting, everything I do impacts on the children's learning and development.

My setting's provision meets the needs of the range of children who attend by planning and ensuring that staff/volunteers deliver individualised and group learning plans, to support learning in interactions with children by providing for a programme that includes reading, writing, painting, drawing, board games, computer games, physical play e.g. ball, outings to sites (parks, the cinema etc.) and events.

My staff plan the learning environment to help children progress towards the early learning goals: to be healthy through physical play and dietary choice (any snacks and meals are brought by the children from home and must be healthy); to stay safe through keeping the facility secure and teaching basic safety and self-protection like the Green Cross Code; to enjoy and achieve using outings, games, events, cinema, cultural activities and participation to achieve knowledge and higher standards.

Safety is important, an Accident Record Book is maintained and an accidents/incidents slip/form is issued if a child has a fall, for example. First aid is provided and parents/carers are informed using the accident slip. Children are helped to make a positive contribution through volunteering to do child's play roles; older children mentor younger ones with staff supervision. Staff also develop skills for the future through supervised computer games whereby children can improve their IT skills.

My setting plans children's play and exploration, in/outdoors, with a balance of adult-led and child-led activities that help children to think critically and be active and creative learners, through homework, subject support, cultural activities and recreation. My setting plans for individual children, in view of their culture and background, including any learning difficulties and/or disabilities, and uses English as an additional language, so the service remains inclusive for each child to receive enjoyable/challenging experiences across several areas of learning. My setting's staff/volunteers also work in schools, helping us to use information from regular recorded observation and assessment to plan and personalise support for every child. They identify and provide for additional learning and development needs, including some children who achieve beyond what is expected of them. Therefore, each child in my setting's care achieves as much as they can in relation to their starting points and capabilities. My setting involves the parents and carers as partners and other providers in children's learning and development to offer an inclusive, caring and welcoming service to all children. At my setting we have high expectations for children and enthuse and motivate them, especially through subject support. My setting supports each child in their learning and works with parents and carers as partners in children's learning and development. Parents are encouaged to attend activities when possible.

My priorities for improvement

The priorities for improvement include:

1. Space – my setting's work will be better improved when more space is secured as negotiations with the local authority are ongoing.
2. Sustainability – my setting has the priority of ensuring the sustainability of the foundation standards we have embraced by using regular monitoring and evaluation through self-assessment.
3. Expansion – due to need, we are exploring answers to calls to open branch provisions in other cities due to the culturally-specific needs that my setting addresses.
4. In my local area there is a priority to address the off-site, small group, learning points in many areas.

Building on the current success of the year's work. I would rate my practice as outstanding.

Contribution of the early years provision to children's well-being in my setting.

My setting's staff/volunteers take time with the child. Normally, before the start date, we have an induction session lasting two or three hours where the parent or carer is present with their child(ren). This allows my setting's staff/volunteers to make an initial assessment of where the child is at in their learning and personal development. Then, staff/volunteers plan for their first session, and build on that with the passing of time, ensuring that we build on each child's individual knowledge and ability to identify safety issues and teach children to behave in ways that are safe for themselves and others (e.g. discouraging snatching of toys, but encouraging sharing).

In my setting we enable children to develop an understanding of dangers and how to stay safely, for instance by not allowing them to jump off chairs. My setting uses learning aids appropriate to the needs of children from different ethnic backgrounds, such as using appropriate children's books or stories for any children with learning difficulties and/or disabilities or those learning English as an additional language can learn to stay safe. Whilst helping children to learn to stay safe, my setting also ensures their safety, taking measures and precautions that are appropriate (e.g. they have no access to the kitchen unless accompanied). Through this, my setting helps the children to get the following results:

- Form appropriate bonds and secure emotional attachments with their carers.
- Learn to behave well and develop good relationships with their peers.
- Develop the characteristics of effective learning.

These results impact on the children's healthy development, enabling each child to form appropriate bonds and secure emotional attachments with carers, ensuring that children are happy and enjoy what they do. The children in my setting learn how to behave well, play co-operatively and develop their independence. The children are being helped to learn to listen and act positively. Parents are allowed on site to build bonds and confidence.

My setting has care practices and routines such as arrival and departure time, or for under-8s nappy changing or snack time, which are used to support children's all-round development and well-being. My setting helps volunteers and staff to encourage children to explore their surroundings and use their imagination through art, off-site visits and cultural activities such as dance or henna painting. My setting works with children who have no play areas due to residing in flats or high rise blocks. Therefore we help children to talk and play with each other and the adults that care for them. My setting ensures recreation as a practice of helping children to develop an understanding of the importance of physical exercise and good food for a healthy diet. At my setting all activity supports children to prepare them for their transition into other early years settings and into maintained nursery provision and/or reception class, and higher learning for those aged 15-16.

My priorities for improvement.

The particular areas for improvement include:

- securing memberships with some play centres, e.g.:
    Monkey Play Business
    Jungle Play Mania
- partnerships with:
    local football clubs
    young football clubs
    BAME women's recreational clubs
- work with:
    play house setting up 'items' for play and for both in- and outdoors

To engage more:

- older parents into healthy keep fit drop-in sessions so the young people can learn by example;
- with the parents, strengthening them to join in at homework sessions so they can continue to have an interest in the learning of their children.

Mother-toddler groups take place to ensure that by the time children become school age parents are already used to my setting's provision.

My practice is: Outstanding.

The leadership and management of my setting:

In my setting I look at the effectiveness of the leadership and management; this is all about how well I organise my services for parents and their children.

- My setting must meet the requirements of the Early Years Foundation Stage (EYFS).
- My setting must carry out self-evaluation and improvement planning.
- My setting must have achievable indicators of performance for management and professional development.
- My setting must provide safeguarding.
- My setting must carry out partnership working.

Therefore I would evaluate as follows:

My setting has effective leadership and management. The supervisor, manager, volunteers and staff at all times consider how well my setting functions through the organised childcare service that it provides and how well it, as an organisation, works with others, such as the Out of School Network Business Development Manager, and the Pre-school Learning Alliance Local Coordinator and the Children's University Outreach Manager, plus any other off-site provisions a child attends such as their schools.

My setting considers how well to:

- implement policies by understanding childcare responsibilities in meeting the learning and development and safeguarding and welfare requirements of the EYFS. Thereby, all staff have been trained in safeguarding, using the Pre-school Learning Alliance provisions. (A list of staff who have been certified and their certificates are displayed in the provision.);

- implement and oversee the educational programmes to ensure that all areas of learning are included and that assessment is consistent and used well to inform the provision's planning. Thereby, my setting uses professional and qualified child carers and teachers as staff and volunteers. Children's Individual Learning Plan is based on the need(s) of the child, e.g. homework or subject support;

- implement and promote equality and diversity and have a clear overview of the progress of all the children who attend. Thereby, my setting implements its equality of opportunities policy alongside other policies. Two folders of all policies are available for parents and carers to view in the setting. The policies are updated through my setting's collaborative work with the Out of School Network;

- evaluate the provision, using the evaluation information to identify priorities for development and set challenging targets for improvement for the learning of children and growth of the setting. This enables my setting's management to plan and respond to situations that require intervention, by planning well or by bringing in professional guidance such as that from the Out of School Network or the Pre-School Learning Alliance. This helps my setting to operate transparently and also be supported as appropriate;

- implement and have effective systems for performance management, including how to tackle under-performance and arrange for the continuous professional development of any staff or assistants using monthly staff supervision, and by testing and challenging children;

- ensure work in partnership with parents and others, especially encouraging parents to take an interest in the learning and overall development of their children, but also ensuring that professionals such as OSN, PSLA, social services, GPs, etc., are welcome to work with the provision;

- implement safety and safeguard children, thereby my setting has the management, staff and volunteers trained and certified in safeguarding children and young people. In situations where potential risk is detected my setting will ensure that intervention and action is taken, e.g. marshals will be used for one-on-one accompaniment of the child(ren).

My setting tackles identified weaknesses regularly, ensuring intervention.

My setting is ready for first inspection and deals with any weaknesses.

My priorities for improvement.

My setting will be seeking to:

1. strengthen links with heads of schools in the immediate local area;

2. ensure that it stocks provision-based sportswear so that children have appropriate clothing for outside weather conditions (although my setting requests these from parents/carers but many times they forget);
3. ensure continuity of dietary policy of children bringing their own food or snacks to the provision and ensure they continue to meet healthy standards.

My setting is Outstanding.

In my setting self-evaluation I would also include additional information such as the following:

My setting, through staff and volunteers, ensures to care for (teach) children to:

- be active and understand the benefits of physical activity. We take walks to the park, we also play in parks and also visit indoor provisions such as Monkey Business and Jungle Mania. Staff and volunteer carers talk to the children about keeping fit;
- understand and adopt healthy habits such as good hygiene practices. Staff always ensure they wash their hands after using the toilet and before eating, and we work together to clear up toys and play items nearer to the end of our sessions;
- make healthy choices about what they eat and drink;
- ask for any account of children's individual dietary and medical needs, e.g. allergies, at the signing of contracts at my setting. It takes into account children from different ethnic backgrounds, learning differences and/or disabilities or those learning English as an additional language, ensuring compliance with their religious dietary demands such as Halal or Kosher;
- have made feedback to schools and parents and commend the work of my setting in helping to improve children's learning attainment as a result of attending the provision.

The uniqueness of my setting.

My setting is not only providing childcare, but other elements to support the children, for instance a qualified advice worker is employed to help parents who do not know how to deal with the benefits system.

Parents who are unemployed and seeking employment and have an interview are allowed, on appointment, to leave their child for 2 hours as a 'spot purchase'.

My setting is a social enterprise, which was started with support following rigorous assessment by Key Fund through the Local Community Enterprise Development Unit.

Having self-evaluated, we are now ready to learn the lessons that would put us in an outstanding position. Under normal circumstances, in order to read for the NVQ Level 3 Diploma, one would have done the Level 2 and be in practice at their own provision, or working in employment at a provision/setting.

CHAPTER 1
COMMUNICATION

INTRODUCTION

The first aspect of your work in an NVQ Level 3 Diploma will be on communication. When working in my setting on a day-to-day basis, answers emerge automatically to address communication with children, parents/carers and other agencies. It should be straightforward to work through these.

You should be able to communicate effectively with parents, the children and young people's workforce.

LEARNING OUTCOME 1

Understanding why effective communication is important in the work setting.

1.1 The key to your success in the childcare and young people care industry is communication. This means that you, as a childcare provider, have a duty of communicating with parents, children and young people, as well as communicating with all local and national agencies that have an interest with what you do.

Communication is the means by which messages are conveyed by people. Through communication I am able to establish the individual requirements of each child and provide response services that welcome and value the children. I have found a variety of ways that people use to convey messages or bring about understanding of their issues. I have come into contact with people who communicate in different ways and have varied levels of understanding. Therefore, effective communication is important by allowing for various methods of expression to accommodate the diversity of dis/abilities and choice in the work setting. Such methods as written, verbal, signed or audio and visual are examples of effective communication that can be combined or used singularly. Many people would either use verbal or written, electronic, such as a telephone text message or e-mail, yet other people would prefer printed methods. Some would like robust record keeping for reminding themselves for future reference.

1.2 Communication is the crucial ingredient to success in accessing the services I provide for the children/parents. Therefore, my setting demands various ways of communication. To this end, at the outset of a prospective contract, I hold pre-contract telephone conversations and/or meetings. This enables relationship development and breaks down barriers. It is important to effectively communicate with the children and parents so that I can best help and safeguard the children, supporting them in their requirements and learning needs. I find that regular, accurate and truthful communication reduces potential tensions; it ensures that parents and children are comfortable. This makes one (myself/the worker) approachable on any matter, issue or concern. Regular communication to the parents enables me to provide accurate updates/reports, at every stage, for the learning and development of children. Regular communication is the means for informing parents and enhances my monitoring. To improve confidence, I strictly adhere to a feedback method so that I make in-house reviews of the worthiness of the service. This enables positive communication. If communication is negative it becomes routine and can fail to demonstrate the interest of the relevant parties, creating defensiveness instead of improvements. This would be poor. If there is no good communication parents would not get accurate information about their children. I ensure good practice, to liaise with the children in my setting, so each child's behaviour is monitored depending on the activities we are involved in or what we are going to do.

Demonstration of how to implement 1.1 and 1.2.

I have looked after K for over a year. My relationship with K is increasingly stronger, giving us a strong bond, through verbal communication, using positive clear words that are happy and consistent. We use body language, hugs, touch, on-the-back pats and cuddles. We also use expressions that are facial, like eye contact and body language.

The following breakdown is evidence of the communication I use in a regular day's work.

I collect K from school. In the first instance I meet with the class teacher at the door and exchange pleasantries. The teacher recognises my responsibilities and I ask how K has been. Usually there are no issues, but if there had been concerns, e.g. if K had had a fall or anything else of concern the teacher would inform me in order for me to relay the same message to K's parents. This routine enables my plan of action to care for K. I would incorporate any information into K's care plan so that changes such as 'not eaten well' can be catered for with supplementary favourites or more choice on the food/snack menu. Following the snack, we play games for 45 minutes; these could be indoor or outside, depending on the weather. We rest for 20 minutes and watch children's programmes, and then do homework if there is any. I make my own observations, and compare notes with my assistant. I make notes for the diaries, recording good behaviour, development changes, concentration etc., so the parents can read the experiences of their children when they collect them. The day ends with a final chat with parents/guardian when they collect the child.

LEARNING OUTCOME 2

2.1 Demonstration of communication preferences.

Through communication I, at the very outset, confidently go through the policies and procedures with parents, establishing clear boundaries and safeguards about such things as safety, the gates and locks in places or on doors, the likes and dislikes of the child, help with homework and general play.

2.2 I understand the differences of people, taking into account sight, hearing or language differences (dis/abilities). In some instances I have to ensure language translation and/or interpretation for some parents so that they understand precisely the policies and procedures, but also the issues affecting their children. I worked with L and S whose mother spoke fluent Polish and very little English. I do not speak any Polish. I had therefore to get the mother to convey her messages through her friend who spoke fluent Polish and English. So, starting with informal chats, I had to build a dual good relationship with both in order to meet the children's needs adequately.

2.3 Many times I had to text messages to the friend of the mother, and had to be careful how the message would come across, as it was a written record for reference, or I would have to sit with both the friend and the mother to ensure that all was clear and okay.

2.4 I had an instance once where, due to a language barrier, I spoke loudly to a parent who was talking to me on the mobile phone whilst walking outside in a traffic area. This caused upset as the parent thought I was shouting. We later sat down and discussed things and everything was ok, but this showed me that due to language barriers sometimes things can come across in a way that was not meant. I have a planner for my setting that I use as guidelines to respond to an individual's reactions when communicating.

GUIDELINES TO USE:

- Daily informal chats so I can assess changes to adjust for the adequate care of the child (e.g. had a fall, did not eat well, tired, slightly unwell, been fine etc.).
- Day's diary noting any concerns, with a photo (when possible), to give to parents to share in the development of their child, but also for them to record any comments.
- Final chat when the parents collect the child. This consists of any noticed concerns such as if the child has not played or eaten well or was moody, but also mentioning achievements. I ensure that the tone and body language I use reassure parents.
- Weekly planner – every child has a weekly planner on file, updated daily.
- Update forms that I use, for instance when children have been away on holiday and may have acquired changes in there experience.
- Text messages when I am able to link up with a parent, e.g. "Kate is doing joined up writing in her homework right now."
- Email, when it is necessary for parents who engage in desk-based work.
- Videos and photos are taken and transmitted immediately to parents when appropriate or when urgency is essential.

LEARNING OUTCOME 3

3.1   Be able to overcome barriers to communication.

I overcome barriers to communication. Different people, due to their backgrounds, use and interpret communicated messages using different methods and ways. In my setting I have come across people using gestures where they are unable to say or utter words in one or another language. Children for instance will wave instead, if they cannot yet talk to say bye-bye. I adapt myself, giving time, attention and space to allow these expressions. Sometimes the parents can also gesture in different ways, as due to cultural differences not everyone just says thank you, please etc.

3.2   Identify barriers to effective communication.

As I work with children and parents, in many instances the barriers to effective communication include lack of language, additional needs, lack of confidence, disability in sight or hearing, or people being shy, their cultural background etc.

3.3   How to overcome barriers.

I use a variety of methods to overcome barriers in my setting. For instance, some parents need to have an interpreter if they do not speak English proficiently. I adapt myself where children use signing or gestures or general words to communicate on most common issues. I have also in some cases sat down and learnt the most common phrases and words to overcome these barriers.

3.4 Strategies for clarifying misunderstandings.

Misunderstandings can arise from a failure to understand a sign or mishearing. Therefore, if I felt there was a misunderstanding, I would make sure to calm the situation, and go over the issue again, go through the matter, explaining, clarifying it and providing written information, or call on someone to mediate or interpret. The best strategy is to keep to hand and in mind a list of resources, e.g. telephone numbers for extra support to draw from.

3.5 Accessing extra support.

I keep a list of telephone numbers to hand for accessing interpretation when I need it. For example, when caring for children whose first language is not English. I also contact my childcare mentor. I also research information from 'inclusion services', local groups, libraries, or I take time to learn about the culture of the individual concerned.

LEARNING OUTCOME 4

BEING ABLE TO APPLY PRINCIPLES AND PRACTICES OF CONFIDENTIALITY

4.1 The meaning of confidentiality.

Confidentiality in my setting means the non-disclosure of information to unauthorised people. I would not disclose information about a child or a parent without parental written consent.

4.2 Demonstration of ways to maintain confidentiality.

I maintain a Confidentiality Policy for parents. I practice confidentiality when dealing with personal issues such as discussing children's observations that I keep on file. I speak to each one alone. I provide information in a sealed envelope. I talk to them on phone in private, ensuring that I am not being overheard. But also, if a reference or a request was made about a child or an individual, such requests would have to be written and be consented to by the parent. My policy clearly sets out the parameters of implementing the Confidentiality Policy.

4.3 Potential Tension.

I am aware of the potential tension between maintaining an individual's confidentiality and disclosing concerns. Concerns must be put in context. If I had a safeguarding issue about a child in my care, under the law I would have to share such concern with relevant authorities. This would cause tension with the parent. I have taken measures in my setting to record observations and if, for example, on the parental side I observed serious neglect in the care of a child, I would ensure the collection of witnesses such as schoolteachers' own observations and ensure that all concerned are working together, raising the same concern, as much as the parent may not like it. Those are the sorts of potential tension situations.

Communication will take the largest percentage of all that a childcare provider has to do with children, parents, colleagues and other agencies.

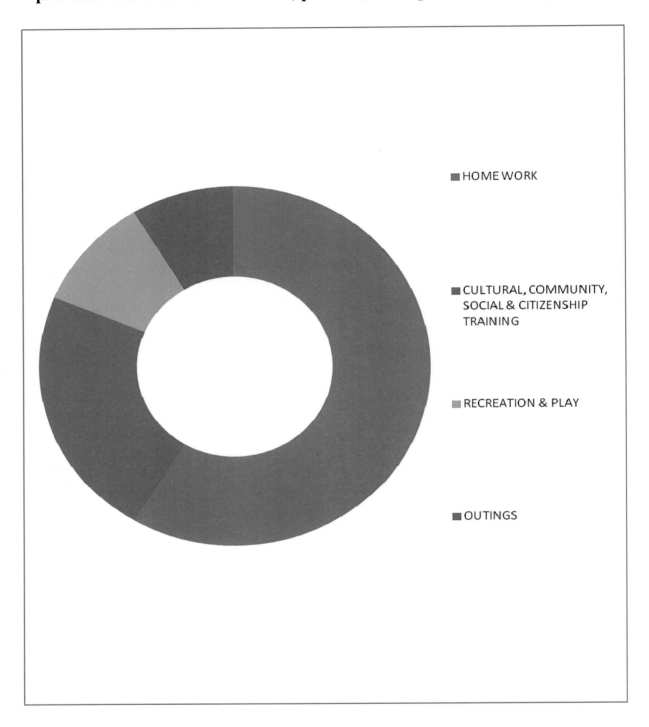

■ HOME WORK

■ CULTURAL, COMMUNITY, SOCIAL & CITIZENSHIP TRAINING

■ RECREATION & PLAY

■ OUTINGS

CHAPTER 2

ASSESSING DEVELOPMENT

PROMOTE CHILDREN'S AND YOUNG PEOPLE'S DEVELOPMENT

This chapter may help the learner to understanding the requirements of assessing the development needs of children or young people and to prepare a development plan.

LEARNING OUTCOME 1

Factors that need to be taken into account when assessing development.

To be able to assess the development needs of a child or young person and prepare a development plan, I always have to understand particular factors that I take into account in order to know the background of the child/young person, so that I can understand their needs and then work on planning their development. The factors I consider include social, economic and cultural, which all have an impact on the lives of children. For instance, housing, community, health status, poverty or being in care are situations that have a bearing on children's development. If a child is brought up in a rough area where the schools are run-down or the family situation is disrupted or where the family is not bothered about upbringing, an assessment and knowledge of the situation can lead to a plan that can be developed.

Assessing a child's or young person's development.

It is important to give children and young people a chance, because if parents do not have much money, children may be fending for themselves. This makes an impact on the development of the child in terms of physical, communication, intellectual/cognitive, social, emotional and behavioural, and moral abilities.

Selection of assessment methods used.

I select my assessment methods of observations using assessment frameworks, standard measurements, information from parent/carers/children and young people, other professionals and colleagues, monitoring and participation. I use these methods taking into account that development is holistic and interconnected, drawing from my Inclusion Policy. In the first instance I make every effort to make my setting into a place of goodness, then I ensure that the children in my care develop into a good gathering. Good gatherings/groups enable a positive outcome, e.g. my own child with an autistic condition is helped in a class of other age-peer children to participate. This makes an impact in a good way. If children/young people are not part of a good establishment/gathering/group, this makes a negative effect on them. Experience shows that early years foundation has an impact on the choices children and young people make in the future.

When assessing development I ensure that I consider and take into account the following factors:

- confidentiality (and when for the safety of the child or young person that confidentiality must to be breached following national guidance, e.g. from Ofsted);
- children's wishes and feelings;

- ethnic, linguistic and cultural background;
- disability or specific requirements and any additional needs;
- reliability of information;
- avoiding bias;
- equality of opportunity;
- being positive;
- being objective.

I record my findings either for reference or as may be appropriate for sharing with parents and colleagues, e.g. my assistant and other professionals.

PROMOTING THE DEVELOPMENT OF CHILDREN AND YOUNG PEOPLE

Implementing the development plan for a child or young person according to their own role and responsibilities, taking into account that development, is holistic and interconnected.

In my setting I use good preparation when planning to implement the development plan. This is because I would have to evaluate the plan and the effect or impact made on the children, in order to ensure improvements that I identify when I evaluate. I therefore implement the development plan for children and young people according to my role and responsibilities as a childminder. I am the senior person in my setting. In my implementation of development I take into account that development is holistic and interconnected. I therefore encourage every child or young person in my setting to take responsibility for their own development as part of the development plan. When I plan implementing development, I would observe the child involved in a physical activity, e.g. using play equipment or apparatus. I implement development as I focus on the physical skills demonstrated by the child/young person. I implement development as I plan that in the assessment I would comment on:

- the child's gross motor skills;
- the child's fine motor skills;
- the child's co-ordination skills;
- the role I play or that of the adult involved in promoting the child's physical development;
- the suggestions for further activities to encourage or extend the child's physical development.

Evaluate and revise the development plan in the light of implementation.

In my setting, 'evaluation and revision of development in light of implementation' is based on the needs of the children. I plan, design and revise my development plan in my setting to meet the needs of the children that I provide for. Through evaluating implementation I ensure that the activities provided are the ones children are interested in, but also those that would benefit their development. Evaluation and revision enables me to give children choices, teaching good morals and manners, healthy eating, etc. My implementation plan would be based on the rate of the child's development or maturity. In my evaluations and revisions of the development plan for each child I have to ensure that I have realistic expectations of the children.

The importance of person-centred and inclusive approach with examples of how I implement this in my work.

In my setting, person-centred and inclusive approach is important because each person is valued and made to feel important in our activities. Person-centred is the approach to assist the children plan their lives and supports. In my setting I base our play and learning on the policy of inclusion. Every child is allowed time to participate, to be involved, engaged and to make choices. I take into account the special needs or learning needs of each child, so those that need personal or individualised support are involved with additional help. For example, on walks outside I ask younger children if they want to hold the hand of an older younger person, or vice versa.

Examples of how I implement person-centred and inclusive approach in my work.

In my setting, person-centred planning is a collection of tools and approaches that I base upon a set of shared values that can be used to plan with the children – not for them. I use these tools to help the children or young people to think about what is important in their lives now and also to think about what would make a good future. For example, I ask the children to help me prepare their own snack, and I ask them what they would like me to include whilst ensuring that there are healthy eating choices that would provide a balanced diet. In my planning I involve the children so they can build their own circle of support and involve all the people who are important in their life. For example, I ask if the children help their parent/carer at home to prepare their snack, e.g. laying the table, clear up toys after play, etc.

Listening to children or young people and communicating in a way that encourages them to feel valued.

In my setting I value every child/young person that I have a duty of care to. Therefore, I always and at all times make sure that myself and my assistant are listening to the children or young people and communicating in a way that encourages them to feel valued. I deal with a range of ages of children and young people. I start with the knowledge that babies come into the world ready to learn and are especially tuned to learn from other people and the cultural and material environment. I am able to adapt the setting to ensure that children are listened to.

Play and other imaginative and creative activities help children to make sense of their experience and 'transform' their knowledge, fostering cognitive development. Language, thinking and learning are interlinked; they depend on and promote each other's development. What children can do is the starting point for learning. Children learn better by doing and saying, so by doing things with other people who are more competent, rather than just by being told, they gain a better understanding.

In my setting I listen. I value every child/young person and I communicate with each and evry one of the children in my care. Therefore, I always and at all times make sure that my assistant and I are encouraging the children to make decisions, so that they feel involved with making choice and decisions. This helps them learn responsibility and allows them to make the rules. This is important because they then learn to own the activity and adhere to the rules they themselves made. I encourage children of different ages to make choices, asking children of the places they would like to go to or visit, activities they would like to do. This way, the children are listened to and feel valued.

Every aspect of work in a childcare setting contributes to the development of children and young people.

GRAPH INDICATOR OF DEVELOPMENT IN ALL ASPECTS

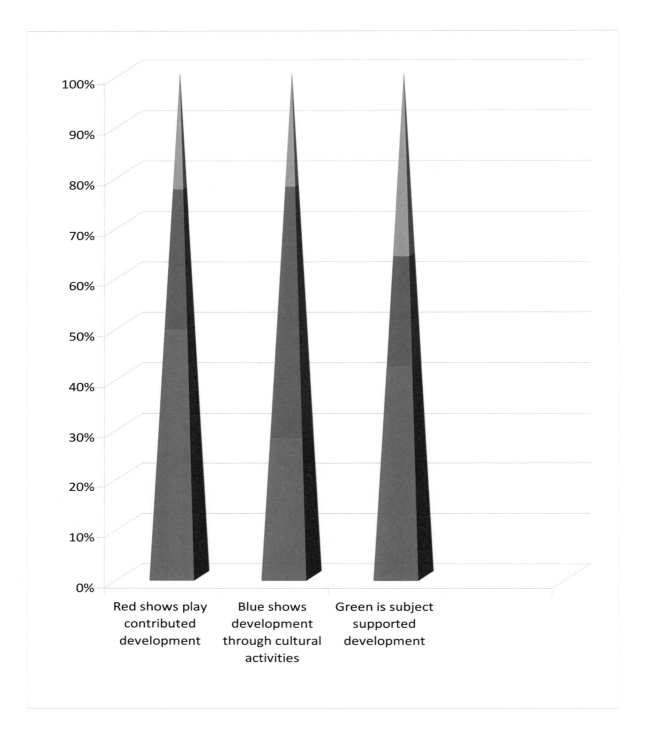

Every childcare provision is different; the development indicators vary accordingly.

CHAPTER 3

PATTERNS OF DEVELOPMENT

YOU SHOULD UNDERSTAND CHILDREN'S AND YOUTHS' DEVELOPMENT.

LEARNING OUTCOME 1

UNDERSTANDING EXPECTED PATTERNS OF DEVELOPMENT FOR CHILDREN AND YOUNG PEOPLE FROM BIRTH TO 19 YEARS.

Understanding unexpected patterns of child development.

BEING ABLE TO PRODUCE A CHILD DEVELOPMENT CHART.

In my setting I generated support and information for the 'Child Development Chart' from the following sources:

- various child development websites;
- my personal experience as a parent and also a childminder;
- discussion with peers, neighbours and parents whose children I care for;
- schoolteachers;
- discussion with my assistant;
- discussion with a trustee of UK KIDZ, a childcare provision.

Introduction to the Chart.

The following table gives me as a childcare worker and parents an idea of how young children develop. It is a summary of my understanding of how each stage of a child's development is part of a continuum, building on the previous stage of a child's development and affecting the next stage. The table is an overview of common traits or signs in most children's development, and is developed through my work experience as a childminder and through the consultations I have made. I am able to recognise that not all children grow and develop at the same pace. For instance, as a parent I have had the test of recognising that slow progress in children's development may be normal or may be due to complications at birth, lack of adequate parental guidance, inadequate nutrition, poor health, lack of stimulation or a more serious problem. However, if problems are noticed by a parent or a childcare worker it is appropriate that those issues are discussed with an appropriate and trained child development worker, health worker, social care worker and/or a teacher.

In my setting, I have understood what all children are normally able to do in terms of communication, intellectually and in actions.

By the age of 1 month	
I have understood and experienced that a baby should be able:	<ul><li>to turn its own head towards a hand that is stroking the child's cheek or mouth;</li><li>to bring both hands towards its own mouth;</li><li>to turn towards familiar voices and sounds;</li><li>to suckle the breast and touch it with its hands.</li></ul>
I have understood that in order to assess the child's development, the advice for parents and/or child carers is to:	<ul><li>make skin-to-skin contact and breastfeed within one hour of birth;</li><li>support the baby's head when holding the baby upright;</li><li>massage and cuddle the baby often;</li><li>always handle the baby gently, even when tired or upset;</li><li>breastfeed frequently and on demand;</li><li>always safely dispose of the baby's faeces and wash hands with soap and water or a substitute, such as ash and water, after changing the baby;</li><li>talk, read and sing to the child as much as possible;</li><li>give consistent love and affection;</li><li>visit a trained health worker with the infant during the first week and again six weeks after birth.</li></ul>
As a carer or parent one should detect the following warning signs to watch for:	<ul><li>poor suckling at the breast or refusing to suckle;</li><li>little movement of arms and legs;</li><li>little or no reaction to loud sounds or bright lights;</li><li>crying for long periods for no apparent reason;</li><li>vomiting and diarrhoea, which can lead to dehydration.</li></ul>

By the age of 6 months	
I have understood that at 6 months babies should be able to:	<ul><li>raise their head and chest when lying on its stomach;</li><li>reach for dangling objects;</li><li>grasp and shake objects;</li><li>roll both ways;</li><li>sit with support;</li><li>explore objects with hands and mouth;</li><li>begin to imitate sounds and facial</li></ul>

	expressions; • respond to its own name and to familiar faces.
I have understood that in order to assess the child's development, the advice for parents and/or child carers is to:	• lay the baby on a clean, flat, safe surface so s/he can move freely and reach for objects; • continue to hold and cuddle the baby every day, giving consistent love and affection; • prop or hold the baby in a secure position so s/he can see what is happening nearby; • continue to breastfeed on demand day and night, and start adding other foods (two to three meals a day starting at 6 months; three to four meals a day from 9 months and beyond); • talk, read or sing to the child as often as possible, not only when she or he is hungry or getting ready to sleep.
As a childminder I am now aware of warning signs to watch for, such as:	• stiffness or difficulty moving limbs; • constant moving of the head (this might indicate an ear infection, which could lead to deafness if not treated); • little or no response to sounds, familiar faces or the breast; • refusing the breast or other foods.

By the age of 12 months	
I have understood that at this stage a baby should be able to:	• sit without support; • crawl on hands and knees and pull him/herself up to stand; • take steps, holding on to support; • try to imitate words and sounds and respond to simple requests; • enjoy playing and clapping; • repeat sounds and gestures for attention; • pick things up with thumb and one finger; • start holding objects such as a spoon and cup and attempt self-feeding.
The advice for childminders and parents to help assess development includes:	• point to objects and name them; • play with, talk, sing and read to the child frequently; • use mealtimes and other family activities to encourage interaction with all family members;

27

	• give consistent affection and be responsive both when the child is happy and when upset; • if the child is developing slowly or has a physical disability, focus on the child's abilities and give extra stimulation and interaction; • do not leave a child in one position for many hours; • make the area as safe as possible to prevent accidents, and keep dangerous objects, such as sharp objects, plastic bags and small items a child can choke on, out of the child's reach; • continue to breastfeed and ensure that the child has enough food and a variety of family foods; • help the child experiment with spoon and cup feeding; • make sure the child's immunisations are up to date and that s/he receives all recommended doses of nutrient supplements; • keep the child's hands clean and begin teaching the child to wash them with soap.
Warning signs to watch for:	• does not make sounds in response to others; • does not look at objects that move; • listlessness and lack of response to the caregiver; • lack of appetite or refusal of food.

By the age of 2 years	
I have gathered information that at this stage a child should be able to:	• walk, climb and run; • point to objects or pictures when they are named (e.g. nose, eyes, ears); • say several words together (from about 15 months); • follow simple instructions; • scribble if given a pencil or crayon; • enjoy simple stories and songs; • imitate the behaviour of others; • begin to eat by him/herself.
I have understood that in order to assess the child's development the advice for parents and/or child carers is to:	• read to and sing or play games with the child;

	<ul><li>teach the child to avoid dangerous objects;</li><li>talk to the child normally – do not use baby talk;</li><li>continue to breastfeed and ensure the child has enough food and a variety of family foods;</li><li>make sure the child is fully immunised;</li><li>encourage, but do not force, the child to eat;</li><li>provide simple rules and set reasonable expectations;</li><li>praise the child's achievements, provide reassurance when the child is afraid and continue to give consistent affection every day.</li></ul>
I have understood that in order to assess the child's development the advice for parents and/or child carers is to watch for warning signs such as:	<ul><li>lack of response to others;</li><li>difficulty keeping balance while walking;</li><li>injuries and unexplained changes in behaviour (especially if the child has been cared for by others);</li><li>lack of appetite.</li></ul>

By the age of 3 years	
At 3 years a child should be able to:	<ul><li>walk, run, climb, kick and jump easily;</li><li>recognise and identify common objects and pictures by pointing;</li><li>make sentences of two or three words;</li><li>say his/her own name and age;</li><li>name colours;</li><li>understand numbers;</li><li>use make-believe objects in play;</li><li>feed self;</li><li>express affection.</li></ul>
I have understood that in order to assess the child's development the advice for parents and/or child carers is to:	<ul><li>read and look at books with the child and talk about the pictures;</li><li>tell the child stories and teach rhymes and songs;</li><li>give the child its own bowl or plate of food;</li><li>continue to encourage the child to eat, giving the child as much time as s/he needs;</li><li>help the child learn to dress, use the toilet or latrine and wash him/herself with soap and water or a substitute, such as ash and water,</li></ul>

	after defecating and before touching food and eating; • listen to and answer all the child's questions; • encourage creative play, building and drawing; • give the child simple tasks, such as putting toys back in their place, to build responsibility; • limit television watching and ensure that violent shows are not viewed; • acknowledge and encourage positive behaviour and set clear limits; • provide consistent affection every day; • if available, enrol the child in an early learning (play) activity with other children.
Warning signs to watch for:	• loss of interest in playing; • frequent falling; • difficulty manipulating small objects; • failure to understand simple messages; • inability to speak using several words; • little or no interest in food.

By the age of 5 years	
A child should be able to:	• move in a coordinated way; • speak in sentences and use many different words; • understand opposites (e.g., fat and thin, tall and short); • play with other children; • dress without help; • answer simple questions; • count 5-10 objects; • wash his/her own hands.
As a childminder my understanding through this learning is that for parents and carers to assess the child at this stage they should:	• listen to the child; • interact frequently with the child; • read and tell stories; • encourage the child (both girls and boys) to play and explore; • listen to and answer all the child's questions and have conversations (with both girls and boys); • encourage creative play, building and drawing;

	• limit television watching and ensure that violent shows are not viewed; • acknowledge and encourage positive behaviour and set clear and consistent limits; • provide consistent affection every day; • enrol the child (both girls and boys) in an early learning (play) programme that helps to prepare the child for school.
Warning signs I should watch out for:	• fear, anger or violence when playing with other children, which could be signs of emotional problems or abuse.

By the age of 8 years	
As a childminder I have now understood that a child's:	• physical development proceeds more gradually and steadily than in the early years; • muscle mass increases, and small and large motor skills improve; • ability to understand and communicate abstract concepts and complex ideas has begun to develop; • span of attention increases, and s/he can focus on the past and future as well as the present; • learning capacity is expanding, and s/he is learning to read, write and do problem solving in a school environment; • friends and interactions with his/her peer group are increasingly important; • interest in friendships includes enjoying time with his/her own peer group and turning to peers for information; • self-control improves, and understanding of more complex emotions increases.
The advice for parents and care givers is to:	• be a good role model, equally for girls and boys; • encourage your child to express feelings and beliefs and to solve problems; • recognise and support your child's strengths and skills as well as limitations; • spend time with your child, and talk and listen to him/her; • find activities you can do together that will

	make your child feel successful, secure and loved; • facilitate and support your child's playtime with friends and in extra-curricular school activities; • acknowledge and encourage positive behaviour and set clear and consistent limits; • show interest and become involved in the child's school – remember that the mother, father and/or other caregiver(s) are a child's first and most important teachers.
As a carer and parent I understand that I must watch for warning signs such as:	• difficulties making and keeping friends and participating in group activities; • avoiding a task or challenge without trying, or showing signs of helplessness; • trouble communicating needs, thoughts and emotions; • trouble focusing on tasks, understanding and completing schoolwork; • excessive aggression or shyness with friends, peers and family.

By the age of 9 years	Physical Milestones: 9-10 years: pulse rate 70 ± 0.6, 9 years: average female weight 63.8lb., height 52in. 9 years: average male weight 61.6lb., height 52in. 9 years: the percent of (male) adult value of thigh 72%, calf 74%, foot 81%, upper arm 72%, forearm 73%, hand 75%. 9 years: muscle width, arm + calf 9.6cm. 9-10 years: bicuspids (8) [permanent]. 9-12 years: childish appearance of face disappears. 9 1/2 years: average female weight 68.2lb., height 53in. 9 1/2 years: average male weight 66lb., height 53in.
By the age of 10 years I have learnt that:	Physical Milestones: 10-11 years: pulse rate 67 ± 0.6. 10 years: average female weight 72.6lb., height

The age between ten and twelve is generally a time when children get a view of approaching adulthood. There are important physical and sexual changes for the child especially if she is a girl. Social relationships can be unsettled for girls and very competitive for boys. Activities, sports and clubs can help them to feel good about themselves and form safe relationships outside the family. The child at this stage needs guidance and safe limits from the carer/childminder but they also need to be a little more independent.	54 1/2in. 10 years: average male weight 70.4lb., height 54 in. 10 years: the percent of (male) adult value of thigh 75%, calf 79%, foot 84%, upper arm 77%, forearm 78%, hand 80%. 10 years: muscle width, arm + calf 10cm. 10 years: the size of testes 1.75ml. 10-14 years: (female) breast development. 10-14 years: (female) pubic hair appears. 10-16 years: (female) growth rate increase. 10 1/2 years: average female weight 77lb., height 56in. 10 1/2 years: average male weight 74.8lb. height 55in.
By the age of 11 years	Physical Milestones: 11-12 years: pulse rate 67 ± 0.6. 11 years: average female weight 81.4lb., height. 57in. 11 years: average male weight 77lb., height 56 1/2in. 11 years: the percent of (male) adult value of thigh 80%, calf 82%, foot 87%, upper arm 81%, forearm 81%, hand 82%. 11 years: muscle width, arm + calf 10.3cm. 11 years: the size of testes 2.5ml. 11-14 years: average female weight 101lb., height 62 in. 11-14 years: average male weight 99lb., height 62in. 11-15 years: 700-1400 ml/day urine production. 11-16 years: (male) pubic hair appears. 11-17 years: (female) menstruation. 11 1/2 years: average female weight 85.8lb., height 58 1/2in. 11 1/2 years: average male weight 83.6lb., height 58 in.

By the age of 12 years	Physical Milestones: 12-13 years: pulse rate 66 ± 0.6. 12 years: average female weight 92.4lb., height 60in. 12 years: average male weight 88lb., height 59in. 12 years: the percent of (male) adult value of thigh 85%, calf 86%, foot 90%, upper arm 83%, forearm 84%, hand 85%. 12 years: muscle width, arm + calf 10.7cm. 12 years: the size of testes 4.0ml. 12-14 years: canines (4) [permanent]. 12-15 years: second molars (4) [permanent]. 12-16 years: underarm hair appears. 12-16 years: (male) penis growth. 12-18 years: (male) growth rate increase. 12 1/2 years: respiration rate 12 to 18 respirations per minute. 12 1/2 years: the forehead becomes more prominent (caused by the growth of brow ridges and air sinuses), both jaws grow forward (lower more than upper). 12 1/2 years: acceleration of penis growth. 12 1/2 years: average female weight 96.8lb., height 61in. 12 1/2 years: average male weight 94.6lb. height 60in.
By the age of 13 years	Physical Milestones: 13-14 years: pulse rate 65 ± 0.8. 13 years: average female weight 101.2lb., height 62in. 13 years: average male weight 99lb., height 61 1/2in. 13 years: the percent of (male) adult value of thigh 89%, calf 89%, foot 91%, upper arm 85%, forearm 86%, hand 87%. 13 years: muscle width, arm + calf 11.3cm. 13-14 years: (male) enlargement of voice box. 13-18 years: (male) underarm hair appears. 13 1/2 years: average female weight 105.6lb., height 62 1/2in. 13 1/2 years: average male weight 105.6lb., height 63in.

By the age of 14 years	Physical Milestones:
	14-15 years: pulse rate 62 ± 0.7.
	14 years: average female weight 110lb., height 63in.
	14 years: average male weight 112.2lb., height 64in.
	14 years: the percent of (male) adult value of thigh 92%, calf 92%, foot 94%, upper arm 91%, forearm 91%, hand 91%.
	14 years: muscle width, arm + calf 12 cm.
	14 years: the size of testes 11 ml.
	14-17 years: (male) deepening of voice.
	14 1/2 years: average female weight 114.4lb., height 63 1/2in.
	14 1/2 years: average male weight 118.8lb., height 65 1/2in.
By the age of 15 years	Physical Milestones:
	15 years: onward (male) 800-2000 ml/day urine production.
	15 years: onward (female) 800-1600 ml/day urine production.
	15-16 years: pulse rate 61 ± 0.9.
	15 years: average female weight 118.8lb., height 63 1/2in.
	15 years: average male weight 125.4lb., height 66 1/2in.
	15 years: the percent of (male) adult value of thigh 93%, calf 93%, foot 95%, upper arm 92%, forearm 92%, hand 93%.
	15 years: muscle width, arm + calf 12.5 cm.
	15 years: the size of testes 15ml.
	15-18 years: average female weight 120lb., height 64in.
	15-18 years: average male weight 145lb., height 69in.
	15 1/2 years: average female weight 120lb., height 64in.
	15 1/2 years: average male weight 132lb., height 67 1/2in.
By the age of 16 years	Physical Milestones:
	16-17 years: pulse rate 61 ± 0.9.

	16 years: average female weight 120lb., height 64in.
	16 years: average male weight 136.4lb., height 68 1/2in.
	16 years: the percent of (male) adult value of thigh 93%, calf 94%, foot 95%, upper arm 95%, forearm 95%, hand 95%.
	16 years: muscle width, arm + calf 13.5cm.
	16 1/2 years: average female weight 120lb., height 64in.
	16 1/2 years: average male weight 143lb., height 69in.
By the age of 17 years	Physical Milestones:
	17-18 years: pulse rate 60 ± 1.4.
	17 years: average female weight 120lb., height 64in.
	17 years: average male weight 147.4lb., height 69 1/2in.
	17 years: the percent of (male) adult value of thigh 97%, calf 97%, foot 97%, upper arm 97%, forearm 97%, hand 97%.
	17 years: muscle width, arm + calf 14.1 cm.
	17-25 years: third molars (4) [permanent].
	17 1/2 years: average female weight 120lb., height 64in.
	17 1/2 years: average male weight 149.6lb. height 70in.
By the age of 18 years	Physical Milestones:
	18 years: average female weight 120lb., height 64in.
	18 years: average male weight 151.8lb., height 70in.
	18 years: the percent of (male) adult value of thigh 100%, calf 100%, foot 100%, upper arm 100%, forearm 100%, hand 100%.
	18 years: muscle width, arm + calf 14.4 cm.
Above Age Eighteen – Adolescence	Physical Milestones:
	19-22 years: average female weight 120lb., height 64in.
	19-22 years: average male weight 154lb.,

	height 70in.
Summary	<ul><li>between birth and 1 years the child is called an infant;</li><li>between 1 and 3 years the child is called a toddler;</li><li>between 3 and 5 years the child is called a preschooler;</li><li>between 6 and 12 years the child is referred to as a school age child; and</li><li>between 12-18 years: the child is called an adolescent.</li></ul>

Explaining the difference between the sequence of development and the rate of development and why the difference is important.

This is important in order to understand 'why children are different but develop in the same sequence', yet there are strengths and weaknesses, which are seen in each child. For instance, Child A may have more physical abilities and Child B may have more communication abilities.

LEARNING OUTCOME 2

UNDERSTANDING THE FACTORS THAT INFLUENCE CHILDREN AND YOUNG PEOPLE'S DEVELOPMENT AND HOW THESE AFFECT MY PRACTICE

There are two types of factors that affect the development of children:

(1) personal and (2) external factors.

Personal factors.

I have had different children in my practice; each child has personal factors. This enables me to understand the personal factors that influence children's and young people's development and how they affect practice. Generally in practice it is acknowledged that such personal factors as genetics, illness, medication, home environment, relationships of parents, parenting, sensory impairment, learning difficulties, disability or, in instances of older children, such things as drugs etc. can impact on the child's or young person's development.

External factors.

Through my work, I have understood the impact of external factors that can affect child development. These factors can include poverty and deprivation, or family environment and background, a household where domestic violence or other type of abuse takes place, or where parents haven't got money to buy books. Also such situations such as a very big or large family and parents haven't got the support and time for all the children. Personal choices also impact on children.

Explanation of how theories of development and frameworks to support development influence practice.

I have compared notes with my tutor's information and websites to understand that there are several theories of development e.g.:

- **Cognitive Development:** Through my work I am able to recognise that children become adapted to circumstances. This is 'cognitive development'. The child recognises, or learns to recognise the familiar and that which they have seen before. Children adapt to their environment (basing my argument on Piaget's development theory that an organism adapts to its environment). Children are born with reflexes that enable them to adapt to environments or situations.

- **Pschoanalytic Development:** Freud's theory of psychoanalytical development consists of:

  1. human behaviour, experience and cognition are largely determined by irrational drives;
  2. those drives are largely unconscious;
  3. attempts to bring those drives into awareness meets defence (resistance) in many different forms;
  4. beside the inherited constitution of personality, one's development is determined by events in early childhood;
  5. conflicts between the conscious view of reality and the unconscious (repressed) material can result in mental disturbances such as neurosis, neurotic traits, anxiety, depression etc.;
  6. the liberation from the effects of the unconscious material is achieved through bringing this material into the consciousness (via e.g. skilled guidance).

- **Humanist Theory:** (e.g. by Jean Watson). This theory is proposed as a childcare/nursing framework, which is philosophically accepted in all health/childcare promotion community approaches. This theory identifies caring, holism and ecology/environment as central to caring for children.

- **Social Learning:** Albert Bandura's Social Learning Theory shows that people learn from one another, via observation, imitation, and modelling. The theory has often been called a bridge between behaviourist and cognitive learning theories because it encompasses attention, memory, and motivation. The necessary conditions for effective modelling include:

  Attention – various factors increase or decrease the amount of a child's attention paid. These include distinctiveness, affective valence, prevalence, complexity and functional value. The child's characteristics (e.g. sensory capacities, arousal level, perceptual set, past reinforcement) affect attention.

  Retention – the child's remembering what s/he paid attention to. This includes symbolic coding, mental images, cognitive organisation, symbolic rehearsal and motor rehearsal.

  Reproduction – the child's reproducing the image, including physical capabilities and self-observation of reproduction.

Motivation – the child's having a good reason to imitate, which includes motives such as past (i.e. traditional behaviourism), promised (imagined incentives) and vicarious (seeing and recalling the reinforced model).

- **Operant Conditioning:** In my practice I call this 'rewarding and unrewarding'. I give stars for good actions or withhold stars for bad action. B.F Skinner believed that the best way to understand behaviour is to look at the causes of a child's action and its consequences. He called this approach operant conditioning, which roughly means changing behaviour by the use of reinforcement, which is given after the desired response. Skinner identified three types of responses or operant that can follow behaviour.

  - Neutral operants: responses from the environment that neither increase nor decrease the probability of a behaviour being repeated.
  - Reinforcers: responses from the environment that increase the probability of a behaviour being repeated. Reinforcers can be either positive or negative.
  - Punishers: responses from the environment that decrease the likelihood of a behaviour being repeated. Punishment weakens behaviour.

- **Behaviourist:** J.B. Watson's theory based on behaviour is that any normal child can be enabled through behaviour to become anything. Behavioural psychology, also known as behaviourism, is a theory of learning based upon the idea that all behaviours are acquired through conditioning. Conditioning occurs through interaction with the environment. According to behaviourism, behaviour can be studied in a systematic and observable manner with no consideration of internal mental states. About Watson's theory of behaviourism I quote the following text from www.psychology.com: 'There are two major types of conditioning:

  (a) **Classical conditioning** is a technique used in behavioural training in which a naturally occurring stimulus is paired with a response. Next, a previously neutral stimulus is paired with the naturally occurring stimulus. Eventually, the previously neutral stimulus comes to evoke the response without the presence of the naturally occurring stimulus. The two elements are then known as the conditioned stimulus and the conditioned response.
  (b) **Operant conditioning** (sometimes referred to as instrumental conditioning) is a method of learning that occurs through rewards and punishments for behaviour. Through operant conditioning, an association is made between a behaviour and a consequence for that behaviour.'

LEARNING OUTCOME 3

UNDERSTANDING HOW TO MONITOR CHILDREN'S AND YOUNG PEOPLE'S DEVELOPMENT AND INTERVENTIONS THAT SHOULD TAKE PLACE IF THIS IS NOT FOLLOWING THE EXPECTED PATTERN.

How I monitor children's development.

I monitor children using different methods through observations, also ensuring that personal checks are made for individual children to ensure that the child is developing along the EYFS guidelines. To monitor, the following should be used:

- assessment frameworks;
- observation;
- standard measurements;

- information from parents/carers/colleagues.

Monitoring tools can include summative and formative assessment methods of children by recording the child's activity and intellectual development. I always record the child's activity and development as part of my feedback to the parents. This monitoring enables both myself and the parents to take appropriate interventions where any deficiency is noticed in the child.

Reasons why children and young people's development may not follow the expected pattern.

I am aware that children's and young people's development may not follow the expected pattern due to various reasons, e.g.:

- children or young people may not have parents;
- poverty;
- broken family;
- birth problems/complications at birth;
- neglect or abuse.

Explanation of how disability may affect development.

Cultural, social, learning needs, and communication are factors that will affect the development of a child with a disability. In addition to restrictions experienced by the child with disability, the child may also:

- be bullied or discriminated against;
- not have the same opportunities as others, e.g. jobs, physical activities;
- cause parents/guardians stress as they may not know how to control the behaviour of the disabled child and may not be able to communicate their feelings as well as they would like to;
- cause sibling rivalry as their sibling(s) may not be receiving the amount of attention they would like and feel neglected. The sibling could also be embarrassed of how their brother/sister is and the condition they are in and may be subject to bullying.

Explanation of how different interventions can promote positive outcomes for children and young people where development is not following the expected pattern.

The child's needs may require intervention from specialist workers singularly or in combination to get positive outcomes. These may include the following:

- social worker;
- speech and language therapist;
- psychologist;
- psychiatrist;
- youth justice system;
- physiotherapist;
- nurse specialist;
- additional learning support;
- assistive technology;

- health visitor.

LEARNING OUTCOME 4

UNDERSTAND THE IMPORTANCE OF EARLY INTERVENTION TO SUPPORT THE SPEECH, LANGUAGE AND COMMUNICATION NEEDS OF CHILDREN AND YOUNG PEOPLE

Analysis of the importance of early identification of speech, language and communication delays and disorders and the potential risks of late recognition.

In any childcare setting early identification of a problem is important because evaluation, diagnosis and treatment can be sought quickly. Early identification of developmental disorders is critical to the well-being of children and their families. It is an integral function of the primary care and an appropriate responsibility of all paediatric health care professionals. Delayed or disordered development can be caused by specific medical conditions and may indicate an increased risk of other medical complications. Delayed or disordered development may also indicate an increased risk of behaviour disorders or associated developmental disorders. Early identification should lead to further evaluation, diagnosis and treatment. Early intervention is available for a wide range of developmental disorders; their prompt identification can spur specific and appropriate therapeutic interventions. Identification of a developmental disorder and its underlying problem may also affect a range of treatment planning, from medical treatment of the child to help the family and school plan their routines for the child/young person.

How multi-agency teams work together to support speech, language and communication.

Once the speech, language and communication needs of children are identified, the various SENCO (Special Educational Needs Coordinators) would come in to intervene using established multi-agency referral methods to assist and support the child and guide the family.

The multi-agency teams may involve the following specialists:

- social worker;
- speech and language therapist;
- psychologist;
- psychiatrist;
- youth justice system;
- physiotherapist;
- nurse specialist;
- additional learning support;
- assistive technology;
- health visitor.

How play and activities are used to support the development of speech, language and communication.

In my setting I have looked after children with learning difficulties and challenging behaviour. My own child has had speech therapy complemented with play and supported classroom intervention due to her autistic learning disability. This has enabled my understanding of how play and activities can be used to support the development of language communication.

Play is activity. Play is a stimulant of all the senses of a child and as a child plays they hear words spoken to them or other people. The child is stimulated to copy or imitate the words associated with the activity they are doing and enjoying. This enables the learning of words and the associated activity.

In this way speech therapy takes place without the strict rigours of therapy, yet used to support the development of speech, language and communication.

LEARNING OUTCOME 5

UNDERSTANDING THE POTENTIAL EFFECTS OF TRANSITION ON CHILDREN'S AND YOUNG PEOPLE'S DEVELOPMENT

How different types of transitions can affect children's and young people's development.

Different types of transitions, e.g. from home to school, change of classes, splitting-up of parents, a new baby in the family, can affect children's behaviour. Some may exhibit such behaviours as not eating or throwing unusual tantrums.

Evaluating the effect on children and young people of having positive relations during periods of transition.

Positive relationships are needed and really important to help with transitions, because this will help to ensure making the routines are kept the same or similar. It is critical for the child or young person to have positive relations during a period of transition. The positive relation will help, e.g. if:

- the transition is emotional. For example where there is bereavement involved, or in instances where a child is entering/leaving care;
- the transition is physical, such as when the child/young person is moving to a new educational establishment, new home/locality, or even from one activity to another;
- the transitional is psychological. For example puberty, or a long-term medical condition;
- the transition is intellectual, such as moving from pre-to-primary school.

CHAPTER 4

LEGISLATION, GUIDELINES, POLICIES AND PROCEDURES

YOU WILL BE UNDERSTANDING THE MAIN LEGISLATION, GUIDELINES, POLICIES AND PROCEDURES FOR SAFEGUARDING CHILDREN AND YOUNG PEOPLE. THEREBY, UNDERSTANDING EXPECTED PATTERNS OF DEVELOPMENT FOR CHILDREN AND YOUNG PEOPLE FROM BIRTH TO 19 YEARS.

UNIT AIM: To provide the knowledge and understanding required to support the safeguarding of children and young people. The unit contains material on e-safety.

LEARNING OUTCOME 1

1.1   Outline of current legislation, guidelines, policies and procedures within the UK affecting the safeguarding of children and young people.

For me, safeguarding includes the Children Act 2004, setting out the process for integrating services to children so that every child can achieve the five *Every Child Matters* outcomes, which are to be healthy, stay safe, enjoy and achieve, make a positive contribution, and achieve economic well-being.

In my work I have over the years familiarised myself with the knowledge and understanding of current legislation, guidelines, policies and procedures affecting the safeguarding of children and young people. I am aware that there is no single piece of legislation that covers child protection in the UK, but rather a lot of laws and guidance that are continually being amended, updated and revoked. In my work, I am now familiar with information that legislation covering child protection can be divided into two main categories: civil law and criminal law.

Civil law is divided into public and private law. Public law puts in place systems and processes in order to minimise the risk of children coming to harm and lays out what action should be taken if children are at risk. Private law deals with family proceedings such as divorce and contact.

Criminal law deals with people who have offended or are at risk of offending against children.

In my setting I constantly refer to notes of my training and my policies in order to make sure that I follow legislation, guidelines, policies and procedures for the safeguarding of children and young people. For instance I ensure inter-agency co-operation, linking my work with the schools where the children in my care go, their GP, social worker etc. I am also able to relate my work with such resourceful organisations as Ofsted, and draw from the history of the establishment of the NSPCC, founded in 1884, to play a key role in influencing legislation to protect children. Here I give an outline of my understanding of current legislation, guidelines, policies and procedures within the UK affecting the safeguarding of children and young people.

The Children and Young Persons Act 1933 is one of the older pieces of child protection legislation, which has parts that are still in force today. It includes a list of offences against children and things to guard against. The Children Act 1989, upon which current child protection system is based, reformed and clarified the existing laws affecting children. It is 'the most comprehensive and far-reaching reform of child law' covering a number of principles. In my setting this helps me so that the most important thing is that a child's welfare is top-most when making any decisions about a child's care. I am also aware that even the law in a court must safeguard the wishes and feelings of the child and shall not make an order unless this is 'better for the child than making no order at all'. In this act it is stated that every effort should be made to preserve the child's home and family links. This act introduced the matter of parental responsibility, which is 'the rights, duties, powers and responsibilities which by law a parent of a child has in relation to the child and his property' (Section 3). The 1989 Act sets out what local authorities and the courts should do to protect the welfare of children, giving them the power of 'duty to investigate if they have reasonable cause to suspect that a child who lives, or is found, in their area is suffering, or is likely to suffer, significant harm' (Section 47).

Local authorities are also charged with a duty to provide 'services for children in need, their families and others' (Section 17). It is Section 31 of the Children Act 1989 that sets out the NSPCC's 'authorised person status', which means the NSPCC has the power to apply directly for a court order if it believes a child is suffering or likely to suffer significant harm. The Children Act 1989 defines 'harm' as ill-treatment (including sexual abuse and non-physical forms of ill-treatment) or the impairment of health (physical or mental) or development (physical, intellectual, emotional, social or behavioural) (Section 31). *The Framework for the Assessment of Children in Need and Their Families* (DH, 2000) is non-statutory guidance, but provides children's carers or professionals with a systematic way of identifying children in need and deciding the best way of helping those children and their families. The guide for anyone working with children is known as *What To Do If You're Worried A Child Is Being Abused* (DfES 2006). This outlines the child protection processes. The Children Act 1989 legislates for England and Wales. The current guidance for Wales is *Safeguarding Children: Working Together under the Children Act* (2004).

The United Nations Convention on the Rights of the Child 1989 (UN, 1989) was ratified by the UK on 16 December 1991. It includes the right to protection from abuse, the right to express their views and have them listened to and the right to care and services for disabled children or children living away from home.

The Human Rights Act 1998 incorporates the European Convention on Human Rights into UK law. Whilst it does not specifically mention children's rights, children are covered by this legislation as they are persons in the eyes of the law, just as adults are. The Education Act 2002 includes a provision (Section 175) requiring school governing bodies, local education authorities and further education institutions to make arrangements to safeguard and promote the welfare of children. Section 120 of the Adoption and Children Act 2002 amends the Children Act 1989 by expanding the definition of 'harm' to include witnessing domestic violence.

After 8-year old Victoria Climbié died in 2000, the government needed to introduce new legislation and guidance to improve child protection systems in England. This resulted in the *Keeping Children Safe* report (DfES, 2003) and the *Every Child Matters* green paper (DfES, 2003), which in turn led to the Children Act 2004. The Children Act 2004 does not replace or even amend much of the Children Act 1989. It sets out the process for integrating services to children so that every child can achieve the five *Every Child Matters* outcomes: to be healthy, stay safe, enjoy and achieve, make a positive contribution, and achieve economic well-being.

Local authorities and their partners (including the police, health service providers and the youth justice system) have to co-operate in promoting the well-being of children and young people and to make arrangements to safeguard and promote the welfare of children. It allows Local Safeguarding Children Boards to be able to investigate and review all child deaths in their area (a requirement laid out in the *Working Together to Safeguard Children* statutory guidance).

I am aware that this act revises the legislation on physical punishment by making it an offence to hit a child if it causes mental harm or leaves a lasting mark on the skin (Section 58), repealing the section of the Children and Young Persons Act 1933, which provided parents with the defence of 'reasonable chastisement'. The Children and Adoption Act 2006 gives courts more flexible powers to facilitate child contact and enforce contact orders when separated parents are in dispute. The Children and Young Persons Act 2008 legislates for the recommendations in the *Care Matters* white paper (DfES, 2007) to provide high quality care and services for children in care. It places a duty on registrars to notify the Local Safeguarding Children Board of all child deaths. The Borders, Citizenship and Immigration Act 2009 places a duty on the UK Border Agency to safeguard and promote children's welfare (Section 55), bringing them in line with other public bodies that have contact with children. The Apprenticeships, Skills, Children and Learning Act 2009 legislates for there to be two lay members from the local community sitting on each Local Safeguarding Children Board. The Sex Offenders Act 1997 requires sex offenders convicted or cautioned on or after 1 September 1997 to notify the police of their names and addresses and of any subsequent changes (known colloquially as the Sex Offenders Register).

I made an indirect contribution when I set up a charity to be known as Agency for Culture and Change Management (ACCM), which lobbied along with others to get the House of Lords to pass appropriate legislation against female genital mutilation. The Female Genital Mutilation Act 2003 extended the existing legislation criminalising female genital mutilation in the UK by making it an offence for UK nationals or permanent UK residents to take a girl abroad, or to help others to take a girl abroad, to carry out female genital mutilation, even in countries where the practice is legal. The Domestic Violence, Crime and Victims Act 2004 closes a legal loophole (whereby defendants in murder and manslaughter cases could escape conviction by claiming each other had killed the child), by creating a new offence of 'causing or allowing the death of a child or vulnerable adult'. The offence establishes a new criminal responsibility for members of a household where they know that a child or vulnerable adult is at significant risk of serious harm.

The Home Office published a circular (16/2005) *Guidance On Offences Against Children* (Home Office, 2005), which contained a consolidated list of offences for all agencies to use in identifying 'a person identified as presenting a risk, or potential risk, to children'. It also discusses the use of the terms 'Schedule One' offenders and offences. The Serious Organised Crime and Police Act 2005 set up the framework for the UK-wide Child Exploitation and Online Protection (CEOP) Centre to be created. It also includes provisions for improving the vetting system to stop adults who pose a risk from working with children (Section 163). The Safeguarding Vulnerable Groups Act 2006, established a new centralised vetting and barring scheme for people working with children (following the 2002 murders of 10-year-olds Jessica Chapman and Holly Wells). The Forced Marriage Act (Civil Protection) 2007, gives courts the power to make orders to protect the victim or potential victim of a forced marriage and help remove them from that situation. The Criminal Justice and Immigration Act 2008 ensures that people who commit sex offences against children abroad can face prosecution in the UK, even if that offence is not illegal in the foreign country in which it was committed.

1.2 Explaining child protection within the wider concept of safeguarding children and young people.

In my setting the wider concept of safeguarding children and young people centres on child protection. I always ensure that I know the background information of where a child comes from. As a childminder I would take into account the environment. For example, how I safeguard children when my own children are at the home in which I also look after the children I care for. Child protection includes keeping children safe from risk of danger or harm. This concept helps a childminder like me to be able to use the following tools to achieve and implement safeguarding, which leads to well-being:

(a) In September 2003 the government produced the *Every Child Matters* green paper to maximise opportunities and minimise risks for all children, young people and their families, and the Children Act 2004 came into force on 1 October 2005.

(b) The *Every Child Matters* green paper identified the following five outcomes as key to the well-being of children and young people: i. Physical and mental health and emotional well-being ('to be healthy'); ii. Protection from harm and neglect ('to stay safe'); iii. Education training and recreation ('to enjoy and achieve'); iv. The contribution made by them to society ('to make a positive contribution'); v. Social and economic well-being ('to achieve economic well-being').

(c) The Children Act 2004 includes Section 10 – a duty to co-operate with the Children's Services Authority (in my case Sheffield City Council) to improve the well-being of children and young people. This is through what care I provide in my setting.

(d) The concept of safeguarding duties relates to children and young people from pre-birth to the age of 19, or 25 if the young person has a learning or other disability. The fact that a child has become 16 years of age and is living independently, working, is in further education, is a member of the armed forces, is in hospital or prison does not change their status or entitlement to services or protection under the Children Act 2004.

(e) The concept of safeguarding is to provide a framework for the safeguarding of children and young people and is consistent with and complements the policies and procedures of my setting. My policies cover all activities and services provided by the setting including my assistant and anyone who come into contact with children and young people, whilst going about their everyday duties. It is also considered that the policy could act as an appropriate reference guide for use by those councillors whose particular role may involve them coming into contact with children and young people.

1.3 Analysing how national and local guidelines, policies and procedures for safeguarding affect day to day work with children and young people.

In my setting, national and local guidelines, policies and procedures for safeguarding affect day to day work with children and young people. This happens in how my policies are implemented and how I use the guidelines. A childminder like myself is at the frontline, delivering the national and local guidelines. For example, I ensure that health and safety procedures are followed, I implement my policies of medication, and comply with the accident guidelines, food, fire drills, etc. I carry out monitoring and child development plans. All these contribute to the overall performance of my duty of care in my setting to ensure the achievement of national and local guidelines, policies and procedures for safeguarding affecting my day to day work with children and young people.

1.4 Why inquiries and serious case reviews are required and how the sharing of the findings informs practice.

In my setting I observe and monitor each child and if I find cause to think that there is a case of abuse or neglect, I would share information appropriately with the relevant person. I carry out observations and case reviews for every child in my setting. As a childminder I have constantly read the relevant information for safeguarding children and young people. I am aware that a serious case review will always be undertaken when a child dies, and when abuse or neglect is the suspected cause of a child's death. The Local Safeguarding Children Board (LSCB) will also consider whether a serious case review should be conducted where a child has been seriously injured through abuse or neglect or been subjected to a serious sexual assault. The reviews are done to see what areas can be improved. For example the case of Victoria Climbié resulted in an inquiry which gave us the Children Act 2004. Eight-year old Victoria Climbié died in 2000, so the government had to respond to the challenges posed and introduced new legislation and guidance to improve child protection systems in England. This resulted in the *Keeping Children Safe* report (DfES, 2003) and the *Every Child Matters* green paper (DfES, 2003), which in turn led to the Children Act 2004. The Children Act 2004 does not replace or even amend much of the Children Act 1989. It sets out the process for integrating services to children so that every child can achieve the five *Every Child Matters* outcomes: be healthy, stay safe, enjoy and achieve, make a positive contribution, and achieve economic well-being. Local authorities and their partners (including the police, health service providers and the youth justice system) have to co-operate in promoting the well-being of children and young people and to make arrangements to safeguard and promote welfare of children. It makes Local Safeguarding Children Boards able to investigate and review all child deaths in their area (a requirement laid out in the *Working Together to Safeguard Children* statutory guidance). I am aware that this act revises legislation on physical punishment by making it an offence to hit a child if it causes mental harm or leaves a lasting mark on the skin (Section 58), repealing the section of the Children and Young Persons Act 1933, which provided parents with the defence of 'reasonable chastisement'. The Children and Adoption Act 2006 gives courts more flexible powers to facilitate child contact and enforce contact orders when separated parents are in dispute. Therefore, to learn lessons and put in place improvements to ensure safeguarding of children and young people is why inquiries and serious case reviews are required and the findings shared to inform practice.

1.5 Explanation of how the processes used by one's own work setting or service comply with legislation that covers data protection, information handling and sharing.

In my setting I have several policies, among which is the Confidentiality Policy, which enables me to follow guidelines on implementing a process of service that complies with legislation to cover data protection, information handling and sharing. On confidentiality I use the following:

Statement of intent – I have this as an introduction to my process:

It is the intention of my setting to respect the privacy of children and their parents and carers, while ensuring that they access high quality care and play opportunities in our setting.

Aim – At the outset of registering new children I explain to parents and carers that:

I aim to ensure that all parents and carers can share their information in the confidence that it will only be used to enhance the welfare of their children.

I explain that my process is to enable me meet the requirements of the Human Rights Act 1998 with regard to protecting the individual's rights to a private family life, home and correspondence. In my setting, my only justification to interfere with this 'right' is where I believe that a child may be at risk of significant harm, to prevent a crime or disorder.

I meet the requirements of the Data Protection Act 1998 with regard to the information I keep about families, including how I gather it, store it and use it. My procedures enable us to meet these requirements.

In my setting I have regard to the Common Law Duty of Confidentiality and only share information with other professionals or agencies on a 'need to know' basis, with consent from parents, or without their consent in specified circumstances relating to safeguarding children.

Personal records – These include registration and admission forms; signed consents; correspondence concerning the child or family; reports or minutes from meetings concerning the child from other agencies; an ongoing record of relevant contact with parents; observations by myself or my staff, i.e. my assistant on any confidential matter involving the child, such as developmental concerns or child protection matters, incident and accident logs; care plans; behaviour plans, etc.

These confidential records are stored in a lockable file or cabinet and are kept secure by myself as the person in charge in a suitably safe place. Parents have access, in accordance with the access to records procedure, to the files and records of their own child(ren) but do not have access to information about any other child(ren). I and my staff will not discuss personal information given by parents with others, except where it affects planning for the child's needs. In providing induction to my assistant I include an awareness of the importance of confidentiality in the role of the key person.

Information sharing concerning child protection issues – There are times when we are required to share information about a child or their family. These are when there are concerns a child is or may be suffering significant harm; there are concerns about 'serious harm to adults' (such as domestic violence or other matters affecting the welfare of parents). I explain to families about our duty to share information for the above reasons. Where I have concerns, I would normally gain consent from families to share these. This does not have to be in writing, but a written record will be made that verbal consent has been given. For good practice I ensure I have them in writing as a signed authority. I do not seek consent from parents to share information where I believe that a child, or a vulnerable adult, may be endangered by seeking to gain consent. For example, where I have cause to believe a parent may try to cover up abuse or threaten a child. Where I take a decision to share information without consent it is recorded in the child's file and the reason clearly stated. Where evidence to support my concerns is not clear I may seek advice from the local social care agency or the NSPCC. I only share relevant information that is accurate, factual, non-judgemental and up to date.

Information sharing concerning a child's development – In my setting I am committed to the development of the children attending. With the introduction of the Early Years Foundation Stage (EYFS) and a higher emphasis on providing high quality care through partnership and collaboration, I am always observing the development of EYFS children during their time at my setting. With the permission of parents I would be sharing this with other services that may be involved in the care of children such as schools and external support agencies. In my setting I am also committed to working with children with additional needs. To achieve this I, with parental permission, gather and share information between services such as schools, inclusion team, health care professionals and other outside agencies. The information is used to provide a consistency of care and offer support suited to a child's needs.

Other records – Issues to do with the employment of my staff, i.e. my assistant, whether paid or unpaid, remain confidential to me as the person directly involved with making personnel decisions. After meeting the necessary Ofsted guidelines, if I were to use a volunteer or a placement of a student undertaking recognised qualifications and training to do observing within the setting, I would ensure that they are informed of my confidentiality policy and required to respect it.

Access to personal records – In my setting parents may request access to any records held on their child and family following the procedure below:

- Any request to see the child's personal file by a parent or person with parental responsibility must be made in writing to me.

- I, as the key person, will inform my assistant of the request and will send a written acknowledgement.

- My setting aims to provide access to requested records within 14 days, although this may be extended.

- I prepare the file for viewing.

- All third parties are written to, stating that a request for disclosure has been received and asking for their permission to disclose to the person requesting it. A copy of these letters is retained on the file.

- 'Third parties' include all family members who may be referred to in the records.

- 'Third parties' also includes workers from any other agency, including social care, the health authority, etc. (I am aware that it is usual for agencies to refuse consent to disclose, preferring the individual to go directly to them.)

- When all the consents/refusals to disclose have been received these are attached to the copy of the request letter.

- A photocopy of the complete file is taken as a record.

- I as the key person will go through the file and remove any information that a third party has refused consent to disclose. This is best done with a thick black marker, to score through every reference to the third party and information they have added to the file.

- What remains is the information recorded by myself in the setting, detailing the work initiated and followed in relation to confidential matters. This is called the 'clean copy'.

- The 'clean copy' is photocopied for the parents who are then invited into my setting to discuss the contents. The file will never be given to the parent, but should be shared by myself, so that it can be explained.

- Legal advice may be sought before sharing a file, especially where the parent has possible grounds for litigation against my setting or another (third party) agency.

- All the undertakings above are subject to the paramount commitment of my setting, which is to the safety and well-being of the child(ren).

LEARNING OUTCOME 2

UNDERSTANDING THE IMPORTANCE OF WORKING IN PARTNERSHIP WITH OTHER ORGANISATIONS TO SAFEGUARD CHILDREN AND YOUNG PEOPLE

2.1 Explaining the importance of safeguarding children and young people.

In my setting the most important factor around which all things happen is the importance of safeguarding children and young people. This is important to me because I am responsible and the children and young people need protection to be safe. Therefore, in my setting I abide by information and guidance as stated in the Children Acts 1989 and 2004 respectively; a child is anyone who has not yet reached their 18th birthday. 'Children' therefore means 'children and young people' throughout. I am aware that the fact that a child has reached 16 years of age, is living independently or is in further education, is a member of the armed forces, is in hospital or in custody in the secure estate for children and young people, does not change his or her status or entitlement to services or protection under the Children Act 1989.

In my setting it is important that safeguarding is set up to assist or care for those who are particularly vulnerable, perhaps because of their age, physical or mental ability, or ill health. Whilst the principal goal of my setting is to care, I have to demonstrate equality of opportunity for all children. Therefore it is necessary to remove, or at least reduce, the barriers that impede care and development or learning. It is about making sure that the right people are recruited as carers and volunteers to work with young people and given DBS (Disclosure and Barring Service, formerly CRB) checks. Also, it is important to create a culture of openness and honesty, and to protect young people from harm and danger without smothering their potential and need for challenge and excitement. Plus, I ensure that my assistant knows the policy and procedures. I achieve this by adopting a child-centred approach in my provision.

2.2 Explaining the importance of a child- or young people-centred approach.

I work clearly to ensure that the children and young people are central to what I offer.

The importance of a child- or young person-centred approach is to understand that every child is different. The national framework of *Every Child Matters* was set up to support the joining up of services to ensure that every child can achieve the five *Every Child Matters* outcomes. Support is offered to children to enable them to be healthy, stay safe, enjoy and achieve, make a positive contribution and achieve economic well-being. All services aimed at children or young people are based around the planning and meeting of the individual needs. Children's wishes should be taken into account during decision making to give them a sense of belonging and not to be made to feel as though its them who's to blame. This should be done in a sensitive manner and they should be listened to, to find out how they are feeling and what they would like. As a result of safeguarding practices in my setting, I have a child-centred approach, which enables me and my assistant to plan and deliver activities for the children that focus on what their care, development and learning needs are. I ensure that the environment is set to enable the child to learn and understand what is being done or taught. In my setting any activity must be in the interest of the child(ren). This allows the child(ren) to stay focussed, and reach their full potential/goals. It can lead to the children developing confidence in what they are learning and their self-esteem improves over the years as they move up in learning. A child-centred approach is about focusing on what the child needs and wants.

2.3 Explaining what is meant by partnership working in the context of safeguarding.

In my setting I have found partnership working essential to the context of safeguarding. Therefore, the importance of partnership working to safeguard is that agencies and other professionals need to work together; it starts with government legislation right through to local working including childminders. Each professional or agency will have a different role of expertise so vulnerable children will need coordinated help from health, education, children's social care and the voluntary sector, and often the justice services so it is important that there is good communication within all the different services available. Safeguarding and promoting the welfare of children depends on effective partnership working between agencies and professionals, all people involved in the welfare of a child have a duty to safeguard them, including the police, health visitors, GPs, hospitals, childminders, nurseries, schools, after school clubs, leisure groups such as football, swimming, brownies, social worker, family, friends, neighbours and the local community. These are all responsible for safeguarding our children and young people and it is important that we all work and communicate together. The common assessment framework provides a way for early intervention for children before it reaches crisis point. It is a shared assessment and planning framework for all communication and that information is shared between different professionals and organisations. The assessment framework centres on child safeguarding and promoting welfare for practitioners who work with children to use.

2.4 Describing the roles and responsibilities of the different organisations that may be involved when a child or young person has been abused or harmed.

I have a duty as a childminder to ensure the safety of children and young people in my care. I am prepared to work with other agencies who also have a role. Therefore I would describe the roles of other agencies as follows:

Social services roles and responsibilities are:

- to provide support for vulnerable children and families.

NSPCC (National Society for the Prevention of Cruelty to Children) roles and responsibilities are:

- to provide support for children and families in situations such as domestic violence or abuse;
- to work with different organisations, e.g. social services, police, family protection, education and health services;
- to provide support via telephone line to home-based childcare workers on whether to refer a situation to social services.

A health visitor's roles and responsibilities are:

- to have crucial skills in protecting children from harm and abuse, as they are one of the first to recognise children who are likely to be abused or neglected;
- to play a big part in all stages of a child protection process including case reviews;
- to support the health of babies and children under the age of five;
- to have contact with many multi-agencies and support the work of the Local Safeguarding Children's Board (LSCB);
- to be trained to a high level to recognise any risks that the child might be in;
- to visit the parents' home so they will gather information such as signs and symptoms that will enable a health visitor to start the process of reporting abuse or neglect. The health visitor will need to have access to ongoing contact with the family if abuse or neglect is suspected;
- to use their own judgement on when to share information with other agencies;
- to support and guide parents of young children;
- to provide developmental checks on under fives.

General Practitioners' (GPs) roles and responsibilities are:

- to maintain their skills in recognising if a child is being abused or neglected;
- to follow all correct procedures if abuse or neglect is suspected;
- to have regular training and update their training when necessary.

Probation officer roles and responsibilities are:

- to supervise offenders to help support them not to re-offend and to protect others from harm;
- to supervise a large amount of offenders that have been identified as presenting potential risk of harm to children and also to protect families of their own, who might be exposed to criminal or anti-social behaviour;
- to liaise with Multi-Agency Public Protection Arrangements (MAPPA) such as safeguarding children, procedures covering sex offenders, domestic abuse, child protection procedures.

Police roles and responsibilities are:

- to prevent crime and disorder and protect all individuals;
- to adhere to legislation to protect children. Children have the right to be fully protected (Children Act 2004 to safeguard and promote the welfare of children);
- to be sensitive in their investigations so the police investigate and work with other organisations such as children's social care to gather information needed;
- to investigate child abuse cases (they have specialist training for this, Child Abuse Investigation Units (CAIUs));
- to access information through IMPACT Nominal Index (INI), which enables them to get accurate information very quickly (including child protection, domestic violence, crime);
- to gather information and work with other agencies in case of criminal proceedings against suspected child abusers. All information will be passed on to the CPS (Criminal Prosecution Services);
- to use their powers to enter premises to ensure that children are immediately protected against significant harm.

School roles and responsibilities are:

- to create and maintain a safe learning environment;
- to identify any concerns and to act upon this information;
- to attend child protection and first aid courses. In cases of special schools staff should have appropriate training on medical issues on safeguarding all children;
- to protect children from harm and abuse (including bullying/cyber bullying);
- to help meet the health needs of children with medical conditions and provide accurate information on the child's educational needs;
- to designate a person that has had specific training to deal with child protection issues;
- to be in contact with multi-agencies to support the child and attend case conferences;
- to have a key role in referring children and providing information to the police for future criminal proceedings that might take place under child protection issues, under the Children Act 1989;
- to manage risks appropriately such as use of the Internet etc.;

- to provide policies and procedures to protect children; child protection, physical contact, safeguarding, risk assessments, outings, injuries, illnesses and emergencies.

SENCO: Schools have a specially designated coordinator for special needs requirements of children and are able to liaise with the wider support agencies as appropriate to support both parents and the children. (I regularly draw from this service due to the special needs of my child who has autism.)

Psychiatric/psychology service roles and responsibilities are:

- to provide support for children who have experienced abuse or harm. They also provide help and support to clarify diagnoses for children with special needs.

School nurses roles and responsibilities are:

- to have regular contact with children from the ages of 5-19;
- to be lead professionals for the CAF (Common Assessment Framework);
- to provide a role in delivering the Healthy Child Programme. They access children and implement their needs such as individual or group needs;
- to work with parents or carers in the care and treatment of vulnerable children. They can provide support to the families to help them achieve better parental skills.

LEARNING OUTCOME 3

UNDERSTANDING THE IMPORTANCE OF ENSURING CHILDREN'S AND YOUNG PEOPLE'S SAFETY AND PROTECTION IN THE WORK SETTING

3.1 Explaining why it is important to ensure children and young people are protected from harm within the work setting.

Within my setting it is important to ensure that children and young people are protected from harm. This is because parents entrust practitioners like myself with their child(ren). As a parent I know that parents would feel reluctant to leave their precious ones in anyone's care if they had doubts about safety.

As a childcare practitioner I uphold the parent's trust to ensure the children and young people remain safe and free from harm, as well as making steady personal development. I am vigilant and aware that failing to uphold this trust is a breach of 'professional values'. In my setting I, and my assistant as staff within the setting, have clear responsibilities to keep children safe and protect children from harm and promote the welfare of children. The process I follow to deliver on safety and freedom from harm is through my policies. That is why I have policies and procedures, as it is my duty to make sure children are not put at risk of, e.g. injury from the surroundings of play equipment, abuse, neglect, bullying or anything at all. I start from the observation that children do not have the capacity, knowledge or know how to protect themselves so I, as the childminder and adult carer, have a duty to help them achieve this. I have learnt a lot from my autistic child, who has no sense of danger and expresses no fear of injury. Such special learning needs must be taken into account when observing to inform care planning in order to protect children and young people from harm. I also put into practice my policies and procedures such as risk assessments, safeguarding (child protection), food hygiene and maintaining children's safety and security on the premises such as cleaning floors and equipment, ensuring locks on drawers and cupboards, maintaining play items and ensuring healthy eating as well as a clean environment of food preparation to avoid food poisoning and cross infection. For instance, I do not allow outside shoes to be brought into areas where babies crawl on the floor. This is why and how I, in my setting, find that it is important to ensure children and young people are protected from harm within the environment.

3.2 Explaining policies and procedures that are in place to protect children and young people and adults who work with them.

1. At present my setting is operated by myself and one assistant. However, in the case of any establishment small or large, all persons employed by a facility that cares for children are under an obligation implied in their contract of employment to give honest and faithful service to their employer. This includes an obligation not to disclose to external sources any trade secrets or confidential information acquired during the course of employment or act in a manner that will undermine the mutual trust and confidence on which the employment relationship is based. I have read information on the Public Interest Disclosure Act 1998, which complements those obligations by providing protection to employees for disclosure made without malice and in good faith of certain specific confidential information to a third party in defined circumstances. These are outlined below in Paragraph 3. The purpose of this policy is to provide a means by which I, as a childminder, and my assistant or a parent or anyone else are enabled to raise concerns with the appropriate authorities if we have reasonable grounds for believing there is serious malpractice within the setting. In my setting I therefore encourage anyone to raise matters of concern responsibly through the procedures laid down in this policy statement.

Scope of the policy

2. In my setting I have a Whistle-Blower Policy, which is designed to deal with concerns raised in relation to the specific issues that are in the public interest and are detailed in Paragraph 3 below, and which fall outside the scope of other policies and procedures. The policy will not apply to personal grievances concerning an individual's terms and conditions of employment, or other aspects of the working relationship, complaints of bullying or harassment, or disciplinary matters. Such complaints will be dealt with under existing procedures on grievance, bullying and harassment, discipline and misconduct.

3. The policy may deal with specific concerns which are in the public interest and may include:

    *   a criminal offence;
    *   failure to comply with legal obligations or with the policies and regulations of the setting;
    *   financial or non-financial maladministration or malpractice or impropriety or fraud;
    *   academic or professional malpractice;
    *   a risk to the health or safety of any individual;
    *   environmental damage;
    *   a miscarriage of justice;
    *   improper conduct or unethical behaviour;
    *   attempts to suppress or conceal any information relating to any of the above.

If, in the course of an investigation, any concern raised in relation to the above matters appears to the investigator to relate more appropriately to grievance, bullying or harassment, or discipline, those procedures will be invoked.

Who can raise a concern?

4. Anyone can raise a concern. Parents, a member of staff, or a member of the public who has a reasonable belief that there is serious malpractice relating to any of the protected matters specified in Paragraph 3 above, may raise a concern under the procedure I have detailed in Paragraph 6 below. The issues raised under the protection list may relate to another member of staff, a group of staff, the individual's own child/work or another part of the setting. Concerns must be raised without malice and in good faith, and the individual must reasonably believe that the information disclosed, and any allegations contained in it, are substantially true. The disclosure must not be made for purposes of personal gain, and in all the circumstances it must be reasonable to make the disclosure. I, as a childminder responsible for my setting, will ensure that any individual, parent or my assistant who is a member of staff who makes a disclosure in such circumstances will not be penalised or suffer any adverse treatment for doing so. However, a member of staff who does not act in good faith or makes an allegation without having reasonable grounds for believing it to be substantially true, or makes it for purposes of personal gain, or makes it maliciously may be subject to disciplinary proceedings.

5. In my setting I would recommend that in view of the protection afforded to a member of staff raising a bona fide concern, it is preferable if that individual puts his/her name to any disclosure. The identity of the person raising the matter will be kept confidential, if so requested, for as long as possible provided that this is compatible with a proper investigation. Anonymous complaints are not covered by this procedure, but may be reported, investigated or acted upon as the person receiving the complaint sees fit (including the use of this procedure), having regard to the seriousness of the issue raised, the credibility of the complaint, the prospects of being able to investigate the matter, and fairness to any individual mentioned in the complaint.

Procedure

6. Initial step – normally any disclosure about a protected matter should be made in the first instance to:

The named child carer (childminder).

If the disclosure is about my setting, myself or my assistant, the complainant may raise the concern with the local authority or Ofsted.

The person to whom the disclosure is made will decide whether the matter should be dealt with under this procedure. If s/he considers that the matter should be dealt with under a different procedure, s/he will advise the person making the disclosure as to the appropriate steps which should be taken.

Process

7. The person to whom the disclosure is made will normally consider the information and decide whether there is a prima facie case to answer. S/he will decide whether an investigation should be conducted and what form it should take. This will depend on the nature of the matter raised and may be:

- investigated internally;
- referred to the external auditors e.g. Ofsted (for those working in the UK);
- the subject of independent enquiry.

Some matters following investigation, will need to be referred to the relevant outside body, e.g. the police, Ofsted, local authority. If the person to whom the disclosure is made decides not to proceed with an investigation, the decision will be explained as fully as possible to the individual who raised the concern. It is then open to the individual to make the disclosure again either to another of the persons specified in the paragraph above.

Investigation

8. In my setting my policy requires that any investigation will be conducted as sensitively and speedily as possible. The person raising the complaint will be notified of the intended timetable for the investigation. The person to whom the disclosure is made may authorise an initial investigation to establish the relevant facts. The investigation may be conducted by me internally or by another person. The investigator will report his/her findings to the person to whom the disclosure was made, who will then decide if there is a case to answer and what procedure to follow. This may include taking steps with the competent authority to set up a special independent investigation or reference to some external authority, such as the police, for further investigation. The decision may be that the matter would be more appropriately handled under existing procedures for grievance, bullying and harassment, or discipline. Where disclosure is made the person or persons against whom it is made will be told at an early stage of it and of the evidence supporting it, and they will be allowed to respond. The individual making the disclosure will be informed of what action is to be taken. Should an investigation or referral lead the appropriate authority to conclude that there has been a breach of discipline, the person, either myself or my assistant may, in addition to any civil or criminal proceedings, be subject to disciplinary action in accordance with the appropriate laws protecting children and young people.

Records

9. An official written record will be kept of each stage of the procedure (see also Paragraph 10 below).

Reporting of outcomes

10. In my setting a report of all disclosures and subsequent actions taken will be made by myself as the person deciding on the issues. This record should be signed by myself and the person who made the disclosure, and dated. Where appropriate the formal record need not identify the person making the disclosure, but in such a case that person will be required to sign a document confirming that the complaint has been investigated. Such reports will normally be retained for at least five years. In all cases a report of the outcome will be made in my Ofsted self-assessment, and I may also refer the report on as appropriately if necessary.

Advice for staff raising a concern

11. In my setting I, as any childminder, should acknowledge the difficult choice a member of staff, a parent or any other person may have to make in raising a concern, as the issues that prompt the concern are likely to be complex. How the member of staff proceeds with his or her concern will vary from situation to situation. The following advice is recommended if a member of staff wishes to make a disclosure:

    - Make any objections to illegal, unsafe or unethical practices promptly so as to avoid any misinterpretation of the motives for doing so.

- Focus on the issues and proceed in a tactful manner to avoid unnecessary personal antagonism that might distract attention from solving the problem.
- Be accurate in his/her observations and claims and keep formal records documenting relevant events.
- The person raising the concern may also wish to seek independent legal advice.
- There may be complaints of retaliation as a result of disclosure.

12. I, as childminder, accept that my setting has an obligation to ensure that staff or anyone who makes a disclosure without malice and in good faith are protected, regardless of whether or not the concern raised is upheld. A member of staff who has made a disclosure and who feels that, as a result, he or she has suffered adverse treatment should submit a formal complaint under the grievance procedure as set out in the relevant way, detailing what has been done to him/her. If it appears that there are reasonable grounds for making the complaint, the onus will be on the person against whom the complaint of adverse treatment has been made to show that the actions complained of were not taken in retaliation for the disclosure.

13. Where it is determined that there is a prima facie case that a member of staff has suffered adverse treatment, harassment or victimisation as a result of his/her disclosure, I am informed by my union, NCMA (now called PACEY, the Professional Association for Childcare and Early Years), that a further investigation may take place and disciplinary action may be taken against the perpetrator in accordance with the relevant procedure.

External disclosure

14. In my setting, if, having exhausted this procedure, a member of staff or the complainant is not satisfied with my responses as a childminder and reasonably believes that the information disclosed, and any allegation contained in it, are substantially true, s/he is at liberty to take the matter further by raising it with certain bodies or persons such as:

- a Member of Parliament;
- a legal adviser;
- other bodies or persons (if any) prescribed by the Secretary of State under Section 43F of the Employment Protection Act 1996, as amended by Section 1 of the Public Interest Disclosure Act 1998.

15. In my setting a member of staff, a parent, or a member of the public who makes an external complaint in good faith to any prescribed body or person after exhausting the setting's procedure, will be protected against victimisation or other adverse treatment. In my setting I have developed several policies, which make 'the procedure' in order to protect children and young people and the adults who work with them, i.e. myself and my assistant. As a childminder practitioner working with children I believe that children flourish when their personal, social and emotional needs are met and where they have clear boundaries to follow for their expected behaviour. My procedures and policies are aiming to enable me to do the right things regarding:

- working in an open and transparent way;
- listening to children and young people;
- exercising the duty of care;
- responding positively when concerns of whistle-blowing happen and to protect the whistle-blower;

- acknowledging my role as one in a position of trust;
- propriety and behaviour/conduct;
- physical care;
- intimate personal care;
- off-site visits;
- photographs and video recording;
- sharing concerns and recording/reporting incidents.

I use my policies so that all children in my care should learn to consider the views and feelings, needs and rights, of others and the impact that their behaviour has on people, places and objects. My assistant and I as staff members will help the children develop these skills with support, encouragement, teaching and setting a good example. In my setting the principles that underpin how we achieve positive and considerate behaviour exist within the programme for promoting personal, social and emotional development.

Positive behaviour procedures

In my setting I am the named person who has overall responsibility for supporting personal, social and emotional development within the setting. This will include challenging or unwanted behaviour. All information is shared between my assistant, the co-worker. As the named person I am required to keep up-to-date with current legislation, research new information on promoting positive behaviour and handling children's behaviour and where it might be necessary to get additional support. I am required to provide my assistant with up-to-date training when necessary on how to support personal, social and emotional development (in-house training or external courses). My assistant, any volunteers and placement students, if any, must provide a positive model of behaviour by treating all persons involved with friendliness, care and courtesy. In my setting I ensure that we work in partnership with parents/carers; they are kept regularly informed about their child's behaviour by their key person. We observe children and use records to help us understand the cause and decide jointly with parents/carers how to respond appropriately.

POLICIES TO USE IN A CHILDCARE SETTING.

THE FOLLOWING ARE SOME OF THE POLICIES TO HAVE AND USE:

Policies keep changing. More and more, new policies are imposed or developed according to either need or new dangers emerging. Policies help to protect children and those who work with them. There is no order of priority as all policies complement one another in safeguarding children and people working in a childcare setting.

1) Fire Safety and Emergency Evacuation Policy;
2) Equal Opportunities Policy;
3) Data Protection Policy;
4) Security against Abduction and Intruders Policy;
5) Record Keeping and Documentation Policy;
6) Physical Environment Policy;
7) Play Policy;
8) Accident and Incident Policy;
9) Meeting Policy;
10) No Smoking Policy;
11) Outdoor Play Policy;
12) Partnership with Parents and Carers Policy;

13) Food Hygiene Policy;
14) Working in Partnership with Schools and Other Agencies Policy;
15) Lost and Missing Children Policy;
16) Maintenance and Replacement of Toys and Equipment Policy;
17) Arrivals and Departures Policy;
18) Behaviour Management Policy;
19) Healthy Eating Policy;
20) Induction Policy;
21) Anti-Bullying Policy;
22) Grievance and Disciplinary Procedures Policy;
23) Cleaning Schedule Policy;
24) Cleaning of Body Fluids Policy;
25) Children Missing from Education/Early Years Policy;
26) Collecting and Escorting Children Policy;
27) First Aid Policy;
28) Complaints Procedure Policy;
29) Confidentiality Policy;
30) Control of Substances Hazardous to Health (COSHH) Policy;
31) Guide to Communicable Diseases Policy;
32) Toys and Play Equipment Policy
(You may need a skipping rope policy, a trampoline policy, football policy or any play item can be singled out and a policy devised);
33) Trips, Visits and Outings Policy;
34) Whistle-Blowing Policy;
35) Risk Assessment Policy;
36) Safer Recruitment Policy;
37) Sun Protection Policy;
38) Staff's Own Children in Setting Policy;
39) Staff Code of Conduct Policy;
40) Volunteer and Student Policy;
41) Administering Medication Policy;
42) Admissions and Fees Policy;
43) Children Settling In Policy;
44) Children's Rights Policy;
45) Children with Additional Needs Policy;
46) Dealing with Harassment Policy;
47) Early Years Foundation Stage (EYFS) Policy;
48) Intimate Care Policy;
49) Involving and Consulting Children Policy;
50) Missing Children Policy;
51) Partnership with Parents and Carers Policy;
52) Positive Behaviour Policy;
53) Suspensions and Exclusions of Children Policy;
54) Uncollected Children Policy;
55) Visits and Outings Policy.

(There are many other appropriate policies which you can develop that have not been listed here.)

3.3 Evaluating ways in which concerns about poor practice can be reported, whilst ensuring that whistle-blowers and those whose practice or behaviour is being questioned are protected.

In my practice the ways in which concerns about poor practice can be reported, whilst ensuring that whistle-blowers and those whose practice or behaviour is being questioned are protected, are set out in my Whistle-Blowing Policy. This policy clearly states as follows: 'I, as a childminder and my assistant, at all times must acknowledge our individual responsibilities to bring matters of concern to the attention of the relevant authority, e.g. to myself as the key person or if appropriate to that of childcare services and/or relevant agencies. Although this can be difficult, this is particularly important where the welfare of children may be at risk. Anyone may be the first person to recognise that something is wrong, but may not feel able to express their/his/her concern out of a feeling that this would be disloyal to colleagues or one/you may fear harassment or victimisation. These feelings, however natural, must never result in a child or young person continuing to be unnecessarily at risk. One must remember it is often the most vulnerable children or young people who are targeted. These children need someone like me/you to safeguard their welfare.'

I encourage anyone involved in my setting to report matters in confidence, not to think, "What if I am wrong – but thinking what if I am right?"

Reasons for whistle-blowing

- Each individual has a responsibility for raising concerns about unacceptable practice or behaviour.
- To prevent the problem worsening or widening.
- To protect or reduce risks to others.
- To prevent becoming implicated yourself.

What stops people from whistle-blowing?

- Starting a chain of events which spirals.
- Disrupting the work or project.
- Fear of getting it wrong.
- Fear of repercussions or damaging careers.
- Fear of not being believed.

How to raise a concern

- You should voice your concerns, suspicions or uneasiness as soon as you feel you can. The earlier a concern is expressed the easier and sooner it is possible for action to be taken.
- Try to pinpoint what practice is concerning you and why.
- Approach someone you trust and who you believe will respond.
- Make sure you get a satisfactory response – don't let matters rest.
- Put your concerns in writing on a Confidential Incident Record form.
- Discuss your concerns with the key worker (childminder) or the manager of Childcare Services of the local authority.
- A member of staff is not expected to prove the truth of an allegation, but you will need to demonstrate sufficient grounds for the concern.

- The childminder (key worker) or manager of Childcare Services will undertake an investigation into your concerns and offer you support.
- I ensure that I protect whistle-blowers using my Confidentiality Policy and the Data Protection Act.

3.4 Explanation of how practitioners can take steps to protect themselves within their everyday practice in the work setting and on off-site visits.

In my setting, myself and my assistant take steps to protect ourselves within the everyday practice in the work setting and on off-site visits by:

- using the Health and Safety Policy within our setting;
- abiding by it;
- not standing on tables/chairs to put up displays;
- ensuring interaction with children;
- not putting ourselves in a position that could be questionable;
- carrying out pre-visits to make risk assessments for off-site visits.

I can only explain this as follows:

Health and safety

I take the maintenance of health and safety extremely seriously as a matter of self safety, also for both legal and moral importance. In my setting I will always strive to go beyond the minimum statutory standards to ensure that health and safety remains the first priority. I aim to ensure the health, safety and welfare of all who come to my setting; my assistant, children, visitors and other individuals. The Health and Safety at Work Act 1974 and the Workplace (Health, Safety and Welfare) Regulations 1992 and their associated Approved Code of Practice (ACoP) and guidance will be complied with at all times. I am aware that it is vital to ensure that all members of my setting and other persons who are affected by the setting/provision's activities take health and safety matters seriously. Any individual in my setting who has been found to have blatantly disregarded safety instructions or recognised safe practices will be subject to the procedures laid out in the Disciplinary Policy. I am responsible for ensuring that the provisions of the Health and Safety Policy are adhered to at all times. As such, I am required to:

Take reasonable care for my own health and safety as well as of other persons who may be affected by my acts or omissions at work.

I must report any accidents, incidents or dangerous occurrences that have led to, or may in the future be likely to lead to, injury or damage, and assist in the investigation of any such events.

I must undergo relevant health and safety training when instructed to do so by the local authority or Ofsted.

Maintain an environment that is safe and without risk to health.

I hold ultimate responsibility and liability for ensuring that my setting operates in a safe and hazard-free manner. The setting will ensure that adequate arrangements exist for the following:

- My setting identifies me, the childminder, as the designated trained Health and Safety Officer who is guided and supported by the assistant.

- Ensuring that myself and my assistant understand and accept their responsibilities in relation to health and safety procedures.

- Encouraging my assistant and any volunteers to undertake health and safety training. Monitoring the effectiveness of the Health and Safety Policy and making/authorising any necessary revisions to its provisions.

- Providing adequate resources, including financial, as is necessary to meet the setting's health and safety responsibilities.

- Ensuring that all accidents, injuries, incidents and dangerous occurrences are adequately reported and recorded (including informing the Health and Safety Executive – The Reporting of Injuries, Diseases and Dangerous Occurrences Regulations 1995 (RIDDOR), Ofsted, where appropriate).

- Reviewing all reported accidents, incidents and dangerous occurrences, and the setting's response, to enable corrective measures to be implemented.

- Information received on health and safety matters is made available to all concerned.

Health and safety inspections and risk assessment

The identification, assessment and control of hazards within my setting are vital in reducing accidents and incidents. For further information I refer to the Risk Assessment Policy. Daily safety checks are carried out, to ensure that the facilities are maintained in a suitable state of repair and decoration. Annual inspections will also be carried out by myself and my assistant coupled with an Ofsted inspection. Any action required as a result of a health and safety inspection is taken as rapidly as possible. An investigation is carried out on all accidents, incidents and dangerous occurrences.

Safety Policy

- My premises are safe, secure and adequately spacious for play and for children to interact freely (a minimum of 2.3 square metres space per child).

- My assistant and any other authorised persons who are regular visitors to the setting are always clearly identifiable at all times while on the premises.

- As childminder I am responsible for ensuring that the premises are clean, well lit, adequately ventilated and maintained at an appropriate temperature.

- My premises comply with all the requirements of the Disability Discrimination Act 1995 and all other relevant regulations and guidance; the ground floor that I use for work is all wheelchairs accessible, I have made several alterations to my house to ensure health and safety.

- There is adequate space for storing all the equipment safely and securely when on site so that I, as childminder, and my assistant and children are protected when accessing toys and equipment.

- Under normal circumstances, I myself will ensure that there is one toilet and one washbasin with hand soap and hot and cold water available for every ten children, ensuring an adequate balance between male and female facilities.

- No child will be left unsupervised in the kitchen area, or outside the premises. I have gates on entering the setting and the rear garden is also protected by gates.

- Myself and my assistant will have access to a work telephone on the premises at all times, however we will only be able to use personal mobile telephone in allotted break periods.

- In the event of snow or ice on pathways on site, myself and my assistant will ensure that these are regularly cleared and kept safe.

- All washing up liquids, soaps or chemicals will be stored in an appropriate way that is inaccessible to children. COSHH regulations will also be observed.

Supervision

Children are supervised appropriately according to the level of risk involved during play and activities. The ages and number of children involved in a given activity is also taken into account. I, as childminder, and my assistant are deployed adequately to ensure general supervision at all times.

Site security

- Parents/carers are encouraged to talk to their children about the importance of remaining safe and not leaving the setting's premises during the care sessions. Myself and my assistant will reinforce this.
- Myself and my assistant will observe and supervise the entrance and exit points when the setting is in operation.
- Visitors will be greeted on arrival and will be asked to sign the visitor's sheet and state the purpose of their visit. Usually visits would be by appointment.
- Visitors to the setting will not be left unsupervised with children at any time.
- If an unexpected visitor has no suitable reason to be on the premises, then they will be asked to leave immediately and escorted from the premises. If the visitor repeatedly refuses to leave, the police will be telephoned immediately.
- A record will be made of any such incidents on an Incident Record Form.
- I, as childminder, (in consultation with my assistant and parents/carers) will regularly review security procedures.

Equipment

In my setting all furniture, toys and equipment are kept clean, well maintained and in good repair and in accordance with BS EN safety standards or the Toys (Safety) Regulations 1995 where applicable. Equipment will be properly maintained and inspected in accordance with the manufacturer's instructions. All electrical toys and equipment are subject to PAT (Portable Appliance Testing). Defective or broken equipment will be taken out of use and stored in a safe place before being disposed of. Flammable equipment will be stored in a safe location away from sources of heat and/or naked flames – I have a garden shade used for this purpose.

Animals

No animal (with the exception of disability assistance dogs) will be allowed on the premises without the prior knowledge and permission of myself. A visit from an animal must be pre-arranged and accompanied by a responsible handler.

Closing the setting at short notice, or in an emergency

In very exceptional circumstances, my setting may need to be closed at very short notice due to an unexpected event. Such incidents could include:

- serious weather conditions (combined with heating system failure);
- burst water pipes;
- discovery of dangerous structural damage;

- fire or bomb scare/explosion;
- death of a close associate or child;
- serious assault on a childminder/assistant or child by a member of the public;
- serious accident or illness;
- chemical contamination.

In such circumstances, I, the childminder, and my assistant will ensure that all steps are taken to keep both the children and themselves safe. All of us and children will assemble at the pre-arranged venue, where a register will be taken. Steps will then be taken to inform parents/carers and the Manager of Childcare Services and to take the necessary actions in relation to the cause of the closure. All children will be supervised until they are safely collected. If, after every attempt, parent/carers cannot be contacted, the setting will follow its Uncollected Children Procedure. A child will never be left alone on my premises. If the registration is affected it is necessary to inform Ofsted of a closure.

Health

I, as childminder, will make sure there is a regular supply of drinking water available to children at all times, especially in hot conditions. In such circumstances, I and my assistant will encourage children to adequately protect themselves from the sun.

Sun protection

I and my assistant understand the dangers posed to children by over exposure to the sun. In hot weather, parents/carers are encouraged to provide sunscreen for their children. This remains the parents' responsibility and I or my setting will not be held responsible where sun cream is not provided. Children will be encouraged to apply the sun cream independently. However, if assistance is needed then it will be given by myself on agreement with the parent. Children will also be encouraged to wear a hat when playing outside in the sun. When deemed necessary, I may apply sunscreen to children who cannot do so for themselves. In hot weather, I will encourage children to drink water frequently. I will also ensure that shady areas out of the sun are always available to children when playing outside.

Hygiene

I, as the childminder registered with Ofsted, and my assistant will be vigilant to any potential threats to good hygiene at my setting. To this end, a generally clean environment will be maintained at all times. I maintain a cleaning rota/timetable. Toilets are cleaned daily and there is always an adequate supply of soap and hand drying facilities for both myself/my assistant and children. This is also monitored throughout the session. I am the first aider who will be mindful of the need to observe the highest standards of personal hygiene when administering any treatment to children. As such, they will wash their hands thoroughly both before and after giving first aid, and ensure that plasters or disposable gloves cover any cuts, wounds or skin damage.

Kitchen hygiene

In all areas where food and drink are stored, prepared and eaten or are prone to the spread of infections, I must be particularly careful to observe high standards of hygiene in such instances. To this end the following steps will be taken:

- Only myself, the child carer, and my assistant trained in food hygiene will prepare snacks. If I had any volunteers or student placements that are not trained in food hygiene they may assist but only when overseen by a food hygiene trained person, i.e. myself.

- Waste will be disposed of safely.
- Food storage facilities will be regularly and thoroughly cleaned.
- Kitchen equipment will be thoroughly cleaned after every use.
- If cooking is done as an activity, all surfaces and equipment involved will be thoroughly cleaned before and after the session.
- Additionally, I will be aware of the provisions set out in the Food and Drink Policy when handling, preparing, cooking and serving food or drink at my setting.

Personal hygiene

In all circumstances, I will adhere to and ensure that children carry out the following routines:

- Washing hands before and after handling food or drink.
- Washing hands after using the toilet.
- Covering cuts and abrasions while at the premises.
- Taking any other steps that are likely to minimise the spread of infections.
- Washing of hands prior to and following first aid.

Dealing with spillages

Spillages of substances likely to result in the spread of infections will be dealt with rapidly and carefully. Blood, vomit, urine and faeces will be cleaned up immediately and disposed of safely and hygienically by double bagging and taken out of the setting. I will wear disposable plastic gloves and an apron while using bleach or disinfectant solution, and wash them thoroughly afterwards. Children will be kept well clear while such substances are being dealt with. I and my assistant are committed to taking all practicable steps to prevent and control the spread of infectious germs, and to uphold high standards of personal hygiene in order to minimise the risk of catching or spreading infections.

Insurance

There are many insurance providers through memberships. I am a member of Pre-School and Learning Alliance, which provides me with insurance cover. The Children Act 1989 and the Health and Safety at Work Act 1974 place a number of legal responsibilities on my setting. Therefore, my setting has insurance cover appropriate to its duties under this legislation, including Employer's Liability Insurance. Responsibility will, in most cases, rest with me as a childminder, but I will as an individual take reasonable care, both for myself and other people who may be affected by their acts or omissions at work. If the setting is held responsible for any incident that may occur, public liability insurance will cover compensation.

LEARNING OUTCOME 4

UNDERSTANDING HOW TO RESPOND TO EVIDENCE OR CONCERNS THAT A CHILD OR YOUNG PERSON HAS BEEN ABUSED OR HARMED

4.1 Describing the possible signs, symptoms, indicators and behaviours that may cause concern in the context of safeguarding.

In my setting, it is a primary duty to safeguard children and young people. In that context we would look for the possible signs, symptoms, indicators and behaviours that may cause concern. When working with children and young people we have a duty to protect them from harm. This could be from being physically, emotionally or sexually abused or even being neglected. If a child is suffering from abuse or neglect this may be demonstrated through what they say (direct or indirect disclosure) or changes in their appearance, behaviour, body language or the way they play. The child could experience more than one abuse. If a child is being sexually abused they may also suffer from emotional abuse.

Physical abuse is the physical injury or maltreatment of a child under the age of eighteen. This is usually carried out by a person who is responsible for the child's welfare under circumstances that indicate that the child's health or welfare is harmed or threatened. For example, types of physical abuse a child could experience include being beaten with a belt, shoe, or other object. Also being bitten, broken bones, being burned with matches or cigarettes. A child could experience being hit, kicked, and deprived of food and drink, having their hair pulled, being scalded with water that is too hot, also shaking, shoving, or slapping. When the child experiences physical abuse, this may be indicated by the child's behaviour as it may alter and become more aggressive and they may have a fear of physical contact or become clingy. They may also refuse to undress out of soiled or dirty clothes due to fear of injuries being detected. Family or those in close proximity to the child could be the cause of the harm the child endures. However, they may falsify explanations as to what really happened.

Recognising signs of child abuse: There is no clear dividing line between one type of abuse and another. Children may show symptoms from one or all of the categories given below. The following is not a comprehensive or definitive list, but gives an indication of situations that should alert me to possible cause for concern.

Physical abuse

In my setting I would look for the following signs:

- bruises in places not normally harmed during play (for example, back of the legs, abdomen, groin area);
- bruising in or around the mouth area (especially in young babies) – Note: 'Bruising to immobile babies' is listed in the LSCB procedures as one of the indicators for which a referral to children's social care should always be made;
- grasp marks on legs and arms – or chest of a small child;
- finger marks (for example, you may see three or four small bruises on one side of the face and none on the other);
- symmetrical bruising, i.e. the same pattern of bruising on both sides of the body/head/legs/arms etc. (especially on the ears or around the eyes);
- outline bruising (for example, belt marks, hand prints);
- linear bruising (particularly on the buttocks or back);
- old and new bruising (especially in the same area, for example, buttocks);
- unexplained injuries, bruises or marks;
- fear, watchfulness, over-anxiety to please;
- bites – these can leave clear impressions of teeth. Human bite marks are oval or crescent shaped. If the distance is more than 3cm across, it indicates that they have been caused by an adult or older child;
- fractures – these should be suspected if there is pain, swelling and discolouration over a bone or joint. As fractures also cause pain it is difficult for a parent or carer to be unaware that a child has been hurt;

- burns/scalds – it can be very difficult to distinguish between accidental and non-accidental burns, but as a general rule, burns or scalds with clear outlines are suspicious, as are burns of uniform depth over a larger area.

I would note the following 2 points:

- It is very rare for a child under one year to sustain fractures accidentally.
- Bruising is very rare in babies who are not yet mobile.

Neglect

In my setting I observe children to look for warning signs which include:

- child frequently appears hungry, asks for food;
- consistently unkempt, dirty appearance, smelly, poor hygiene;
- babies' nappies not being changed frequently enough;
- the child's clothes are often dirty, scruffy or unsuitable for the weather;
- repeated failure by parents/carers to prevent accidental injury;
- medical needs of child unmet – for example, failure to seek medical advice for illness;
- developmental delay;
- behaviours such as head banging or rocking;
- the child is exposed to risks and dangers, such as the home being unsafe or drugs or needles being left around;
- the child is left alone with unsuitable carers;
- the child has lots of accidents;
- no one seeks medical help when the child is ill or hurt.

Sexual abuse

In my setting I have been made aware through training that some possible signs of sexual abuse will include:

- explicit or frequent sexual preoccupation in talk and play;
- hinting at sexual activity or secrets through words, play or drawing;
- sexualised behaviour – for example, pretend sexual intercourse during play;
- sexually provocative relationships with adults;
- itching, redness, soreness or unexplained bleeding from vagina or anus;
- bruising, cuts and marks in the genital area;
- repeated urinary tract or genital infections.

Emotional abuse

In my setting I observe children and would look for signs which may include:

- the parent/carer giving the repeated message to the child that he/she is worthless, unloved or inadequate;
- the parent/carer having wildly unrealistic expectations of their child's abilities, taking into account the child's age and stage of development;
- the child showing serious difficulties in his/her emotional, social or behavioural development;

- the parent/carer frequently causing the child to feel frightened or in danger.

Some possible signs

In my setting I observe children and would look for signs which may include:

- very low self-esteem, often with an inability to accept praise or to trust adults;
- excessively clinging, withdrawn anxious behaviour;
- demanding or attention-seeking behaviour;
- over-anxious – either watchful, constantly checking or over-anxious to please;
- withdrawn and socially isolated;
- unwillingness to communicate;
- sudden speech disorders;
- repetitive, nervous behaviour such as rocking, hair twisting.

4.2 Describing the actions to take if a child or young person alleges harm or abuse in line with policies and procedure in own setting.

Supporting a child who tells about abuse: In my setting I have a written plan of action. Should a child or young person in my care tell about abuse, I put in to action the following plan:

- I stay calm.
- I ensure that the child is, and feels safe.
- I seek necessary medical treatment without delay.
- I tell the child they are not to blame – it's not their fault.
- I tell and show the child that they are being taken seriously – do not express disbelief.
- I explain to the child that they have done the right thing to tell you.
- I do not promise that I will be able to keep secret the things the child has told you – be honest and explain that it will be necessary to tell someone else.
- I keep questions to a minimum and ask only open questions. For example, after noticing a mark on a child, ask, "How did that happen?" and NOT "Did Daddy do that?", which is a 'leading' question.
- I use the child's own words but check out with the child what they mean if this is unclear (for example, the child may have particular words for parts of the body).
- I repeat back to the child (as accurately as possible) what you have heard to check your understanding of what the child has told you.
- I ask the child if he/she has told their mum/dad/other person these things.
- Any child old enough to communicate directly should be asked how s/he hurt himself/herself. In younger children it is perfectly normal to ask the parent/carer what happened where an injury is clearly visible.
- I tell the child what will happen next and what I intend to do.
- I write down what the child has told me as soon as possible after the event. Ensuring that records are recorded factually, and signed and dated. They should be countersigned by the designated person for child protection in my setting.

I do not:

- Put it off.

- Press the child for explanations.
- Leave it to someone else to help the child.
- Be afraid to voice my concerns, the child may need urgent protection and help.

I remember!

- Any child anywhere can be abused at any time.
- Children with disabilities are especially vulnerable.
- Child abuse can be committed by anyone – adults or children.

My responsibility as a childcare provider

I implement the Childcare Act 2006. The Childcare Act which requires that group care providers must:

- have a written safeguarding children policy and procedure in place, in line with the Local Safeguarding Children Board (LSCB) local guidance and procedures, and implement it effectively;
- ensure through induction that all members of staff (including volunteers) understand the policy and procedure;
- ensure the policy and procedure have been explained to and are accessible to all parents;
- have a designated member of staff, with appropriate child protection training, to take lead responsibility for safeguarding children within the setting and to liaise with local statutory children's services agencies, as appropriate;
- have procedures in place to be followed in the event of an allegation being made against a member of staff and that all staff are aware of these procedures.

School-run provision

Schools that directly manage childcare may use the school's safeguarding policy and procedure for their childcare provision, as long as it meets Childcare Act requirements. However, as a childminder I also provide a school-run service as part of my work.

Childminders must have a thorough understanding of safeguarding policy and procedure. Therefore, I must always ensure that my assistant is aware of and understands the policy and procedure. As a childminder I am able to clearly define the policy and procedure for parents and take the lead responsibility for safeguarding children in my setting.

I am the designated person (DP) for child protection and I attend refresher training every 3 years. I am aware that a setting should have more than one trained DP, if the DP works part-time or is absent from the setting for long periods. So my assistant has also received appropriate training including first aid.

My responsibility as a childcare provider: Recording concerns about children.

In my setting, if I have concerns then I must:

- write down everything that has given cause for concern and why. I do this as soon as possible;
- record any dates and times of incidents or observations and any contact with the child's parents/carers, making sure they are factual and do not include personal opinions or assumptions, unless they can be supported by facts;

- record any explanation for the injuries or behaviour given by the child and/or parent/carer;
- record who the child has come into contact with since the disclosure or injury (if known);
- ensure that records containing information on individual children are stored in a secure place on the premises. In the case of group care facilities (for example, nurseries, pre-schools, etc.) records should be kept in a locked place and arrangements made for designated persons to gain access to them. It will not be sufficient for keys to locked storage to be held by only one member of staff;
- my record of the disclosure or injury in the accident/incident record should be cross-referenced to all other records or files that are held about the individual child concerned.

Seeking advice and reporting to the local authority. I am aware that I can seek advice and can take action by reporting suspected abuse/making a child protection referral. I must make a referral to Children's Social Care Services by telephone, where a social worker trained in child protection will support me. The social worker will check whether the family is known to social care services already and will discuss the case with a senior officer.

Enquiries will often begin by asking other people in contact with the child, such as teachers, health visitors or doctors, if they have any concerns for the child. In most cases there will be a discussion between the social worker and the parents and child. Sometimes it soon becomes clear that there is nothing to worry about, but if concern remains about the welfare of the child, the formal Child Protection Enquiry procedures will begin immediately. Because of the confidential nature of this work, I may not be kept informed as the enquiry continues, but my alertness as the childminder will have been the important first step in protecting the child.

- A 'referral' is simply a report of a concern or a request for a service to the Local Authority Children's Social Care Team by a member of the public, a person who has contact with children in a professional capacity or a relative of the child.
- When making a referral, I would need to be aware that the Local Authority Children's Social Care Team may already be involved with the family.
- Before making a referral, I will normally be expected to have spoken to the parents/carers about my intention to refer to the Local Authority Children's Social Care Team, unless (following prior discussions with a social care professional and/or my assistant) it is believed that this will place the child at risk of significant harm.

Whether or not I have sought advice beforehand from a social care professional, making a referral to the Local Authority Children's Social Care Team will involve providing the following information:

- The child's name, address, date of birth, parents'/carers' names, GP's name.
- My (the referring person's) details, for example, position in the setting, address, etc.
- What the concerns are. How and why they have arisen. What appear to be the needs of the child.
- The parents'/carers' reaction to the concerns that have been expressed (if parents/carers are aware of the concerns).
- Any recent changes in the child's behaviour or presentation.
- Whether there are any other children in the household (if known).
- Whether there are any other agencies currently involved with the family (if known).
- Whether there have been any previous concerns about this child or other children in the household.
- Whether the child has any disabilities or special needs.

Also:

- Whether any immediate action is necessary to protect the child.

- Clarify who knows about this referral.

- Clarify which information I, as the referrer, is being reported directly and which information has been obtained from a third party. I can speak to my mentor, Early Years Foundation Stage Adviser (EYFSA), Childcare and Playwork Adviser (CAPA) or Childminding Support and Development Officer (CSDO) for advice. This can be useful if I am unsure, but it is not a substitute for a referral and it is essential that it does not delay the reporting process. In the event that I seek advice in this way, my adviser will contact me the next day to check if a referral has been made, and in some cases make a third party referral. The need for a third party referral could signal that you have not acted in accordance with your setting's child protection policies and procedures and may require further investigation.

Communicating with parents and carers

- Every parent/carer should be made aware of my (the childcare provider's) Child Protection Policy. Parents/carers must be informed that I (the childcare provider) have a duty to report suspected child abuse or neglect. This information is included in safeguarding policies and can be included on the setting's registration form.

- If my concerns are that the child may have been deliberately harmed or sexually abused, or I feel that the child may be at greater risk of harm by discussing with the parents, then I should contact the Local Authority Children's Social Care Team immediately, without informing the parents that I am doing so (as they may be implicated in the abuse).

- Any injury visible on a child (accidental or non-accidental) is recorded as soon as the child arrives in my setting. Parents should be encouraged to tell me about injuries that have happened outside the childcare setting. If an injury is clearly visible on a child, it is appropriate to ask the parents/carers about the injury, which may be accidental. I do not have to be afraid to ask open questions or make observations, such as, "What happened?" or "I noticed when she got changed that X had a bruise on her leg". Similarly, changes in a child's behaviour causing me concern need to be discussed with the parents and carers using open questions such as, "Has anything happened at home as I've noticed that X seems very unruly and not his normal self?"

- If I am concerned about signs of neglect in the child or a damaging emotional relationship observed over a period of time, I will normally have discussed these concerns with the parent. If there is no change and I remain concerned about the welfare of the child I should then tell the parent/carer that I am contacting the local authority. (It might be helpful to remind the parents/carers of my duty to report concerns in line with my Safeguarding Policy, which the parents/carers will have seen.)

4.3 Explanation of the rights that children, young people and their carers have in situations where harm or abuse is suspected or alleged.

In my setting, I have the awareness that:

1. A child or young person has a right not to be subjected to repeated medical examinations following any allegations of abuse, whether of a physical or sexual nature. A child has the right to be protected against significant harm (Children Act 1989; *Every Child Matters*, 2004; United Nations Convention on the Rights of the Child etc.). Children should contribute their own account of their own views. They should be listened to and within certain circumstances these should be applied, but when a child is

in significant harm then you would look at the child's best interest to make them safe. They should be fully informed of everything that is happening to them and they should be consulted sensitively.

2. Carers and/or family members normally have the right to know what is being said about them and to respond or contribute to important decisions. The carers/parents of the child have the right to seek legal advice and to be kept informed of any allegations against them and all that is going on.

3. Children should be kept fully informed of processes involving them. If the child/young person is able to, they should be allowed to say what they wish to see resulting from the issues surrounding incidents of abuse, e.g. young people will often want to leave the environment of their abuse/neglect.

LEARNING OUTCOME 5

UNDERSTANDING HOW TO RESPOND TO EVIDENCE OR CONCERNS THAT A CHILD OR YOUNG PERSON HAS BEEN BULLIED

5.1 Explaining different types of bullying and the potential effects on children and young people.

Bullying is not always easy to recognise as it can take a number of forms. A child may encounter bullying attacks that are:

- physical: pushing, kicking, hitting, pinching and other forms of violence or threats;
- verbal: name calling, sarcasm, spreading rumours, persistent teasing;
- emotional: excluding (sending to Coventry), tormenting, ridiculing, humiliating;
- Cyber bullying: In recent years, a new form of bullying known as 'cyber bullying' has become increasingly common. Studies show that one in five children were cyber bullied in 2008. Cyber bullying may be emotional, racist or sexual forms of abuse. It happens through emails, text messages or telephone calls. Information about someone may also be shared by putting it on to social networking sites. This can include the sharing of private photographs.

The potential effects of persistent bullying can result in:

- depression: low self-esteem, shyness, poor academic achievement;
- isolation: threatened or attempted suicide.

In my setting I look for the following signs that show if a child or young person may be being bullied:

Coming home with cuts and bruises, torn clothes, asking for stolen possessions to be replaced, losing dinner money, falling out with previously good friends, being moody and bad tempered, wanting to avoid leaving their home, aggression with younger brothers and sisters, doing less well at school, sleep problems, anxiety, becoming quiet and withdrawn. These definitions and indicators are not meant to be definitive, but only serve as a guide to assist me as a childminder. It is important too, to remember that many children may exhibit some of these indicators at some time, and that the presence of one or more should not be taken as proof that abuse is occurring. There may well be other reasons for changes in behaviour such as a death or the birth of a new baby in the family or relationship problems between parents/carers. In assessing whether indicators are related to abuse or not, the authorities will always want to understand them in relation to the child's development and context.

5.2 Outline of the policies and procedures that should be followed in response to concerns or evidence of bullying and explaining the reasons why they are in place.

This is to ask, "What would I do in my setting if a bullying incident occurred?" Children spend almost half their waking hours in my care or school, so that childminders and schools have a particular responsibility to look for signs that abuse may be happening. NSPCC 2002 reported that 1 in 6 children had experienced serious maltreatment. It is likely that among the children I support that there will be children who have experienced some form of abuse. Therefore, as a childminder, I build special relationships with children. I may regularly work with children in small groups or on a one-to-one basis. I, or my assistant, am likely to be the person who the child feels more comfortable to talk to when the rest of the children are not around. It is important that I know how to recognise when abuse may be happening and what action you should take. In my setting, I avoid jumping to conclusions. I must always be observant. I may notice physical signs or changes in a child's behaviour, or the child may hint or disclose to me that they are being abused or bullied. I must also think about how I would respond if a child were to hint or disclose this to me.

I always:

- report concerns about possible signs or changes in behaviour to the designated person or appropriate agency;
- take what children say seriously – it will take a lot of courage to tell, so children will rarely lie about abuse;
- reassure children that they are not to blame if they tell me they have been abused;
- tell children that I will have to tell someone who can help them;
- write down what I have observed or what has been said – but keep the information secure.

I never:

- promise to keep information a secret;
- investigate further or ask questions;
- appear shocked;
- make promises to children.

I always ask myself, "Do I know what action to take if I recognise abuse is happening to a child?"

I remember that:

- it is not my responsibility to draw conclusions – only report what I have noticed or have been told;
- I have a statutory duty to report concerns under the Education Act 2002;
- I can receive support from my adviser/mentor, the designated child protection officer or through the appropriate organisations.

5.3 Explaining how to support a child or young person and/or their family when bullying is suspected or alleged.

In my childcare setting I support a child or young person and/or their family when bullying is suspected or alleged. It is good practice that practitioners and the child's or young person's parents/carers should work together to identify any such behaviour. I would support the child or young person who needs help to improve personal and social skills, including assertiveness techniques and conflict resolution. I am able to provide support for a child or young person who is being bullied by:

- encouraging the child or young person to talk;
- listening to their problems;
- believing them if they say that they are being bullied;
- providing reassurance that it is not their fault; no one deserves to be bullied;
- discussing the matter with a senior colleague;
- taking appropriate action, following the setting's policy on anti- bullying.

In my childcare setting I have to be aware that children and young people who are experiencing bullying may be reluctant to attend the setting and may therefore be often absent. They may be more anxious and insecure than others, have fewer friends and often feel unhappy and lonely. They can suffer from low self-esteem and a negative self-image; seeing themselves as failures, stupid, ashamed and unattractive. Possible signs that a child or young person is being bullying include:

- suddenly does not want to go to the setting when s/he usually enjoys it;
- inexplicable cuts and bruises;
- possessions have unexplained damage or are persistently 'lost';
- becoming withdrawn or depressed but refusing to explain.

While the above signs may indicate that a child or young person is being bullied, they may also be symptomatic of other problems such as child abuse (see above). We have already looked at factors that make bullying more likely. The behaviour of some children and young people can also lead to them experiencing bullying, although this does not justify the behaviour of the bullies. For example, some children and young people may:

- find it difficult to play/enjoy leisure with others;
- be hyperactive;
- behave in ways that irritate others;
- bully other children and young people;
- be easily roused to anger;
- fight back when attacked or even slightly provoked;
- be actively disliked by the majority of children and young people using the setting.

The other element is that as a carer I also have a duty to ensure that the bully is made aware of their inappropriate actions and helped to a positive outcome of respect for others and acknowledge the variety of humanity. The size of a human body does not call for bullying. Age does not give anyone a right to bully others. Therefore I would also support parents and work together with them and the young people/children to resolve matters positively.

LEARNING OUTCOME 6

UNDERSTANDING HOW TO WORK WITH CHILDREN AND YOUNG PEOPLE TO SUPPORT THEIR SAFETY AND WELL-BEING

6.1 Explaining how to support young people's confidence and self-esteem.

In my setting, I am the key person. I support young people's confidence and self-esteem. I work in a way that shows that self-confidence and self-esteem in young children can be greatly boosted by a strong key person approach in the setting. I am the key person. Many aspects of this approach support the safeguarding of children. I would take the following points of action:

Listening and tuning in to a child: This will include (me) the key person noticing changes in a child's behaviour and emotional well-being, and developing a trusting relationship so that the child can tell me if things are upsetting him/her. Taking a child's concerns seriously is important. Often, when a child has been bullied or abused in some way, s/he will try to communicate what has happened. The child needs to know that I am there to listen and, most importantly, that I will believe what s/he tells me.

Allowing a child to express his or her feelings: If a child is allowed to express sadness and anger as well as happiness and enjoyment, s/he may feel more confident that s/he can have a range of emotions. The child will therefore be more likely to tell other people how s/he is feeling.

Increasing a child's confidence: This would involve making the child feel a sense of belonging, and that s/he is special for many unique qualities. It is important to show a genuine interest in what a child has to say, and to praise her/him for any achievements. To say a quick, "That's lovely X", is really not enough to show a child that I value him/her.

Observing a child and keeping regular records of behaviour: I am in a strong position to note any changes of behaviour or signs of insecurity that could result from child abuse.

Working with parents: The emphasis is in the childminder's (key person's) approach on developing a close relationship with parents, which is also important. As the key person I can:

- help a parent to appreciate that a child is finding a particular situation upsetting or difficult;
- support a parent with practical advice on general care and clothing;
- offer emotional and practical support in cases of family conflict or domestic violence.

6.2 Analysis of supporting resilience in children and young people.

In my setting I support resilience in children and young people. I am able to draw from a number of information resources, e.g. in the UK one can get resources from Barnados and/or the National Society for the Prevention of Cruelty to Children (NSPCC). I am therefore able to start my analysis by asking the following questions:

- What is resilience and why is it important to child welfare services?
- Why are some children and young people more successful than others at resisting and overcoming stressful episodes?
- How can child welfare services promote resilience?

To provide a good analysis I draw from the resources mentioned above and I answer those questions as follows. As a child minder I realise that the weight of evidence amongst practitioners of childcare suggests that incorporating resilience-promoting strategies in services to children and young people can make a real difference.

Principles of resilience and practical applications (I got this information from NSPC):

- Risk factors are cumulative – the presence of one increases the likelihood that more will emerge.
- Transition points in children's lives can be both threats and opportunities.
- Where the cumulative chain of adversities can be broken, most children are able to recover from even severe exposure to adversities in early life.
- Managed exposure to risk is necessary if children are to learn coping mechanisms.
- Key factors promoting resilience in children are support from family and/or peers, good educational experiences, a sense of urgency of self-efficacy, and opportunities to contribute to family or community life by taking valued social roles.
- Acute episodes of stress are less likely than adversities to have long-term effects on children's development.
- The promotion of resilience involves trade-offs – the goal is effective adult adjustment rather than eliminating the legacy of all childhood difficulties.
- Children and young people who have experienced difficulties report more often being helped by non-professional supporters (friends and family), rather than by professionals. Social care professionals should avoid weakening informal sources of support.

Effective strategies for the early years (antenatal to 4)

I have sourced information from various parents, drawn from experience and learned that effective strategies for healthy development include:

1.   In the antenatal period:

   - adequate maternal nutrition throughout pregnancy;
   - avoidance of maternal and passive smoking;
   - moderate maternal alcohol consumption;
   - social support to mothers from partners, family and external networks;
   - good access to antenatal care;
   - interventions to prevent domestic violence.

2.   During infancy:

   - adequate parental income;
   - social support for mothers, to moderate prenatal stress;
   - good quality housing;
   - parent education;
   - safe play areas and provision of learning materials;
   - breastfeeding to three months;
   - support from male partners;
   - continuous home-based input from health and social care services, lay or professional.

3. During the pre-school period:

- high-quality pre-school day care;
- preparatory work with parents on home-school links;
- pairing with resilient peers;
- availability of alternative caregivers;
- food supplements;
- links with other parents;
- local community networks and faith groups;
- community regeneration initiatives.

Effective strategies for middle childhood (5 to 13)

- reception classes that are sufficiently flexible to accommodate a range of cultural and community-specific behaviours;
- creation and maintenance of home-school links for at-risk children and their families, which can promote parental confidence and engagement;
- positive school experiences – academic, sporting or friendship-related;
- good and mutually trusting relationships with teachers;
- the development of skills, opportunities for independence and mastery of tasks;
- structured routines, and a perception by the child that praise and sanctions are being administered fairly;
- in abusive settings, the opportunity to maintain or develop attachments to the non-abusive parent, other family member or, otherwise, a reliable unrelated adult;
- maintenance of family routines and rituals;
- manageable contributions to the household that promote competencies, self-esteem and problem-solving coping;
- in situations of marital discord, attachment to one parent, moderation of parental disharmony and opportunities to play a positive role in the family;
- help with resolving minor but chronic stresses as well as acute adversities;
- provision of breakfast and after-school clubs.

Effective strategies for adolescence and early adulthood (13 to 19)

In my setting I use:

- strong social support networks;
- the presence of a least one unconditionally supportive parent or parent substitute;
- a committed mentor or other person from outside the family;
- positive school experiences;
- a sense of mastery and a belief that one's own efforts can make a difference;
- participation in a range of extra-curricular activities;
- the capacity to re-frame adversities so that the beneficial as well as the damaging effects are recognised;
- the ability, or opportunity, to 'make a difference' by helping others or through part-time work;

- not to be excessively sheltered from challenging situations that provide opportunities to develop coping skills.

6.3 Explaining why it is important to work with the child or young person to ensure they have strategies to protect themselves and make decisions about safety.

In my setting, it is important to work with the child or young person to ensure they have strategies to protect themselves and make decisions about safety. My role as a childminder is to empower children and young people to support their own well-being and safety. I have an effective child and young person protection policy that promotes a caring and supportive environment in the setting and creates an atmosphere in which children and young people feel that they are secure, valued, listened to and taken seriously. The setting's Child Protection Policy supports children's and young people's development in ways that foster their security, confidence and independence. I encourage and use the following strategies:

Protecting themselves – in my setting, child protection not only involves the detection of abuse and neglect but also the prevention of abuse by helping children and young people to protect themselves. As part of this preventive role I help children and young people to do the following:

- understand what is and what is not acceptable behaviour;
- stay safe from harm;
- speak up if they have worries and concerns;
- develop awareness and resilience;
- prepare for their future responsibilities as adults, citizens and parents.

In my setting I am always actively involved in prevention activities, e.g. information sessions for childminders. This enables me to engage children, and in turn helps children and young people to keep safe both now and in the future. Children and young people need to know how to take responsibility for themselves and to understand the consequences of their actions. I ensure that children and young people in my care know and understand:

- that they all deserve care and respect, to know their rights and how to assert them;
- how to do things safely and how to minimise risk, how to deal with abusive or potentially abusive situations, when and how to ask for help and support.

In my setting I criticise myself, reflect on my work, seek other practitioners' opinions, and find that critical thinking and decision making are also essential for helping children to keep themselves safe. I help them to develop these skills by encouraging them to participate in decision making within the setting and providing opportunities for co-operation. I also encourage children and young people to trust their own feelings and judgement in difficult situations.

By learning to trust their inner feelings, children can avoid many potentially risky situations. In my setting I also use role-play to help them think about what they should do if their friends want them to do something they dislike or feel uncomfortable about, such as going to a party, getting drunk, having sex, shoplifting, taking drugs, etc. I know that peer pressure can be very strong, so I encourage the children to decide and set limits about what they will or will not do, so that they know how to cope before the situation arises. I make sure that children understand the dangers of situations that may put their personal safety at risk, such as:

- being left at home alone;
- playing in deserted or dark places;

- being out on their own;
- getting lost, for example on outings;
- walking home alone, especially in the dark;
- talking to strangers;
- accepting lifts from strangers, including hitchhiking.

Risk-taking and developing independence: In my setting, I observe that as children and young people get older, they need opportunities to explore their environment and to develop their independence. To do this safely they need to know and understand about acceptable risk-taking. I explore this through stories (such as *Jack and the Beanstalk* for young children) and television programmes. Children can think about and discuss the risks taken by their favourite characters. I encourage them to identify some of the risks they take in their own lives and look at ways in which they can minimise risk. I use puppets and role-play to help them deal with potentially risky situations. I ensure that the children and young people know and understand. The Keep Safe Code (see www.kidscape.org.uk) has useful advice.

Seeking help: In my setting I make things clear. Children and young people need to know where to go for help and support in difficult situations. I encourage children to identify people in the setting and the local community who can help them to keep safe. For example, worries about bullying or problems at home may be discussed with a trusted adult; if they get lost they can ask a police officer for assistance. I encourage children and young people to think of a trusted adult (such as parents or carers, another relative, best friend, teacher, key worker) to whom they could talk about a difficult situation (for example, abuse, bullying, negative peer pressure, etc.). I ensure that children understand that if they go to an adult for help, especially within the setting, they will be believed and supported. I provide children with information about other sources of help and support, such as Childline or The Samaritans.

LEARNING OUTCOME 7

UNDERSTANDING THE IMPORTANCE OF E-SAFETY FOR CHILDREN AND YOUNG PEOPLE

7.1 Explaining the risks and possible consequences for children and young people of being online and of using a mobile phone.

I create a scenario here

In a country like the UK the majority of settings have websites. In countries like Uganda, South Sudan or Kenya the majority will not have a website, yet it is easy for children to become exposed to Internet use either from home or an internet cafe.

E-safety for the setting

I do not have a website, but a setting may have its own website, which demonstrates the work of the setting, provides a source of information to parents and develops links with the wider community. The setting website should protect the identity of children. Where a child's image appears, the name should not, and vice versa. Parental permission should be obtained before using images of children on the website.

Understanding the importance of e-safety for children and young people

In my setting I have to understand the importance of e-safety for children and young people. This is due to the continuing development of new and mobile technologies. My setting has a responsibility to help children and young people to stay safe online. E-safety is a safeguarding issue as part of the wider duty of care for all who work with children and young people. I have a good understanding of e-safety issues and risks, and how these might relate to the children I work with, including data protection and child protection.

Child protection and ICT

In my setting I have a duty in relation to children and young people to monitor their use of the Internet and email in order to protect them from inappropriate, malicious or offensive material, as well as to protect them from paedophiles preying on children via the Internet.

Chat rooms and social networking sites

In my setting I ensure that children and young people should only be given access to educational chat rooms, which should be moderated to ensure that discussions are kept on-topic, and that there is no language or behaviour that is inappropriate. I have guidelines for using chat rooms or social networking sites in the setting that are included in the setting's policy for using ICT. Children and young people are taught never to give out personal details that would identify who they are, and never to arrange to meet anyone they have 'met' in a chat room or social networking site. Additionally, children and young people are taught not to rely on anyone they have met in a chat room or social networking site for important advice, and if anything makes them feel uncomfortable, not to reply to the message but instead seek advice from a familiar adult such as their childminder, key worker, teacher, parent or carer.

7.2 Describing ways of reducing risk to children and young people from:

- social networking;
- Internet use;
- buying online;
- Using a mobile phone.

In my setting I describe to children and young people that there are possible risks to children and young people including:

- accessing potentially harmful content such as pornography;
- possible dangerous contact with strangers in chat rooms;
- commercial pressures like spam and intrusive advertising.

UK mobile phone operators have taken steps to help protect children and young people from potentially harmful content accessible via their mobile phone, including the following:

- All UK mobile phone operators have to provide an Internet filter on their phones to help block accessing material that is potentially harmful to children, such as pornography. However, in most cases parents will need to ask their operator to activate the filter.

- Being registered as a child user will mean that the child cannot access material provided by the mobile telephone operator or its partners that is rated as 18+. All mobile phone users are considered to be children by their mobile operator unless or until they have proved to their mobile operator that they are 18 years old and over.

- Bluetooth allows a mobile telephone to find and 'talk' to other Bluetooth-enabled mobile phones nearby and vice versa. So when activated on a child's or young person's mobile phone, they may receive unexpected and unwanted messages from other Bluetooth-enabled phone users nearby, and any personal information stored on their phone (such as their contact list) could be vulnerable. Mobile operators therefore advise that Bluetooth is not enabled on children's and young people's phones.

- Chat rooms or games (where you can chat to other users), which are provided by a mobile operator or its partners and which do not have 18+ age-restrictions must be moderated. Different mobile operators may have different moderation policies and systems that may affect the level of safety, so ask the mobile operator about this. I always remember that chat rooms accessed on the Internet via mobile phone (that is, which are not provided by the mobile operator or its partners) may not be moderated.

- The mobile operator should have systems and procedures in place to help deal with nuisance and malicious phone calls. It is important to let the mobile operator know if their system is failing, both in order to protect children and others using the same service.

- The mobile operator will take action against spam, whether it is text, picture or email. I would find out what action the mobile operator is taking and report any spam received on the phone to them.

Using the Internet

My approach would be that in my setting I would have filtering systems in place to prevent children and young people from accessing inappropriate materials. There are procedures in my place for children and young people to report accidental access to inappropriate material. My setting provides appropriate opportunities within the service/care plan to teach Internet safety. There are procedures in my setting to deal with 'personal alleging' by a child or young person as a result of Internet safety education. In my setting I am the nominated member of staff with responsibility for child protection issues. Children's and young people's use of the Internet, email and/or chat rooms is regularly monitored to ensure that inappropriate use is not being made. There are sanctions in place to deal with children and young people who deliberately access inappropriate sites or post bullying or offensive messages.

In my setting I can help children and young people to understand the importance of e-safety by giving them the following tips:

- Think about whom you give your mobile phone number to – you do not know where it might end up.

- If you start receiving annoying, nasty or rude texts, remember, do not reply, but do keep a record of it. If any of these things bother you, talk to an adult you trust or report it to your school or mobile phone operator.

- A growing number of viruses are attacking mobile phones, so be careful with what you download onto your mobile.

- If you often receive spam (junk mail) texts from random numbers, report it to your mobile phone operator.

- If you are taking photos or film of your friends and want to upload them to the Internet, always check with them first.

- Remember to keep control of your own image too. Once a picture is posted online, it can be copied, changed and distributed without your knowledge. Only upload and exchange photos that you would be happy for everyone to see.

Buying online

I am aware that with a number of Internet payment options to choose from (such as debit cards, top-ups and pre-paid cards), children and young people can buy goods and services online even if they do not own a credit card. It is important that they know about e-safety when buying online, especially possible dangers such as being tricked into buying something on a fake website or accidentally giving their personal information to a fraudster. In my setting young people should be made aware of the following important points about buying online:

- Be aware of the potential risks of online shopping such as identity theft and security issues.

- Criminals could install malicious software (malware) on anyone's computer that might damage data, cause a PC to run slowly, gather personal information, harm one's reputation or be used to steal money.

- Ensure that your computer has up-to-date anti-virus software and a firewall in place, to provide protection against the potential risks of shopping online.

- Only use online retailers you trust or ones that have been suggested by friends or family.

- Shop around to get the best deals and to check a website's returns and privacy policy before buying anything. When buying things online, always read the small print!

- Ensure that you have strong passwords (a combination of letters, numbers and symbols) on websites you use to shop online.

- Know what a secure website looks like – look for the padlock symbol in the bottom right of the browser window, and for website addresses which begin with https (the 's' stands for security).

- Print out a copy of any online orders and check your bank statements after you have bought anything online.

Mobile phones

In my setting, I am aware that Internet access is now available on most mobile phones. While this provides opportunities for communication, interaction and entertainment, there are possible risks to children and young people.

Safeguarding is like a web, everything in the business of childcare is designed for safeguarding the children.

CHAPTER 5

PROFESSIONAL PRACTICE IN EARLY YEARS SETTINGS

The following is experience drawn from my setting to deal with:

PROFESSIONAL PRACTICE IN EARLY YEARS SETTINGS.

THE AIM: This chapter introduces to you the competence required for the application of principles and values in day-to-day practice. The unit includes the importance of evidence-based practice. It revisits the issues of professional practice, reflection and review and professional development in areas identified as challenging.

LEARNING OUTCOME 1

UNDERSTAND THE SCOPE AND PURPOSE OF THE EARLY YEARS SECTOR

1.1 Explaining how the range of early years settings reflects the scope and purpose of the sector.

My setting is one of a range of early years settings that reflects the scope and purpose of the sector. I have discovered through work experience that the early years sector in the UK is complex; unlike many European countries it was not developed by government policy with specific aims but came about in response to families' requirements, which were based on changing economical and social factors. In the second half of the 20th century public expenditure on early years provision focused on families with social needs and difficulties. Local authority day nurseries catered mainly for children who were at risk from harm in deprived areas. There was early years provision available in the private sector in the form of childminders, nannies and private nurseries.

I have learnt that during the 1960s the playgroup movement developed, where parents set up and ran provision for their own children to learn through play in village halls and other community facilities. This was originally the way many settings were formed. Families' requirements for their children vary. Some parents want care for their children so that they can return to work, some parents want to stay with their children while they socialise, some parents want their children in a setting that offers services aimed at learning, some parents want their children to be in a home-based environment and some families cannot afford to pay fees for provision. This is why the early years sector has various forms of provision to meet the needs of families. Provisions in the sector include nurseries, childminders, pre-schools, crèches, children's centres and parent and toddler groups. I am aware that over the past 10 to 15 years the early years sector has been at the forefront of government agenda and there has been huge changes in response to social and economic developments.

LEARNING OUTCOME 2

UNDERSTANDING CURRENT POLICIES AND INFLUENCES ON THE EARLY YEARS SECTOR

2.1 Identifying current policies, frameworks and influences on the early years sector.

In my setting I follow guidelines on legislation to safeguard children: I ensure that I implement the government identified current policies, frameworks and influences on early years. The frameworks are: Early Years Foundation Stage (EYFS), Children Act and the United Nations Convention on the Rights of the Child (UNCRC). Also, current equalities legislation, current research, social and economic influences such as work patterns and financial constraints, *Every Child Matters* (ECM) outcomes, how the Education Act introduced free childcare provisions and also about Dame Claire Tickell, the independent chair of EYFS's review of 2008.

The framework and influences on early years offer a principled approach. In my setting I therefore identify current policies, frameworks and influences on the early years through taking the principled approach the EYFS has set. The EYFS principles, which guide the work of all practitioners, are grouped into four distinct but complementary themes:

- A Unique Child;
- Positive Relationships;
- Enabling Environments;
- Learning and Development.

Effective practice in the EYFS is built on these four guiding themes. They provide a context for the requirements and describe how practitioners should support the development, learning and care of young children. The themes are each broken down into four commitments describing how the principles can be put into practice. The EYFS *Principles into Practice* cards explain how I, as a practitioner, can use these in their day-to-day work.

A Unique Child recognises that every child is a competent learner from birth who can be resilient, capable, confident and self-assured. The commitments are focused around development, inclusion, safety, and health and well-being.

Positive Relationships describes how children learn to be strong and independent from a base of loving and secure relationships with parents and/or a key person. The commitments are focused around respect, partnership with parents, supporting learning, and the role of the key person.

Enabling Environments explains that the environment plays a key role in supporting and extending children's development and learning. The commitments are focused around observation, assessment and planning, support for every child, the learning environment, and the wider context – transitions, continuity, and multi-agency working.

Learning and Development recognises that children develop and learn in different ways and at different rates, and that all areas of learning and development are equally important and inter-connected.

This principled approach ensures that the EYFS meets the overarching aim of improving outcomes and reflects that it is every child's right to grow up safe, healthy, enjoying and achieving, making a positive contribution, and with economic well-being.

I therefore identify current policies, frameworks and influences as 'Setting the Standards'. The EYFS sets standards to enable early years providers to reflect the rich and personalised experience that many parents give their children at home. Like parents, providers should deliver individualised learning, development and care that enhances the development of the children in their care and gives those children the best possible start in life. Every child should be supported individually to make progress at their own pace and children who need extra support to fulfil their potential should receive special consideration. All providers have an equally important role to play in children's early years experiences – for example, a childminder who sees a child for two hours a day should consider what a child's individual needs are at that time of day, and ensure that the provision they deliver is both appropriate to those needs and complementary to the education and care provided in the child's other setting(s). All types of providers have the potential to deliver the EYFS to an excellent standard.

In my setting I identify current policies, frameworks and influences as 'Providing for Equality of Opportunity'. As a provider I have a responsibility to ensure positive attitudes to diversity and difference – not only so that every child is included and not disadvantaged, but also so that they learn from the earliest age to value diversity in others and grow up making a positive contribution to society.

As a practitioner I should focus on each child's individual learning, development and care needs by *removing or helping to overcome barriers* for children where these already exist, by being alert to the early signs of needs that could lead to later difficulties and responding quickly and appropriately, involving other agencies as necessary, stretching and challenging all children.

I recognise that the purpose and aims of the EYFS is to influence policy and practice in my setting. As a result I therefore know that every child deserves the best possible start in life and support to fulfil their potential. A child's experience in the early years has a major impact on their future life chances. A secure, safe and happy childhood is important and it provides the foundation for children to make the most of their abilities and talents as they grow up. When parents choose to use my setting's early years services they want to know that my provision will keep their children safe and help them to thrive.

Through my training I understand that EYFS is the framework that provides that assurance. I have learnt that the overall aim of the EYFS is to help young children achieve the five *Every Child Matters* outcomes of staying safe, being healthy, enjoying and achieving, making a positive contribution, and achieving economic well-being by setting the standards for the learning, development and care for young children, which they should experience when they are attending a setting outside their family home, ensuring that every child makes progress and that no child gets left behind; providing for equality of opportunity and anti-discriminatory practice and ensuring that every child is included and not disadvantaged because of ethnicity, culture or religion, home language, family background, learning difficulties or disabilities, gender or ability; creating the framework for partnership working between parents and professionals, and between all the settings that the child attends; improving quality and consistency in the early years sector through a universal set of standards that apply to all settings, ending the distinction between care and learning in the existing frameworks, and providing the basis for the inspection and regulation regime; laying a secure foundation for future learning through learning and development that is planned around the individual needs and interests of the child, and informed by the use of ongoing observational assessment.

In my setting I follow the identified current policies, frameworks and influences on early years because they are providing for equality of opportunity. As a provider I have a responsibility to ensure positive attitudes to diversity and difference – not only so that every child is included and not disadvantaged, but also so that they learn from the earliest age to value diversity in others and grow up making a positive contribution to society.

As a practitioner I focus on each child's individual learning, development and care needs by removing or helping to overcome barriers for children where these already exist. I am alert to the early signs of needs that could lead to later difficulties and respond quickly and appropriately, involving other agencies as necessary, stretching and challenging all children. In my setting all children, irrespective of ethnicity, culture or religion, home language, family background, learning difficulties or disabilities, gender or ability should have the opportunity to experience a challenging and enjoyable programme of learning and development.

In my setting I follow the identified current policies, frameworks and influences on early years.

Creating the framework for partnership working

Partnership working helps successful delivery of the EYFS in a number of different ways. In my setting I am aware of children who receive education and care in more than one setting, so practitioners must ensure continuity and coherence by sharing relevant information with each other and with parents. Patterns of attendance are a key factor in my planning. Close working between early years practitioners and parents is vital for the identification of children's learning needs and to ensure a quick response to any area of particular difficulty. Parents and families are central to a child's well-being and practitioners should support this important relationship by sharing information and offering support to learning in the home. In my setting I frequently need to work with professionals from other agencies, such as local and community health services, or where children are looked after by the local authority, to identify and meet needs and use their knowledge and advice to provide children's social care with the best learning opportunities and environments for all children.

Improving quality and consistency

The identified current policies, frameworks and influences on early years bring together and simplify the learning and development and welfare requirements, in addition to ending the distinction between care and learning and between birth-to-three and three-to-five provision. Most requirements are applicable to all types of setting so that, wherever they send their children, parents can be assured that essential standards of provision are in place.

Laying a secure foundation for future learning

The identified current policies, frameworks and influences on early years make it crucial to the future success of children's earliest experiences to help to build a secure foundation for learning throughout their school years and beyond. Practitioners must be sensitive to the individual development of each child to ensure that the activities they undertake are suitable for the stage that they have reached. Children need to be stretched, but not pushed beyond their capabilities, so that they can continue to enjoy learning. The keys to achieving this are ongoing observational assessment to inform planning for each child's continuing development through play-based activities. In my setting I follow the identified current policies, frameworks and influences on early years as a flexible approach that responds quickly to children's learning and development needs, and I encourage the coherence of learning and development across different settings and related to the child's experience at home.

2.2   Explaining the impact of current policies, frameworks and influences on the early years.

In my setting, due to where I am located, we have put an international outlook to the work as a result of the diversity of cultural backgrounds that the children come from. This helps to put in practice some aspects of the impact of current policies, frameworks and influences on the early years. The impact is traced from The United Nations Convention on the Rights of the Child. In 1989 world leaders decided that children needed a special convention just for under-18s because they often need special care. The four core principles are: (1) non-discrimination; (2) devotion to the best interests of the child; (3) the right to life; (4) survival and development and to respect the views of a child. These also protect children's rights by setting the standards in health care, education and legal, civil and social services.

The impact puts in place international law and standards of expectation that all children have a right to adequate food, shelter, clean water, education, health care, leisure and recreation.

Then there is the Children Act. This act protects all children up to the age of 18 regardless of race, religion, gender, culture, whether they are rich or poor, have a disability, what they do and don't say and what language they speak, no child should be treated unfairly. The best interests of the child must always come first when making decisions that can affect them.

Then there is the EYFS, which I find to work at setting the standards for learning, ensuring that children make progress and no child gets left behind.

The government has a responsibility to take measures to make sure children's rights are protected, respected and fulfilled. In this instance we have the impact through Ofsted.The Education Act introduced free childcare provisions for under-5s and since September 1st 2010 this rose from 12 and a half hours a week to 15 hours a week. The free entitlement provides access to education and care and the hours can be flexible over the week. All childcare provisions must use the EYFS and help young children achieve the five *Every Child Matters* outcomes. Local Education Authorities (councils) are adopting a single-term entry into reception class. However, in my setting this is not applicable as I have open-ended time as a childminder to take on children as long as I have vacancies. However, reception classes started in September 2011 where they only have one intake of children means that some of the children would have recently turned 4 years old. If I have nursery or reception age children in my setting I try to link with local schools and nurseries because reception classes and nurseries work closely together covering the same themes each term. This enables me as a childminder to use more play, as I am aware that all reception classes will need to do more learning through play because of the young age of the child.

I have discovered that single funding formula has been introduced and this gives parents greater flexibility of childcare provisions and have a greater choice of how they use their free 15 hours entitlement. Settings will be funded on the basis of participation, not places and this will be done on a term-by-term basis. Funding can now be split/shared between a maintained nursery and the private, voluntary or independent sector, so some of the funding can be used to pay for childcare to a childminder. The current EYFS has six areas of learning and 69 learning goals. Dame Claire Tickell is recommending they reduce the early learning goals children are assessed against at age five to 17 from 69. She recommends that parents receive a summary of their child's development, along with the health visitor check at age two to help early identification of any problems or special educational needs. She would like to see less paperwork so more time can be spent interacting with the children and that all practitioners have a Level 3 qualification. £4 million has been given to 15 local authorities to provide nursery places for the most disadvantaged two-year olds. This is a pilot scheme which ran until March 2012. Their aim was to make sure places and staff are available in the right areas.

These examples I have used clearly show the impact of current policies, frameworks and influences on the early years.

2.3 Describing what is meant by evidence-based practice and give examples of how this has influenced work with children in early years.

In my setting I would describe what is meant by evidence-based practice and give examples of how this has influenced work with children in early years, starting with what I have in place such as documents. I have progress records and observations. I complete forms such as Ofsted reports in order to reflect on the work I do and this influences the work I do. Such evidence has been set by the Early Years Framework to guide practice. Further, as a childminder, I have been made aware that evidence-based practice is practice that is influenced by objective evidence derived from research. In my practice, I believe that my everyday work is likely to have been influenced by many factors – my qualifications and training, my experience of working with children, learning from colleagues, research I carry out by reading, and my personal experiences. In my setting I recognise that professional practice requires me to keep up-to-date with researched findings and to consider how these can be applied to my own setting, although care needs to be taken when interpreting what research tells us. Some studies are superficial. Some forms of research contradict others and the media often poorly report on research. I have been directed to an example of how research has influenced work with children. This research is *The Effective Provision of Pre-School Education* (EPPE), which is a comprehensive report investigating the effects of pre-school provision. Its findings found that children who had attended early years provision were more likely to have better cognitive, social and behavioural skills when they started formal education than those who had no early years provision. EPPE also confirmed the value of early learning through 'play', especially from low-income families. *Key Elements of Effective Practice* (KEEP) is another example. This document emphasises that effective learning in children is dependent on secure relationships. Learning through play and forming secure relationships are both key elements to the EYFS.

LEARNING OUTCOME 3

UNDERSTANDING HOW TO SUPPORT DIVERSITY, INCLUSION AND PARTICIPATION IN EARLY YEARS

3.1 Explaining what is meant by:

- diversity;
- inclusion;
- participation.

Diversity means:

Different or diverse people, having a variety of differences between individuals in a group of people, e.g. varying backgrounds, experiences, styles, perceptions, values and beliefs. In my setting this may be where the children are of different age groups, different cultures, or even the foods they eat at snack time.

Inclusion means:

The act of including, the act of taking part and getting involved. This may be helping a child who is not keen to play either due to disability or language. In my setting I would take steps to observe and reflect in order to provide resources so that the child becomes included in the activity.

Participation means:

The process of identifying, understanding, and breaking down the barriers to involvement and belonging. In my setting I believe that participation can be for the parents to be involved in the setting. Active participation gives children and families a say in how provision is made for them. Skills to promote participation include listening actively to what children and families say and being ready to respond by changing day-to-day practice or the way that a setting is organised. Communicating with parents and being ready to respect their opinions is an important element of participation.

3.2 Explaining the importance of anti-discriminatory/anti-bias practice, giving examples of how it is applied in practice with children and carers.

The importance of anti-discriminatory/anti-bias practice is where I, as a childminder, must have policies in the setting that support anti-discriminatory practice, which will say that all children are treated equally regardless of ethnicity, gender, religion or ability. In my setting I ensure that services must be all-inclusive. Thereby, children with special education needs have access to all areas and activities. Equipment must reflect diversity. Dressing up clothes should be for boys and girls – I have clothing from different cultures and they are accessible to all. Girls should be encouraged to play with traditional 'boys' toys, and boys encouraged to use traditional 'girls' toys. Toys should reflect all races and sexes, such as having black dolls, boy dolls, etc. Books, toys and posters should show ethnic minorities and disabled people in positive roles such as working as doctors, teachers, policemen/women etc., and not stereotyped according to race, ability and gender.

Equality and equal opportunities

Eqality and opportunities is about giving each child in the setting the chance to participate in all activities, trips, stories, role play, etc.

Legislation

I wish to mention the legislation in relation to equal opportunities in settings. These laws include the Children Act 1989, the Human Rights Act 1998, and the Disability Discrimination Act 1995. In my setting I am aware of and implement the Race Relations Act 1976 and the Sex Discrimination Act 1975, particularly if one has an interest of going into work in a nursery as a practitioner.

Implementation

I ensure in my setting that practice isn't just about not discriminating and stereotyping against the children. I also have to remain unbiased about children's parents and their way of life. For example, if a 17-year old mother walked into my setting, I cannot jump to the conclusion that she had unprotected sex at 15, got pregnant, lives in a council house, takes tax payers' money and sits around smoking and drinking. If this happened anywhere, or a practitioner saying something very similar, this would be extremely unprofessional and an unfair comment to make. I believe that this issue is about actively challenging discrimination in practice, e.g. if a childminder is not part of the solution then s/he must be part of the problem. Therefore, in my setting, I clearly say to the new parents bringing in children that all children will be included and valued no matter what ethnicity, gender, ability, culture and beliefs they have. I never have preconceived ideas. For example, boys can play with dolls, girls can be truck drivers or builders, white people can be cleaners, black people can be doctors. I ensure that I challenge any stereotypes and/or discriminative words and gestures if I hear children use them.

Examples of how it is applied in practice with children and carers

Celebrating a variety of religious celebrations such as Diwali, Christmas, Easter, Chinese New Year, etc. I also prepare activities around these religious celebrations to raise the children's own awareness of why that religion celebrates a certain event or time of the year.

Disability

If there is a child with behavioural problems, bad parents, disabilities or are multicultural, I as a childminder must have understanding and empathy.

Culture

I ensure that I know about their culture and background, e.g. some children in Asian or Arabic societies have gender roles in the home and so a boy may not understand what tidy-up time is, as it may be his mother and sisters' role at home. I ensure that I balance the rules of the setting and his right to follow the child's culture and the legislation.

Safety

I also balance the issues of safety. For example, is a sari suitable for a climbing frame game?

Equipment

I take the step of looking at the toys and images in books and posters – are they giving out the right vibe? For instance, are all children from an African background pictured wearing traditional clothing or is it showing the African culture in the UK (western clothes like jeans and coats)? I make sure that toys are suitable, e.g. not too easy and not too hard, so a wide range of children can access them.

Age

I ensure and update my understanding that 1-3 year olds are a product of their home life, so they need understanding and patience.

Policies

I have an Equalities Policy, and I have an anti-discriminatory statement of intent.

In my setting I have a statement of intent to promote anti-discriminatory/anti-bias practice by implementing my policy. The following is my anti-discriminatory/anti-bias statement of intent, which I use as a pattern for good practice:

MY CHILDCARE SETTING
ANTI-DISCRIMINATION/ANTI-BIAS STATEMENT OF INTENT
I take great care to treat each individual as a person in their own right, with equal rights and responsibilities to any other individual, whether they be an adult or a child. Discrimination under sex, race, religion, colour, creed, marital status, ethnic or national origin, or political belief, has no place within my setting. Should any person believe that this policy is not being totally complied with, it is their duty to bring the matter to my attention at the earliest opportunity. My setting and staff are committed to:
1. Encourage positive role models, displayed through toys, imaginary play and activities that promote non-stereotyped images. Books will be selected to promote such images of men and women, boys and girls.
2. All children will be encouraged to join in activities, i.e. dressing up, shop, home-corner, dolls, swing, climbing on large apparatus in parks, bikes, etc.
3. Regularly review childcare practice to ensure the policy is effective.
4. My setting aims to ensure that individuals are recruited, selected, trained and promoted on the basis of occupational skill requirements. In this respect, my setting will ensure that no job applicant or employee will receive less favourable treatment on the grounds of age, gender, marital status, race, religion, colour, cultural or national origin or sexuality, which cannot be justified as being necessary for the safe and effective performance of the work or training for the work.
5. Service Provision: No child will be discriminated against on the grounds of sex, race, religion, colour or creed. Wherever possible those designated disabled or disadvantaged will be considered for a place, taking into account their individual circumstances and my ability to provide the necessary standard of care.
6. My setting will strive to ensure that all services and projects are accessible and relevant to all groups and individuals in the community within the targeted age groups.
7. I will strive to promote equal access to services and projects by taking practical steps, such as ensuring access to disabled people and producing material in relevant languages and media.

3.3 Explaining how the active participation of children in decisions affecting their lives promotes the achievement of positive outcomes.

If children are able to participate in choice, this enables them to feel ownership. This enables the children to want to do the things set out for them, from which they make choices, the choosing becomes an achievement for them, and they feel that they own the choice and the achievement.

In my practice I allow active participation of children in decisions affecting their lives so that this promotes the achievement of positive outcomes. I provide a setting and a service that is for all. Therefore I always ask parents at the outset about each child's individual needs. This enables me to plan for the choices the child might make. Through the choices children make, there are decisions that appeal to each child's individual needs.

In my setting active participation of children in decisions affecting their lives promotes the achievement of positive outcomes. I always make sure that I find out the likes and dislikes of children so that I can provide an environment where I can give the children choice. By giving the children choices my setting allows them to make decisions building on their confidence, self-esteem and social skills. For example, in my setting we have golden time once a week and the children get to pick the weekly set activities in different areas of the setting and also which ones they want to attend each week.

I have learnt through practice that children need to actively participate in decisions that will affect their life. Children that are young need to make simple choices that enable them to find out their likes and dislikes. It can be as simple as having a choice between an apple and a pear, or a cheese sandwich and a packet of crisps. This will enable them to express their needs and wishes. Letting the children make choices builds each child's confidence, self-esteem and their social skills.

In my setting the children make choices all the time. This will be when a child makes a choice on what they want to do or who they want to do it with; these are simple choices that a child of pre-school age can make for themselves. This will enable the child to develop more and make choices later on in life that are more important, such as relationships, whether to gain a qualification, which career to follow, when to get married, when to have children, what course at college, or what job they may undertake. These will all be big decisions that could affect the rest of their life. I, as practitioner, need to actively listen to the child's choices and other ways that they may be able to communicate their wishes such as pointing, pictures or signing (which are non-verbal). I always need to understand that children have voices and that they should be heard and providing that they or others are not in any significant harm, then their wishes should be listened to and followed.

Example of how children in my setting actively participate in their own choices

At my setting I open at 8am, and for the safety of all the children, when they first come in, myself and my assistant are in one room. Then, at 9am, I open up another room and the garden and then at 11am it is pack away time and at 11.30 we separate all three rooms with different choices, such as one room might have a computer, another room might have stories and the last might have singing and the children make their choices about which activity they would like to join in. Then, at 12.30, I allow the children to lay the table for their lunch as I supervise. There is a variety of fruit and choices in sandwiches. In my setting children also make choices on all activities during free flow. By giving them these choices it helps them to make small decisions in life and will enable them later in life to extend this to bigger decisions that affect their lives more and will help for future experiences. This is how the active participation of children in decisions affecting their lives promotes the achievement of positive outcomes.

LEARNING OUTCOME 4

BEING ABLE TO REVIEW ONE'S OWN PRACTICE IN PROMOTING DIVERSITY, INCLUSION AND PARTICIPATION IN EARLY YEARS SETTINGS

4.1 Explaining the importance of reviewing own practice as part of being an effective practitioner.

In my setting I have found that there is great importance in reviewing one's own practice as part of being an effective practitioner. I have learnt that 'reflective practice' is the term used to describe the way in which professionals evaluate their own work and consider ways of improving their work. It is important to do this, as each year a different set of children and parents join the setting. They may have different needs and expectations or interests. Activities, routines and polices may have to be changed or updated to accommodate the new families. Reflecting on practice will help to see where changes need to be made. In most settings, staff are developing all the time too. Their knowledge and skills may change due to extra training or new staff having new ideas. I am aware that national standards and frameworks may also change so this may have an impact on how the setting is run.

To reflect on practice I always need to be able to critically question what I do and see whether what I am doing is working or whether there is room for improvement. This may mean observing the reactions of children and other people to help me think about my effectiveness. In my setting in areas I think are working well, I think about what skills and knowledge are helping me to do well and whether I can become more effective. In areas I think there are weaknesses, I would also think about ways to improve, which may mean more training in a certain area.

Reflecting on my practice will help me to have a clearer picture of what I actually do within my work role. It will help me to feel more confident about how I work with children and to be clearer on the things I may not be so sure about. It will also help me to reach higher standards in my work and to provide a better service to children. Therefore, I have found that there is great importance in reviewing one's own practice as part of being an effective practitioner.

4.2 Undertaking a reflective analysis of one's own practice

Practice is the implementation of standards and policies that I have set for my setting. Therefore, all own-setting reflective analyses examine how well I implement my setting and the standards expected by such quality upholding bodies as Ofsted and the local education authority. Part of my reflection is through the annual review of self-evaluation required of me by Ofsted. In my setting I evaluate how I assess my work. I use the various systems of accountability to allow me to stand back to measure how I am practising. In order to undertake a reflective analysis effectively it has to be done in the work setting. My work setting is that of a childminder. There are a range of types of early years sector, which include the following: pre-school, LEA nursery, day nursery, children's/family centre etc. All these are to be found in the Local Education Authority (LEA), private, voluntary or independent sector. My setting would be under the private sector. I am aware that the voluntary sector includes faith and community groups that set up childcare provisions, whilst the LEA also has pre (nursery) facilities. They all offer context for childcare.

The purpose for which I undertake a reflective analysis in my own practice is to care and educate children, and all the above settings including mine will cater for babies and children that are placed there or into a day nursery for parent/s to go back to work. As I undertake this reflective analysis of my own practice I bear this background in mind in order to cater for children taken to sessional settings for social/education needs or purposes. I bear in mind all of these reasons and know that children come to me for a mixture of care, education and other reasons. Therefore as I care, I reflect. Reflection can be like moving furniture around my playroom or home. Once it's moved I stand back and take a look, to see if things are better, or I ask myself, can I still get to the TV and door/small toys, car boxes and garage? If I find that I cannot do what I need, then I move and rearrange things again. Reflection for practice is the same, the way things are done may not always be the only way to do them. Reflecting to see this helps identify gaps and areas that can be improved. As I analyse reflectively I can state that when it is during practice, i.e. when I am in action, I make on-the-job decisions, observations and judgements. When it is after practice, in hindsight – on action, I analyse theoretically – what happened, and could have happened, enabling me to identify the change that made the transition between what did happen and what could have happened.

Reflection on my own practice is important because it allows me to assess what I am doing well and identify areas where I might like or need more training or guidance to ensure that I am performing to the best I can and am meeting all the standards and expectations within the setting's policies and procedures. It helps me think about what I am doing and to always be aware of how I work with the children, families and colleagues. Through my reflection I am learning from things I am doing well and identifying areas to improve on. In my analysis I have found that reflecting on one's own practice can enhance and improve my confidence and self-esteem, because I can look at what I am doing well, the things I have learnt and achieved and feel good about myself, especially if I have done something with ease that I used to find difficult or if I have done something I never thought I would do. This then gives me confidence to continue working well and to aim to try other new things or to use what new skills or knowledge I have gained in my practice. For example, I have done this NVQ 3 course and I look back to where I started the testing, the values, my tutor's many hours of helping me to comprehend and apply material to my setting, and how much knowledge I have secured through it and it makes me feel proud. So I am now able to make an analysis of what reflective practice is in my own setting.

What is an analysis of reflective practice in my own setting?

I have learnt that the most important characteristics of reflective practice are the process of reflecting on action that I have taken, either during an activity or after an activity itself. I have learnt that Donald Shön first coined the phrase 'reflective practice'. He argued that the ability to reflect on action was part of the process of continuous learning. I now know that reflective practice can be used as a learning opportunity across a range of activities, projects and experiences by individuals and teams. I understand and apply this in my setting. Reflective practice is best undertaken by me standing back and examining success or lack of it, or I could use a facilitator or coach such as my tutor who can support and challenge my actions or the learning. The outcomes of reflective practice can help inform the learning and development needs of a practitioner.

What is the process of reflective practice in my setting?

In order to undertake an analysis of reflective practice in own setting:

- I gather data on what has/is occurring/what I have done in my setting.
- I analyse what has worked well and what needs to improve, stop or change in my setting.
- I commit to a set of changed actions and behaviours in my setting.
- I put these into practice within my setting.
- I review the effectiveness of these actions in my setting.

In many respects, therefore, reflective practice is linked to the action learning cycle. Reflective practice has many similarities with action learning, which means doing something about things already done, taking action to improve after lessons have been learned by myself, the practitioner.

What is the link to learning practice and Learning Needs Analysis?

Within this undertaking of an analysis of reflective practice in my own setting I have learnt that the output of reflective practice should be a greater awareness of my behaviour and actions and their impact on the children and parents in relation to my setting, or my links with others in external agencies, and how I implement and act on my policies. Also, the result of reflective practice is often the identification of development areas; aspects of my skills, knowledge or behaviour that need to be enhanced. This learning can apply both to teams as well as individuals. Therefore, reflective practice should focus on what I, the childminder or the team or individuals, need to continue and what needs to change. I have through this analysis understood that it is essential, just like with other techniques for identifying learning needs, that I as a childminder take responsibility for my own development. For those who work in organisations, some of the learning and development requirements may be met by the organisation, such as the provision of courses or funding for professional development. Alternatively, the individual, together with their line manager, may identify opportunities on or off the job for development. Reflective practice should then encourage the individual to think about what they have gained from the development they have undertaken and what they need to do next.

4.3 Developing of strategies to deal with areas of difficulty and challenges encountered in professional practice in early years settings.

Quality assurance is a clear strategy to deal with areas of difficulty and challenges encountered in professional practice in early years settings. I have a template form that I use to address and develop strategies. Further to that I have for this question also set out how I would respond to an identified difficult situation encountered in an early years setting.

In my own setting I have experienced difficulties and challenges. My setting is an early years practice. In order to develop appropriate strategies, I have to use good practice as the first strategy upon which to build everything else that follows. Therefore I take into account the 'feelings and behaviour' of the children and use it as a creative approach or springboard to develop strategies to deal with areas of difficulty and challenges encountered in professional practice in my early years setting.

Feelings and Behaviour – A Creative Approach

In her book, *Feelings and Behaviour – A Creative Approach*, published by Early Education, Anni McTavish provides further information on how to use puppets, stories and responsive behaviour skills to respond creatively and compassionately to the various incidents, emotions and behaviour that young children display. I have found this book helpful as a practitioner to respond to young children's feelings and behaviour, which are posing difficulty and challenges. The book provides a step-by-step guide and practical suggestions, supported by examples of good practice. I have used it to develop positive strategies for dealing with difficulties that can arise in any early years setting. Parents and children expect qualitative services. Therefore, my strategies are to prevent and defuse difficult situations as part of my EYFS implementation of principles.

In my setting I have seen that behavioural issues commonly encountered in an early years setting include biting, fighting and conflict, problems with sharing and tantrums. Creative strategies to deal with these can be implemented in any setting, significantly improving the day-to-day experiences of both children and adults.

The following form shows the date(s) of an incident; indicating what the incident relates to (in this case a health and safety matter, and shows what guidance has been complied with – applied as relevant Actions:

MY CHILDCARE SETTING

Quality assurance form:

Date	Incident	Action
COMPLIANCE	HEALTH & SAFETY	Ofsted GUIDANCE
		EXPECTED STANDARD SAFEGUARDING
MANAGEMENT	KEY WORKER	PARENT
IN SETTING PLAN		
THE PROBLEM		
STRATEGIES		
PERIOD OF IMPLEMENTING STRATEGIES		
RESULTS		
IF STRAGY HAS NOT WORKED WHEN CHILD IS REFERRED TO PARENT & EXTERNAL AGENCY		
Here I am taking three examples for this exercise showing what strategies to use to defuse the difficult and challenging situation that could arise in my early years setting. (a) Biting; (b) Fighting; (c) Serious incident.		

Incident: Biting

I have seen that biting is a common behaviour in young children between the ages of 14 months to two and a half years of age. Most biting occurs in toddlers, who have little or limited language, but usually stops as language and social skills develop. To know this helps with the development of strategies to deal with it. I am aware that children may also bite because of hunger, teething, anger or boredom. They may not have enough space, be overcrowded or not have access to enough favourite toys. Biting may be initiated by transitions, such as a new baby in the family or giving up a dummy, by worry or stress, or because they are in an inappropriate environment or expectations are too high. I have learnt some useful questions to ask: When and where did it happen? Who with? What happened before? What happened afterwards? Why do I think it happened? What is 'behind' the behaviour – how do I think the child feels? As a childminder I have learnt to avoid to feel awkward, or defensive, in response to questions from parents of 'bitten' children. For example, do I tell them who the 'biter' is? I may also be unsure of how to support the parent/s of the child who is biting. This shows how a difficult situation arises for me as a practitioner, yet I have to deal with it. Hence, the need to be ready, armed and equipped with strategies that can resolve the situation peacefully.

If a child bites: I have learnt to comfort and take care of the child who has been bitten, in a 'low-key' calm way. (The biter may not realise how much it hurts.) Strategically I tell the bitten child, "That must be sore, let's get a cold cloth." To the biter, I have to say in a firm, but gentle voice, "It's not OK to bite, biting hurts. If you want to bite, you can bite a cracker or a toy, but I can't let you bite Tom." I have to strategically encourage the biter to 'make amends' in some way, to help get a cold cloth, a tissue or teddy for comfort. I strategically do not insist on 'sorry', unless the biter genuinely wants to do so. I strategically support the bitten child to say, "No, don't do that", and to ask for a hug/soft touch.

Strategies to use:

In my setting I make a point of giving positive attention and affection to the 'biter' throughout the day. I strategically would provide snacks and drinks regularly. I make sure there is more than one of a favourite toy. I arrange furniture and resources to make space and room for play. I am always on hand to help children set simple limits – say 'mine', or 'no, my toy', and model for them how to negotiate and take turns. I am aware of changes taking place at home, and help children to deal with these by talking, "You miss your dad while he's away", "It can be a bit scary when you move to a new house". I discourage 'play-biting' at home, but I do share concerns and strategies with parents. My target is strategically that behaviour will change if everyone works together.

Never bite a child back: In my setting I teach children how to gain positive attention. I would develop a 'biting policy', and a leaflet with guidelines to support parents and my assistant. I reassure parents that biting is a common occurrence, and a phase that their child will move through. (I guard against saying things like, "This is one of the worse cases I've seen" – even if it is!)

Creative ideas to try: In my setting I provide crunchy snacks – apples, carrot sticks, cucumber, toast, rice and corn crackers. I would strategically introduce a puppet or persona doll story about biting, along with the idea of a 'biting' basket containing objects that are safe to bite or mouth – jam jar lids, flannel, new plastic dog toy, rubber door stop, tough beanbag, etc. I would also provide a treasure basket for seated babies (six to ten months) and heuristic play resources for one- to two-year-olds. I would ensure I have sanitation to sterilise provided teething rings of all shapes and sizes. I would plan simple rhyme and singing sessions for short amounts of time with small groups of children. I would provide interesting natural play materials to pinch, poke and squeeze such as play dough and clay. Strategically I would model how to say sorry appropriately with my assistant/children. I would acquire or take photos of children being caring, gentle or respectful of each other, and make a display, perhaps linking to the themes of the EYFS – Positive Relationships, Learning and Development. I would strategically act, if biting persists, by asking the child's parents to visit a dentist or a paediatric osteopath.

Incident: Fighting

Fighting and conflict: One of my own children has autism and learning difficulties, so I have had to learn both through my training and as a parent. In my setting, learning how to deal with conflict is a necessary skill for children to acquire. Children are also learning to 'self-regulate' – becoming able to tolerate a feeling of distress. This involves a child to learn waiting until the need is met (for example, feeling hungry, but being able to wait for lunch in five minutes), or in being creative and beginning to problem solve. I strategically have learnt that providing a structured, predictable environment, with warnings for changes in routine, and then appreciating children when they manage to 'self-regulate', will all help: "Well done for waiting your turn so patiently." In my setting, I work strategically to help with conflict – the most common reason is over toys or resources – to be on hand with a non-judgemental commentary, along the lines of, "You really wanted the toy, and when you grabbed it, Alia hit you, and now you are so mad you want to hit her back! I can't let you hit Alia, but I can help you talk to her about what you would like." I have found that as children learn to tolerate some frustration and anxiety, they will be less reactionary, and impulsive. Strategically I am always ready to step in and model for children how to wait for a turn: "Let's wait here by the table, until they're finished, then we can have a go." I have learnt and practise the key, which is to be a child's ally, the friend in these situations, rather than the rule-maker who says, "Stand there and wait your turn!"

Incident: Serious Incident

Where conflict is more serious: For example, children are being verbally abusive or racial comments are being made, I help them see things from a different perspective through the use of a story. I have had a child who used to racially abuse other children, and I had to deal with this matter by ensuring that she understood that people are different but are all valuable and worthy. I made myself her ally and showed her that we can be different races, different sexes, different ages, but we value one another and live together. I also had to speak to the parents as some of the language the perpetrator used was adult-like. The habit died almost as quickly as it appeared. Strategically this will also give children some 'emotional distance', making it safer for them to begin to consider their actions.

Recognise children's physicality: In my setting I always strategically examine a child's behaviour where there is lots of throwing, hitting or kicking. I provide ways for the children to express this through games and activities such as throwing wet sponges against the wall, hitting balls or targets, building with blocks, banging with saucepans and wooden spoons, squirting runny paint onto large pieces of paper, kicking balls. I also sing songs or play movement games to practise stopping, starting and waiting, encouraging children to work in pairs, on their own or as part of a group. I strategically know through my training that as long as children are not hurting each other, it can be useful to wait before stepping in – to see if they come up with their own solutions, however small. Therefore, I strategically praise them if they manage this, and talk about it later in a small group, so other children have the opportunity to learn.

Sharing: I am aware that young children are not always ready to share. Strategically I look at this as not always ready to do 'turn-taking', and if I am inventive with games to facilitate this, some sharing is possible. I strategically work to allow children time to develop and experience the concept of 'ownership'. I strategically set up a space or small table in a corner where children can place special toys from home. I allow them to show others what they brought and find this is ideal. I can strategically use a simple photographic game of baby photos on a flap, with the 'grown-up' picture beneath. This can help to explain 'who belongs to whom'. Once a child learns that sharing does not necessarily mean they have to give their one precious toy away, sharing becomes more of a possibility.

In my setting I help children develop confidence in turn-taking with simple games and songs like *Two Little Dickie Birds*. I would use cardboard cut-outs or six plastic birds in a bag. I sing the song and share the game with six children. Or I can sing *Five Little Monkeys Jumping on the Bed*. I can also use other things like asking children to hand round plates of fruit, where there is plenty for everyone to have three to four pieces. I model politely, saying 'please' and 'thank you' as I do this. I would positively reinforce any spontaneous turn-taking, but rather than saying, "Good boy or good girl", I would say, "I like how you're taking turns, well done!"

In my setting I work hard to help children to join in and develop friendship skills, I ask them to do things like, "Could you deliver this 'letter' to Sarah in the house?" or, "I think they need some more blocks for the train they're building… here are some."

Strategies and ideas

I provide pots of bubbles to blow in the wind. I pave colourful ribbons to dance and sing with. I include simple board games that are fun to share with one other. I try using kites or parachute games. I can use a well-resourced role-play shop, with plentiful supplies of boxes, tins, paper bags, tills, pens and paper that provide lots of opportunities for sharing and turn-taking. I help children to negotiate how turn-taking can work. I always talk and say things like, "Adam loves the trains, can he have the green train for one minute, as long as he gives it back? I can put the egg timer on for you." or, "Let's write a list of names of who wants to have a go. How long shall we each have – two, three or four minutes?" I tell a simple story about two children or puppets fighting over a toy, and invite children to help 'sort it out', and come up with ideas to solve the dispute.

Tantrums

I am aware that a child's screams and hitting can be alarming, but tantrums can be common in many young children under the age of five, or if the child has learning disabilities such as autism and may be under-developing. I remind myself this is a normal development and stay calm. Tantrums are a bit like a rainfall with too much rain falling at once. Likewise, emotions can be too much for a child to hold, and they overflow. I, the adult, have to deal with myself first and help the child appropriately, hence this training. I have learnt that tantrums can happen when a child, used to a relaxed approach at home, joins a setting with clear limits and well-defined boundaries. Children are learning to deal with their emotions, and need our help to do so.

Ideas to try

When dealing with difficulties or challenges from a child I now know to consider the 'useful questions to ask': When and where did it happen? Who with? What happened beforehand? What happened afterwards? Why do you think it happened? What is 'behind' the behaviour – how do you think the child feels? I try distracting a child if I know a tantrum is brewing. I utilise the outdoor area fully. I remind myself that limits are important; it's OK to stick to them. I am aware that children find it hard to wait too long, so I make sure routines run smoothly. I ask myself questions such as, could they be hungry, tired, or becoming ill? I always use the friendly ally approach. I offer cuddles, a cosy story time or gentle songs to ward off a tantrum. But because nothing can be predictable with children, if a tantrum occurs I make sure the child is safe and keep other children 'out of the line of fire'. It may help to avoid eye contact. I reassure visitors and other children that this is normal and the child needs to express some strong feelings. I do not try to reason with or have a conversation with a child in the heat of a tantrum. (I have to calm him/her down first.) I may, depending on the child, be able to hold him/her, rock him/her or reassure him/her to help him/her calm down.

Ideas for promoting positive behaviour

I have a child with learning difficulties. I have through this experience learnt that I can use awards/rewards such as a star-sticker award chart. So I can develop or have a celebration tree – I record individual children's achievements on paper 'leaves' and hang them onto the tree. I can use children's names and simple language to appreciate behaviour I like. I can say that, "I like how you put all those blocks away Mariam!"

I talk to the parents/guardians

To provide guidelines for parents and my assistant about how to support positive behaviour, and make sure they use children's correct names, I report achievements and positive behaviour to parents within earshot of their child. This will also help to build positive relations with parents. A simple statement like, "Ambar has been a very good partner today", is enough to lift the spirits of both child and parent, yet it is a report. In my setting I stick to three or four general rules, such as, 'Walking indoors, running outside', 'Respectful and gentle touch', 'Listen when someone speaks'. I am on guard that myself and my assistant need to model these appropriately. I can reinforce these 'good' behaviours throughout the day. I ensure communication. I make a point of saying what I want, rather than what I do not. I say, "Yes, we can get the toys out, once we've finished tidying up these blocks", instead of, "No, we must tidy up first!" I always consider the effects of too much stimulation, colour and sound in the environment, and aim to keep the setting as calm as possible, with soothing colours, and natural resources. I always smile at children, and tell them how much I like them, their clothes and enjoy spending time with them. I always make time for fun, laughter, jokes and special treats.

Unique Child

In my setting, whilst I believe that as an adult, and a parent, I have a well-developed understanding and implement strategies to deal with areas of difficulty and challenges encountered in professional practice in early years settings, I am also aware that all behaviour needs to be taken in context. Although there are some general rules and guidelines, it is important that each child's individual situation is considered, and any plan to deal appropriately with behaviour must begin with observation.

I take time to get to know a child, for example, what's happening at home, their interests and passions, as well as spending time with them. In my setting I also consider how adult responses might be affecting behaviour. I ensure that I take care of myself by talking through concerns with my mentor, colleagues and consulting parents, and access training and specialist help where necessary. It is important that when dealing with the feelings and behaviour of early years children, childminders and teachers should try looking at creative ways to approach and deal with problems in order to develop strategies to deal with areas of difficulty and challenges encountered in professional practice in early years settings.

CHAPTER 6

SUPPORTING CHILDREN'S SPEECH, LANGUAGE AND COMMUNICATION

When addressing issues relating to:

SUPPORTING CHILDREN'S SPEECH, LANGUAGE AND COMMUNICATION

UNIT AIM: I found that this unit aims to provide a basis for understanding the importance of speech, language and communication for a child's overall development and explores the ways in which those working with children can support the development of speech, language and communication skills.

LEARNING OUTCOME 1

UNDERSTAND THE IMPORTANCE OF SPEECH, LANGUAGE AND COMMUNICATION FOR CHILDREN'S OVERALL DEVELOPMENT

1.1   Explain each of the terms:

- speech;
- language;
- communication;
- speech, language and communication needs.

In my setting I understand the importance of speech, language and communication for children's overall development. These components are so vital that I use them in every aspect of my dealing with children.

- Speech – voicing or verbalising language.
- Language – structured communication with rules and a set of symbols that are spoken, written or signed.
- Communication – a way of sending signals to other people, i.e. body language, facial expression, gesture and language.
- Speech, language and communication needs – the need for these three areas refers to any difficulty that a child might have in their development, or in these areas themselves. These three areas are closely linked to other areas of development. Being able to communicate opens doors with the overall development.

In my setting therefore, cognition refers to the information that we gain and store for future experiences, i.e. touching something hot, the child will then make a connection with said object. A child with difficulties in any of these areas will need support to aid with their development. I have seen this many times, sadly with my own child who has a disability and does not recognise and has no fear of danger. She wants to walk to the gas stove and wants to touch the fire. I have to be on guard to support her and protect her to increase effective communication for safeguarding purposes.

In my setting I see how children come into school with spiky profiles – some can speak fluently and others a mixture of words. In my setting I have provided care for children whose first language may not be English. In my setting I always ensure that before children join my provision I make or do a home visit to get to know the child's communication needs. This is also useful before the child attends schools. In these visits I usually ask the parents about the child, and get to know basic information, likes and dislikes, communication and language or speech needs. This initial communication helps my planning – I get to know what name the child likes because James may like Jimmy or Edith may prefer to be called Edy. To generate communication rapport, I usually show some pictures of the activities I provide in my setting and ask which ones the child likes.

One-to-ones

For me asking questions that start with 'what' and moving onto questions with 'how'. I always start with "what is your name?", even if the parents have already given me information of who the child is. This helps the child to know that I want to know him/her. Therefore, in my setting I understand the importance of speech, language and communication for children's overall development. I also would agree with the English dictionary meanings as follows:

- Speech – something that is spoken; an utterance, remark, or declaration.
- Language – communication by voice in the distinctively human manner, using arbitrary sounds in conventional ways with conventional meanings; speech.
- Communication – the imparting or interchange of thoughts, opinions, or information by speech, writing, or signs.

In my setting I have learnt that speech, language and communication begin from birth; simply engaging in eye contact and smiling is communication. Speech is started with noise and sounds. Language starts by a child listening, so even from very young ages children learn and communicate with us.

I have learnt that speech is vocalised language. It is usually learnt before the written language. In speech the symbols are not written or signed but are actual spoken language as sounds. Usually from the age of 6 weeks babies will make cooing sounds to show pleasure. The babies make these sounds as the mouth has not yet fully developed properly. From 6-9 months the baby will babble as if they are practising sounds. By 9-12 months the range of sounds that babies produce becomes more limited and reflects the sound used in the language they are hearing. At around 12 months babies repeatedly use one or more sounds that have a meaning for them. The number of sounds that children will need to learn depends on the language they are hearing. English has over 40 different sounds.

Therefore, I have found that research sets out that language is a set of symbols either spoken, written or signed that can be used and understood between people. Language can be quite abstract. Linguists also suggest that the main feature of a language is a series of roles that users employ.

In communication, a baby or child that cries so much may be unable to draw attention to need or pain, such as a soiled nappy or ailment, and the adult may need to observe and check for signs or symptoms or seek external agencies support.

That is how I understand the importance of speech, language and communication for children's overall development.

1.2 Explain how speech, language and communication skills support each of the following areas in children's development:

- learning;
- emotional;
- behavioural;
- social.

Speech, language and communication (SLC)

In my setting, SLC is used when children are learning. For example, listening, communicating, etc. and how these help us learn. In educational settings, children and young people need to learn. This is when they develop. Therefore, speech, language and communication skills support each of the following areas in children's development:

Learning – This is when children are able to:

1. listen to and understand information they are given;
2. make sense of concepts and ideas they are learning;
3. learn a whole range of new words and use them well;
4. share their ideas with others and answer questions;
5. use language to solve problems and ask for help or explanations;
6. read, write and learn to spell, interact with others, play and socialise.

Emotional – Speech, language and communication skills support children's development and if they understand, they are less likely to throw tantrums when their skills in speech, language and communication have grown and they are understanding more.

Behaviour – Speech, language and communication skills support children's development in how the child behaves. Once a child understands language they can begin to understand the consequences of their actions. The child responds positively when spoken to through behaviour or actions.

Social – Speech, language and communication skills support children's development in social activity. This allows children to understand the feelings of others and the ways we may interact.

In my setting, this is how speech, language and communication skills support children's development emotionally, behaviourally, and socially.

1.3 Describe the potential impact of speech, language and communication difficulties on the overall development of a child, both currently and in the longer term.

In my setting there is great impact from speech, language and communication. Therefore, if there were any speech, language and communication difficulties this would impact negatively on the overall development of a child both currently and in the long term. I always work with each child to gauge how they are using communication so they can benefit from support, which may require speech therapy or other external agencies' support. Speech, language and communication needs in children vary with each individual child. As a practitioner I must constantly assess and contribute in all aspects of communication, speech and language. I must listen to the child and try to understand the things the child is trying to communicate to us. In my setting I always work to ensure that I am helping children improve things like language. I can take some measures that are fairly simple, such as by having patience. I repeat the words often and praise the attempts and successes a child makes. I can ask the child to point out something or encourage saying words or sounds. I encourage the child to take my hand and lead me to something the child needs or wants. This is a good way of helping communication and means that I can say the thing they need so they learn it. I find that in my setting encouragement is essential, as I do not want the child to feel silly or ashamed if they struggle with the correct word. In all settings speech, language and communication skills are vital for all children. I have learnt that without these skills they will not reach their full potential. Early years practitioners are crucial to supporting children, and identifying when they might be having difficulty. One in ten children have speech, language and communication needs, so all early years workers need to understand how to better support these children.

In my setting, and I know that in educational settings too, children and young people need to:

- listen to and understand information they are given;
- make sense of concepts and ideas they are learning;
- learn a whole range of new words and use them well;
- share their ideas with others and answer questions;
- use language to solve problems and ask for help or explanations;
- read, write and learn to spell and interact with others, play and socialise.

Children with different speech and language abilities will need different support to help them to be able to do all of the above. This is how I describe the potential impact of speech, language and communication difficulties on the overall development of a child, both currently and in the longer term.

LEARNING OUTCOME 2

UNDERSTANDING THE IMPORTANCE AND THE BENEFITS OF ADULTS SUPPORTING THE SPEECH, LANGUAGE AND COMMUNICATION DEVELOPMENT OF THE CHILDREN IN ONE'S OWN SETTING

2.1 Explaining the ways in which adults can effectively support and extend the speech, language and communication development of children during the early years.

In my setting I understand the importance and the benefits of adults supporting the speech, language and communication development of the children. Therefore I explain the ways in which adults can effectively support and extend the speech, language and communication development of children during the early years, as it is seen through the way I communicate with each child. I use words and levels of language for instance (different language and words for babies compared to 3- and 4-year olds). I use the following methods:

- Questions – this I find is an important part in stimulating and extending children's speech, showing the children that I am interested in what the child is doing/thinking.
- Rhetorical questions – this I find very useful when working with babies and toddlers as it helps me and any other adults sustain commentary whilst busy with a child who may not be able to say very much. It helps babies and toddlers to feel included as long as eye contact is kept throughout by both parties.
- Closed questions – I use closed questions, i.e. expecting short answers such as 'yes' or

'no'. This I find good for babies and toddlers so that they can feel part of the decision making and for children who do not yet feel comfortable with adults yet.

- Open questions – I use this expecting longer answers, so as to help children to think more about what they are going to say.

I would like to emphasise that in my setting I explain to my assistant and the parents the ways in which adults can effectively support and extend the speech, language and communication development of children during the early years, ensuring that words and levels of language are age/stage appropriate. I give children plenty of time to answer as a child takes longer to process the information given to them. I look at them and they look at me, I get down to their level, maybe I kneel, I speak at a normal pace and use language that they understand. I use questions such as rhetorical, closed and open. I am sensitive as to when to use questions (age/stage) so that the desired conversation/interaction is not above the understanding of the child. I use appropriate information and activities. I develop or search for such activities based on the child's interests. For example, I can allow sharing a book as the children always love listening to the story in a book and joining in with the words. Children can then experience the factual side of books, for instance if there are leaves in the story, I can allow the children to come with me in the garden and collect a leaf each, to feel and know. This way, by watching and exploring, I am supporting the learning of new words such as leaf. I always try to provide designing, drawing and mark making equipment in the creative area to encourage children to write as a form of communicating (mainly for the older children but some younger children participate too). I can also incorporate songs for a child to communicate with actions; if they don't want to participate in singing, the actions usually make them join in.

In my setting I also work with parents, to ensure that there are opportunities such as reviews with parents emphasising how important communication is. I am aware that there are many times that parents communicate with their child, e.g. on the way home in the car, dinner time, bath time, bed time. I am aware that the strong secure relationships with parents can come out of the communication the parent has with the child.

External agencies: I am also aware that if there are difficulties of speech, a speech therapist would be a referral point through the GP. In school, a SENCO will support a child with communication difficulties, referrals, parents' permission, Speech and Language Therapy (SALT). Therefore, in my setting I understand the importance and the benefits of adults supporting the speech, language and communication development of the children. The above is how I explain the ways in which adults can effectively support and extend the speech, language and communication development of children during the early years.

2.2 Explain the relevant positive effects of adult support for the children and their carers.

In my setting I am aware that positive effects may include improvements in:

- speech, language and communication skills;
- social interaction;
- behaviour;
- emotional development/self-confidence.

Relevant positive effects in my setting will involve encouraging children to develop self-confidence, which impacts on their communication with others – the positive effect is that children can become more socially comfortable. I work towards self-confidence in order to build self-esteem, which enhances well-being, a positive outcome of *Every Child Matters*, and builds their ability to be resilient, knowing adults support their learning and communication positively in opposition to negatively judging, criticising, ridiculing/teasing. There will be a decreasing need for aggression or frustration where communication difficulties may otherwise have proved too much for them or had been overwhelming. The positive effect is that children learn to manage their behaviour through communication skills. With increased communication skills children take more enjoyment and learning from their interests, speaking and listening activities leading to enrichment. A major effect is the potential for reducing the number of referrals for specialist speech, language and communication support. I am aware that there are the *Talk to Your Baby* resources. These are a good resource for supporting parents – I am aware that these resources are good to build relationships, support children's engagement of communication at home and in the setting. In my setting I use daily activities to open up opportunities to develop children's communication, speech, language and vocabulary, for example, whilst playing ducks and boats in the water tray, on the carpet with small vehicles and tracking, at the jigsaw table, or during a snack time of breadsticks, fruit, milk and water. Adult support can also be from external professional agencies, e.g. contact with a speech therapist can have positive outcomes for both the child and the carer, using eye contact, getting down to the level of the child when talking with them, providing information to parents/carers about events taking place in their local community, praising and encouraging children and also allowing them to express their emotions.

In my setting, I am aware that there are several key areas of development, which can be remembered by the acronym PILES: P = physical, I = intellectual, L = language, E = emotional, S = social. These are the aspects of development that I target for positive results of development. I am aware that if adults in my setting and/or school do not give good support in these areas, children do not learn the correct way of communicating and carers with problems in this area also do not have a role model. In my setting I also use picture books that provide for reading books without words; this enables a child to 'tell' the story using pictures as clues. This develops language and different ways to communicate using voice. There are several stages that show various signs of a child's development:

1. **From the moment they are born:** Babies will recognise the mother's voice – and probably the father's – from inside the womb. I have learnt that in fact, it is good to sing and speak to the baby before birth – in pregnancy women are encouraged to talk to their bump. Following birth, one should be sure to make eye contact and smile. As a childminder I am able to do this so as to get the relevant positive effects of adult support for the children and the child's carers.

2. **From birth to age two:** I have learnt that in order to get the relevant positive effects of adult support for the children and their carers, I should know and be able to explain to carers or parents that it is estimated that we are born with 20% of our brain capacity, but before our third birthday it is up to 80%. If carers and parents know this, it will result in the relevant positive effects of adult support for the children and their parents/carers.

3. **Before they start talking:** The relevant positive effects of adult support for the children and their carers can be evidenced through communication. Communication is more than just words, it is also gesture, eye contact, body language, touch, music, smiles. Babies can understand long before they can talk. Therefore, I am able to give the relevant positive effects of adult support for the children and their carers because if a child learns something good through me, it makes the carer's work easier.

4. **Communication:** I have learnt that communication is a two-way exchange – you smile, s/he smiles; you sing, s/he opens her mouth wide; s/he babbles and you respond. This is the start of conversation. Through this knowledge I am able to give the relevant positive effects of adult support for the children and their carers.

5. **Say it back the right way:** The child learning to speak will say things the wrong way round. I say it back the right way, and extend it. S/he points and says, "ay aw" and I say,

"Yes, it's your toy car, isn't it? Your lovely red car". Therefore, I am able to give the relevant positive effects of adult support for the children and their carers because if a child learns something good through me, it makes the carer's work easier.

6. **Allow TV for limited periods:** I have learnt that children can be allowed to watch television, but as guided learning. In my setting I allow children to watch television but with them so that I can talk about it. Nobody learns words by passively watching TV, so I limit the time the television is on and use the time to play, which enriches exploration and discovery for the young mind. I give this advice to parents and carers. This way I am able to give the relevant positive effects of adult support for the children and their carers.

7. **Talking can happen at any time:** I am aware that talking can happen at any time for children, but it is recommended not to keep up a running commentary, as young minds need time to process what they are hearing and also need space to babble themselves. This is advisable for childminders and carers. Therefore, I am able to give the relevant positive effects of adult support for the children and their carers because if a child learns something good through me, it makes the carer's work easier.

8. **Using Conversation:** Conversation is a two-way process. You speak, leave space, hear a babble or see some pointing, and then you respond. In my setting, according to age, this is what I would do with a talking child, so I start the habit and it grows for them to speak, listen and understand. Therefore, I am able to give the relevant positive effects of adult support for the children and their carers because if a child learns something good through me, it makes the carer's work easier.

9. **Allowing response:** I am aware that by all these things, by responding I am showing respect for what the children are trying to say and encouraging them to stay engaged with me or any involved adult whilst I carry on my conversation.

10. **Helping develop their communication and social skills**. In my setting, adult support is the most important start to the children's later learning, plus it helps social and emotional development. Although it cannot be guaranteed it is also likely to discourage crying. If a child is supported and can get what s/he wants by pointing or speaking s/he would not need to cry to get attention. Therefore, in my setting I am able to give the relevant positive effects of adult support for the children and their carers because if a child learns something good through me, it makes the carer's work easier.

2.3 Explaining how levels of speech and language development vary between children entering early years provision and the need for this to be taken into account during settling and planning.

In my setting the levels of speech and language development vary between children entering early years provision and there is a need for this to be taken into account during settling and planning. I am aware that settling children into their day is of great importance. The learning opportunities available are amplified when children are confident, happy, motivated, engaged and supported in their play and exploration, through their active participation or through natural observation – this is known as vicarious learning (first coined by Bandura in 1986 to refer to observation learning).

In my setting I follow the EYSF. This is due to the fact that planning for children's needs is a requirement of the early years framework in supporting the positive outcomes of EYSF through the *Every Child Matters* (ECM) outcomes. Ensuring human and children's rights is an effective way to proactively support children's development of communication, speech and language needs. Planning also provides occasions for understanding reactive strategies that expand communication, speech and language skills in response to each child's individual interests. In my setting I am aware that levels rely on a scale of the expected speech and language development for babies and children. I have learnt that in the UK children are expected to absorb and assimilate language that enables 'school readiness' for children aged 5. So a child will be ready by that age to enter into school. I have also learnt that for older children the development sequence will help for communication, speech and language.

For children entering early years provision the variation in development can be evidenced by asking as a way of assessment: How old are you? What class do you like? This being the stage of development they are at. I am aware that babies need more exaggerated facial expression with clear gestures to objects in order to help meaning and communication understandable. Whereas a 4-year old needs a more complex language to help development progress, it is important to take into account various stages/aspects of the child's development. How much stimulation and encouragement have they experienced? What is their first language and language spoken at home? Are there any individual speech, language or communication needs/difficulties/gaps? I always take into account these assessment factors, which could be asked and answered formally in writing/audio – I can always do these as part of my setting's welcome to new families and children through their enrolment and settling-in policy/procedure, and professionally informal, observing information that supports my practice. The suggestions I help make for the child's individual development and how I can involve myself in their play and learning may be good for my assistant or in other settings such as schools. It is good for temporary or agency staff who are less permanent in an early years settings. Therefore, that is how levels of speech and language development vary between children entering early years provision and need to be taken into account during settling and planning. It is also necessary in my setting to be aware of the self-confidence and self-esteem of the individual children.

I have experienced this particularly with my daughter who has learning difficulties. She has fears and her self-confidence can be low. In speech she will misuse the context more than for a child of her age. So she is easily misunderstood. Therefore, being aware of a child's self-confidence and self-esteem is important. I am aware that the child's ability to settle may highlight a need for reassurance, transitional awareness and an understanding of attachment theory.

In my setting if a child is struggling to settle, I invite the parent to wean the child into the setting, allowing me to visit him/her at home so s/he gets used to me. This helps for adaptation for a childminder/staff, parent activity. I have come across the suggestion that it will help to have some knowledge of the *Every Child a Talker* project/programme (2008). This is designed to help early years practitioners create a developmentally appropriate, supportive and stimulating environment in which children can enjoy experimenting with and learning language. It can be implemented whether children are in early years settings, with a childminder, or at home with their parents. I have learnt that there is something called 'scaffolding' children's language by helping with grammatical constructs and extending understanding. Also, 'recasting' the information children give can involve the child, e.g. "We done sand today." – "Yes, we did play with the sand today, how did you make that sandcastle?" "Adam coat, your coat" "Yes, that is Adam's coat and this is my coat, who am I?"

My role as a childminder becomes one that enables 'facilitating' communication between children – this helps them with understanding each other, forming positive relationships, and demonstrates ways each can utilise negotiation and conflict resolution by waiting, listening and expression. This is how levels of speech and language development vary between children entering early years provision and the need for this to be taken into account during settling and planning.

LEARNING OUTCOME 3

BE ABLE TO PROVIDE SPEECH, LANGUAGE AND COMMUNICATION
DEVELOPMENT OF THE CHILDREN IN ONE'S OWN SETTING

3.1 Demonstrate methods of providing support taking into account the:

- age;
- specific needs;
- abilities;
- home language where this is different to that of setting;
- interests of the children in own setting.

In my setting I can demonstrate the methods of providing support taking into account the age, specific needs, abilities, home language where this is different to that of my setting, and the interests of the children.

Methods may include:

- adapting own language;
- scaffolding the child's language;
- giving children the time and opportunity to communicate;
- facilitating communication between children with each other;
- learning through play;
- working with parents or carers;
- implementing the UN Convention on the Rights of the Child.

Age

In my setting I support children through provisions and my services. My expectations of children's behaviour take account of their age and stage of development. Expectations that consider children's age and stage of development are evident where in my setting I implement and demonstrate a broad understanding of child development and developmentally appropriate behaviours in young children – this helps to modify the children's behaviour and programming to address the needs of individual children, including those with disabilities or learning difficulties or developmental delay. In my setting I demonstrate awareness that children's behaviour is influenced by their temperament, abilities, experiences, culture and family context. Therefore, I encourage children to understand one another in the setting, so they become aware of factors that may influence other children's behaviour and to respond using appropriate strategies – I always tell children for instance, "Joelia is younger than you, so she may not understand some things, do not fight with her if she is holding your toy." I also encourage families to contribute their ideas and experiences about their own children's behaviour.

Specific needs

In my setting the provisions and my expectations take account of children's specific needs, which impact on their behaviour. I take account of their age and stage of development, I take account if the child has specific needs.

In my setting it depends on the age and (if applicable) the educational level (school grade) of the child(ren) in question. Parents often have their child(ren) with disability issues given an

Aptitude Test at a Children's Treatment Centre at an early age. My own child has had to undergo that exercise to secure a working guide statement for school and all the agencies involved. The results of that testing can be shared in such ways to improve the setting in which one is working. In order to better integrate children with specific needs or disabilities into a setting or a school classroom there are many meetings with primary caregivers, home care workers, (special) educators, and potentially some of the officers (including the person who did the Aptitude Testing) from the Children's Treatment Centre. It might help to stress aiding children with disabilities to build self-esteem. This is how I would demonstrate methods of providing support, taking into account the specific needs.

Abilities

In my setting I demonstrate methods of providing support taking into account the age specific needs and the children's abilities. I recognise that children have different abilities, either according to age or other personal circumstances, such as learning differences (do not perceive them as difficulties – they are just different). I am aware that the process of communicating with others begins at birth and continues to develop throughout life. I have seen in my setting that primary school children are at an age when their abilities to express themselves, listen to others and successfully communicate their thoughts and feelings undergo rapid change. They are often eager to learn how to communicate better.

I recognise that people of all ages can have trouble expressing what they think and feel. Sometimes humans just find it difficult to find the right words. Sometimes a situation seems intimidating and one can feel shy to say what they really feel. Sometimes we are afraid that others will make fun of us or reject us. All of these difficulties are particularly common with young children. In my setting therefore, I recognise that communication is a two-way process. The ability to listen is vital in effective interpersonal communication and is linked to being sensitive and empathetic with others. Again, some young children find it difficult to listen carefully. Therefore I implement as a method a few simple rules that can help young children to communicate effectively:

- I think before I speak.
- I don't shout.
- I speak clearly.
- I tell the other person how I feel.
- I say all I want to say.
- I listen carefully.

I have learnt that communication patterns and abilities vary greatly from one child to another and depend to a large extent upon experiences before entering my setting or the school. For example, some children may be used to communicating a lot with parents or older brothers and sisters, while others may have had little social interaction. Some children talk a lot and are very excited when they communicate, whereas others either don't talk much or seem uninterested. In a new setting for all children, this is a time when their communicative abilities are increasing dramatically. They are learning to differentiate. Where a younger child simply yells, a six- or seven year-old can often understand and explain the cause of his/her frustration or pain. I know that a very young child may call all animals 'dog', but an older child differentiates between 'dog' and 'cat' – and eventually learns to tell the difference between different breeds of dog. The child's view of the world becomes more sophisticated. My child used to refer to dogs as giddy up horses.

In my setting, while the child's vocabulary is expanding, I am aware that the vocabulary is still fairly unsophisticated. Starting school and learning to read introduces children to many new words, but they often find themselves unable to say exactly what they mean. For example, a child will have experienced feelings of jealousy and being nervous but may not be able to describe them in words.

In my setting, regardless of the different communication abilities or patterns that they have established, children of six- and seven-years old are aware of the power that communication gives them. For example, they may have learned that one way to express displeasure is to sulk and not to respond to questions or attempts to engage them in conversation. Sometimes children do this with parents, and may get pleasure and a sense of control from seeing how upset their parents become. On the other hand, children at this age can become frustrated when they are not able to communicate effectively and need to be supported to say what they want to say.

In my setting it is part of the service that I make it important to help children understand that the ability to express oneself directly does not give licence to say anything one thinks or feels in any situation. I support children – good communication involves being conscious of other people's feelings. I do not encourage children to just say whatever they want to say, regardless of how hurtful or inappropriate it may be. When infants first learn to speak, they do little to censor what comes out of their mouths, whether what they say has a specific purpose (such as getting something to eat) or is simply produced for the pleasure of making sounds. By the time children are six or seven though, they have learned that there are certain things that are said in some social contexts which are not to be expressed in other situations. For example, children tell other children things they would not say to a childminder or teacher.

I therefore encourage children to think about what they want to express in different social contexts. Then, when they do try to say something, they should communicate it clearly and directly. In the process of coping, one of the central elements is the ability to use available resources in order to obtain help. Children vary greatly in the extent to which they seek support and help on a daily basis. Some children appear to seek help all the time, even when it is not needed. Others rarely ask for help, possibly because they lack practice in communicating requests for help to others. For many children, the fact that the potential helper is an adult and an authority figure can make it more difficult to ask for help.

In my setting I am aware that learning to read and write opens up a whole new world for children. In early childhood, communication with and by children mainly involves the spoken word, but most six-year olds are beginning to rapidly expand their reading skills. The standard of skills is still very uneven, with some children managing a few words and others able to read simple books on their own. Reading allows children to access knowledge on their own, without relying on anyone else, and gives them power. It is another example of how children in this age group are rapidly expanding their communicative abilities. This is how I demonstrate methods of providing support taking into account the age, specific needs and abilities of children.

Home language where this is different to that of setting

In my setting I demonstrate methods of providing support taking into account the age, specific needs and abilities of children and in situations where home language is different from that of my setting. I have for instance looked after a number of children from the Polish population settling in the area of my work.

Many come to the UK without any or much spoken English, they mainly use Polish in their homes with the children. I had to support the children and parents by breaking the language barrier and sought friends of the parents/families who spoke some English in order to have appropriate and trusted communication. I could have used an official interpreter, but the trust would not really be there, so I used community networks and friendships to translate. During the process of looking after the children I found myself acquiring some spoken Polish language. Whilst the idea of having a child in your childminding setting who does not speak English, or your own home language, may seem daunting, I found that supporting a child's home language, even when I cannot speak it myself, is not impossible. I use a bit more extra care, so that bilingual and multi-lingual children can be accommodated and thrive in what was a mono-lingual childminding setting and their inclusion has many positive benefits to all children involved.

One of the most important things is for me to maintain a balance between helping children to acquire new language skills and supporting their home language. I find it essential that children who speak alternative languages can get help and feel able to use their home language even in my setting. Children need to feel that their language and culture is welcomed, valued and respected by having it acknowledged and visibly supported. I, as childminder, should be careful not to provide transitional bilingual education that shifts the child from speaking their home language to the dominant majority language, i.e. English, but to maintain and enhance the child's first language. In order to achieve this, the whole environment of my setting should reflect a multi-cultural and multi-lingual approach. I am lucky that my family is multi-cultural and dual heritage.

Settling in period

When I discuss a placement with prospective parents I am able to find out more information about a child's home language and experience with other languages. Children may be initially shy and rely on their first language or be able to understand more words than they can speak. Discussing what words a child can speak or understand helps build a more accurate picture of their current language skills. It may also help to find out why parents have chosen a setting with a different language. Some parents may deliberately choose a setting to help their child acquire an additional language; others may have been forced into their decision by a lack of alternative childcare facilities. I am aware that the reason for their choice may influence how they feel about the setting and language support. If they are hoping a child will develop new language skills I may need to discuss why I want to incorporate their home language too. In my setting I can allow a settling in period where the child attends with a parent or other family member that can act as a translator; this period will be particularly important. During these I and the other children present can learn and use key words and phrases such as greetings, toilet, yes, no, mummy, daddy, drink and eat. They also allow the child to learn your daily routines such as preparing for a school run or a meal. Having predictable routines and behaviour expectations will help children to settle more easily.

I can enhance these using photographic representations of the timetable and expected behaviour. These photographs are examples of the visual and contextual clues that enable children to interact. Other examples include conceptualising environmental print by the addition of photographs, for example, for the contents of boxes. While a child is settling in, it can be beneficial to introduce the child to another child through an activity they can share, as this will be less intimidating than being immersed in the larger group and expected to interact. Children will need support as they learn and make sense of new cultural values and behaviours. A positive attitude from both myself and the other children present leads to more success in becoming bilingual. Incorporating their home language is essential to their self-esteem and to help them settle quickly into my setting. I demonstrate methods of providing support taking into account the age, specific needs and abilities and home language where this is different to that of setting.

Multilingual environment and resources

I use resources to create a multi-lingual environment. I provide multi-cultural events and resources and real life experiences and activities children can make sense of and identify with. I do this because my setting is a mono-lingual childminding setting providing opportunities to communicate with adults, parents, peers, older children and others from the community who speak their home language and encouraging children's use of the home language. When planning I try to use familiar topics, songs, stories, rhymes and artefacts. Suitable artefacts might include dressing up clothes reflecting the child's own culture, cooking implements, tableware, calendars, pictures, leaflets, newspapers. I find it helpful to provide activities that demonstrate the purpose and function of items. For example, using a wok and chopsticks for stir frying if I have a Chinese child in my setting. I know that this allows children the opportunity to see their own culture reflected and other children have the opportunity to learn about different cultures in context. I can also experiment with role play with structured areas to represent home experiences to encourage interaction and engagement. Literacy materials can also be provided so children can use print in a relevant and purposeful manner, e.g. recipe books, menus and magazines. I always try to use some songs, stories and rhymes in the children's home language. Stories from their own culture help children with their emotional security. I know that older, more confident bilingual children, parents and family members can help support me and the children by helping to teach songs, dances, stories of other cultures, rhymes and legends in both English and the cultural language of the story. I share these activities with the whole group and not just those speaking the language. Props, gestures and facial expressions can be used to help their understanding. I can get books and toys to reflect the diversity of society in positive ways and represent language in addition to English, particularly children's home languages. I am aware that dual-language books and story and song CDs are available to borrow from libraries, or I borrow from the parents who may have some to share. Other appropriate books include those depicting stories and people from other cultures, legends and folk tales from the children's home culture.

I know that books for bilingual children beginning to read need to be chosen with illustrations that match the text and of concepts that the children are familiar with. Abstract concepts may be more difficult to grasp. Abstract phonics in a foreign tongue may be more difficult for bilingual children to achieve.

When I use graphic or mark-making activities they should contain all the usual provisions used for monolingual children, with additional alphabet books and picture dictionaries in the emergent bilingual child's first language. I always ensure that examples of scripts familiar to all the children should be provided and early attempts at mark-making encouraged and discussed. Adults could be invited to model writing and could include family and community members. In my setting I have learnt over the years as a childminder that parents, older siblings and family members are the most valuable source of multi-lingual tutors, artefacts, songs, stories and recipes. They will be able to tell me what resources are relevant to them; never assume that just because a child identifies with a particular culture they will follow all the practices. For example, just because a child is Chinese, does not necessarily mean at home they eat with chopsticks. Including parents and families informs me and other childminders about home and community-based languages and experiences and the literacy experiences of the children and their parents' expectations. That way I demonstrate methods of providing support, taking into account the age, specific needs, abilities, and home language where this is different to that of setting.

Interests of the children in own setting

In my setting the interest of the children is the basis and ultimate aim. I am also aware that all of the national frameworks are based on the UN Convention on the Rights of the Child

(CRC). What are the child's best interests? I understand that the CRC does not explicitly define a child's best interests. The term is imprecise, as is 'welfare of the child' and many other concepts. Even so, some points are very clear from the CRC. In the case of actions and decisions affecting an individual child, it is the best interests of that individual child that must be taken into account. It is in a child's best interests to enjoy the rights and freedoms set out in the CRC. For example, it is in children's best interests to develop respect for human rights and for other cultures (Article 29.1(b) and (c)). It is in a child's best interests to maintain contact with both parents in most circumstances (Article 9.3). It is in the best interests of indigenous children to be raised in the indigenous community (Articles 5, 8.2 and 30). A child capable of forming a view on his or her best interests must be able to give it freely and it must be taken into account (Article 12).

Parents have primary decision-making responsibility on behalf of their children (Articles 5 and 18.1) but, if they fail to make the child's best interests a basic concern, the state may intervene to protect those interests (see Article 9.1 for example). Usually and normally any parent would have their child's interests at heart even when choosing a childminder. In my setting I implement 'best interests of the child' to mean and describe the set of principles or factors that guide a provision's policies and deliberation when assessing what decisions would keep a child safe and how best to meet a child's needs; this in court could include custody. This term is used differently in each country. I have found useful the following examples of principles and factors applied in different settings or systems that include:

✓ importance of birth family bonds and attachments including siblings;
✓ importance of bonds with other care givers in a child's life;
✓ health and safety of a child including hygiene;
✓ the special needs of a child;
✓ the mental and emotional health of the birth parents or others seeking custody;
✓ the length of time the child has spent waiting for permanency;
✓ what the child wants, usually with an age or level of maturity attached to the suitability of listening to the child's wishes.

In my setting I strive to uphold, and protect the 'best interests' of the child using the following methods that may include:

• adapting own language;
• scaffolding the child's language;
• giving children the time and opportunity to communicate;
• facilitating communication between children with each other;
• learning through play;
• working with carers;
• implementing the UN CRC recommendations on the rights of the child;
• upholding the Ofsted standards set out in EYFS framework.

This is the way that I demonstrate methods of providing support, taking into account the age, specific needs, abilities, and home language where this is different to that of my setting.

3.2 Observation.

Usually observation aspects are practical ways in which you demonstrate how to do what is required of you. But if your tutor wants you to write up what you do, simply emphasise in what you write on the phrase 'I do'.

3.3 Evaluate the effectiveness of speech, language and communication support for children in one's own setting.

In my setting I reflect on my practice so as to evaluate the effectiveness of speech, language and communication support for children as follows. Language intervention is effective and the earlier treatment is initiated, the better the outcome. In my setting we use speech, language and communication every day with the children. Also, when doing activities we are communicating, talking and using language. I am aware that in many settings there are children who communicate using Makaton when they do not know how to say certain words or when in a noisy environment. I think it is important to let children express themselves through language. I have learnt that for schoolchildren with weak language skills, language services that are integrated into the education setting by school speech-language therapists/pathologists have resulted in important educational outcomes, including significant gains in reading skills for primary school children. I now know that meaningful improvements in adaptive behaviour in the setting comes about through one-to-one support to help for the child. I have to observe children, and where I find that there are shortcomings in a child's development of speech, language and communication I offer effective support, discussing with the parent my concerns and, where appropriate, agree to make referrals. When considering services for communication disorders in my setting, I have found that some parents wait too long before taking action. I am aware that many school boards provide good services that build on the pre-school/childminders' efficiency and effectiveness in supporting the children and families to access help prior to entering school. In my own local area I am aware that services are deployed by speech-language pathologists and supervised supportive personnel using the most educationally current and innovative techniques and service delivery models. In my setting I know that language is not just another subject. It is the means by which all other subjects are pursued. I have learnt that the only sensible and practical solution to educating the children with communication disorders is integrated, not fragmented, educational services administered by educational speech-language pathologists in educational settings.

In my setting I therefore review evidence about the key factors that provide a supportive speech, language and communication environment. (Key factors: physical environment, staff roles and responsibilities, training needs and opportunities, views of children, appropriate involvement of carers.) In this exercise I am standing back and I am reflecting on my delivery and content not on the effectiveness of it. Are the children learning? Do they enjoy it? Can I see changes or not? Since to evaluate is to measure, how I do this? I look at the key factors in detail:

1. My rooms/setting layout – I ask myself, what does my physical environment look like? What is the noise level? Are there quieter and noisier areas, planned times or activities? Quality of light – are play areas well lit for children to see and communicate well with each other, see mouth movements, resources and staff (myself and my assistant)? Is there enough space to move, expressively, with whole bodies, with and without speed? Resources and toys – is there a varied selection available for both indoor and outdoor play?

2. Staff, involvement/roles – How does everyone interact with children to promote communication, share observations that 'worked well', "She does have two eyes, two ears and very jumpy feet", share information about choices, e.g. snack foods, range of activities, are we making introductions? "Joelia's mum is in today to help make sandwiches." Have I clarified staff responsibilities? I ensure that all involved know me as the key person; this system operates to support the children. How do I monitor, check children's language needs?

   I ask myself, have I got a system for planning daily routines? Are there times of the day to support communication, e.g. greetings and goodbyes, hygiene practices, toilet asking times? Small, large group and individual activity? Do I evaluate my training opportunities? For example, this course, or possibly for Makaton, baby signing, other language, SLT, disabilities/impairment, development, activity intervention and awareness.

3. I evaluate the children's own views – How do children tell me what they like to do, what they would like to play with and how is that recorded/actioned?

4. I evaluate the effectiveness of how I engage parent and carer involvement – How does my setting engage with parents to share activity ideas, rhymes, resources, books, event dates, news, parents' language needs, knowledge and expertise?

5. Language itself – I identify the types of language/methods of communication used in the setting, such as facial, body, creative, expressive, behavioural, ESL or EAL, sign, Braille and see if anything needs updating, renewing, reorganising to meet the needs of everyone who accesses my provision. I evaluate to identify if there are any gaps in languages. These are words that are used to discuss and describe objects and activities spoken in English within the setting but home language versions are unknown so that they can't be shared with parents/carers outside of the setting, e.g. sand, play dough, book corner, snack time. In my setting I have heard what is known as 'in reverse'. In reverse are the words used at home not known in English so children are unable to share events or items with everyone within the setting, e.g. cultural clothing names, musical instruments, cooking utensils, event and festival names. I therefore am constantly adapting ways to communicate, such as pointing, increasing the use of facial expression, simplifying and shortening sentences, text, email, large print.

This is the way I evaluate the effectiveness of speech, language and communication support for children in one's own setting.

LEARNING OUTCOME 4

BE ABLE TO CONTRIBUTE TO MAINTAINING A POSITIVE ENVIRONMENT THAT SUPPORTS SPEECH, LANGUAGE AND COMMUNICATION

4.1 Explain the importance of the environment in supporting speech, language and communication development.

In my setting the environment is important in supporting speech, language and communication development. This makes the children strong, they become more confident in using speech, language and communication. I am able to contribute to maintaining a positive environment that supports speech, language and communication. I explain this as follows. I use the physical environment, making opportunities available through planning and, throughout the day, including a range of child and adult-led activities, using communication and developing 'friendliness'. For example, I use my space, light and layout noise levels, visual support, clear and consistent routines, supporting notes. I know that many different resources describe 'communication friendly' or 'communication supportive' environments, settings or spaces. I use these to support the children. In my policies and work plan I use relevant materials to design activities for my setting, showing why and how the environment is important in supporting children's speech, language and communication development. I use the EYFS principles into practice. The importance of the environment in supporting speech, language and communication development is that it enhances EYFS, 'enabling environments' for the children. Therefore:

*   I provide a stimulating environment in which creativity, originality and expressiveness are valued.

- I include resources from a variety of cultures to stimulate new ideas and different ways of thinking.

- I offer opportunities for children with visual impairment to access and have physical contact with artefacts, materials, spaces and movements.

- I provide opportunities for children with hearing impairments to experience sound through physical contact with instruments and other sources of sound.

- I encourage children who cannot communicate by voice to respond to music in different ways, such as gestures.

This is how I explain why and how the environment is important in supporting children's speech, language and communication development.

4.2 Review evidence about the key factors that provide a supportive speech, language and communication environment.

In my setting I review evidence about the key factors that provide a supportive speech, language and communication environment. (Key factors: physical environment, staff roles and responsibilities, training needs and opportunities, views of children, appropriate involvement of carers.) In order to review my evidence, I am standing back and I am reflecting on my delivery and content, not on the effectiveness of it. I ask myself: Are the children learning? Do they enjoy it? Can I see changes or not? Can I see evidence and show it to others or share it with parents or carers? Since to review evidence is to re-assess, look at it again and measure how I do this, I look at the key factors in detail.

KEY FACTORS THAT PROVIDE A SUPPORTIVE SPEECH, LANGUAGE AND COMMUNICATION ENVIRONMENT IN MY SETTING ARE:

1. My rooms/setting layout – After setting up, I review evidence by asking myself, what does my physical environment look like? What is the noise level? Are there quieter and noisier areas, planned times or activities? Quality of light – are play areas well lit for children to see and communicate well with each other, see mouth movements, resources and staff (myself and my assistant)? Is there enough space to move, expressively, with whole bodies, with and without speed? Resources and toys – is there a varied selection available for both indoor and outdoor play?

2. Staff, involvement/roles – I review evidence of how everyone interacts with the children to promote communication, share observations 'that worked well', "She does have two eyes, two ears and very jumpy feet", share information about choices, e.g. snack foods, range of activities, are we making introductions? "Joelia's mum is in today to help make sandwiches." Have I clarified staff responsibilities? I ensure that all involved know me as the key person; this system operates to support the children. How do I monitor children's language needs? I ask myself, have I got a system for planning daily routines? Are there times of the day to support communication, e.g. greetings and goodbyes, hygiene practices, toilet asking times? Small, large group and individual activity? Do I evaluate my training opportunities? For example, this course, or possibly for Makaton, baby signing, other language, SLT, disabilities/impairment, development, activity intervention and awareness.

3. I review evidence and evaluate children's own views – how do children tell me what they like to do, what they would like to play with and how is that recorded/actioned?

4. I review evidence and evaluate the effectiveness of how I engage parent and carer involvement. How does my setting engage with parents to share activity ideas, rhymes, resources, books, event dates, news, parents' language needs, knowledge and expertise?

5. Language itself – I review evidence of the identified types of language/methods of communication used in the setting such as facial, body, creative, expressive,

behavioural, ESL or EAL, sign, Braille and see if anything needs updating, renewing, reorganising to meet the needs of everyone who accesses my provision. I evaluate to identify if there are any gaps in languages. These are words that are used to discuss and describe objects and activities spoken in English within the setting but home language versions are unknown so that they can't be shared with parents/carers outside of the setting, e.g. sand, play dough, book corner, snack time. In my setting I have heard what is known as 'in reverse'. In reverse are the words used at home not known in English so children are unable to share events or items with everyone within the setting, e.g. cultural clothing names, musical instruments, cooking utensils, event and festival names. I therefore am constantly adapting ways to communicate pointing, increasing the use of facial expression, simplifying and shortening sentences, text, email, large print. This is the way I review evidence about the key factors that provide a supportive speech, language and communication environment for children in my own setting.

SUGGESTED BIBLIOGRAPHY:

Seek a Tutor's Guidance
Read EYFS *Every Child Matters*
Read upon UN CRC Notes
Use the policy documents and work plans
Search various websites on education and childcare
Find and read the *CACHE Level 3 Child Care and Education Student Book* (CACHE Child Care and Education 2007)

The best practice helps children by seeing their differences not their difficulties. Always see a challenge not a hinderance.

CHAPTER 7

CHILDREN WHO HAVE DIFFERENCES OR SPECIFIC REQUIREMENTS

In my setting I have tackled issues relating to

SUPPORTING CHILDREN WHO HAVE DIFFERENCES, CHILDREN AND YOUNG PEOPLE WITH SPECIFIC REQUIREMENTS

UNIT AIM: The unit is designed to assess competence in supporting disabled children or young people and those with specific needs in partnership with their carers. It also includes partnership working with other agencies and professionals.

LEARNING OUTCOME 1

UNDERSTAND THE PRINCIPLES OF WORKING INCLUSIVELY WITH DISABLED CHILDREN AND YOUNG PEOPLE AND THOSE WITH SPECIFIC REQUIREMENTS

1.1 Outline the legal entitlement of disabled children and young people for equality of treatment and the principles of working inclusively, placing the child/young person in the centre.

Once I receive an expression of interest for a place for a child, I visit the home of the child to meet the child and the parents. This enables me to plan for the needs, and specific needs of that child so I can meet the legal entitlement of disabled children and young people for equality of treatment and the principles of working inclusively, placing the child/young person in the centre. Using the EYFS my role would involve:

- removing of or helping to overcome barriers for children where these already exist;
- being alert to the early signs of needs that could lead to later difficulties, and responding quickly and appropriately, involving other agencies as necessary;
- stretching and challenging all children.

I am aware that the EYFS establishes four overarching principles to inform our thinking and practice in order to meet all young children's entitlement to learning. What materials I use must be organised according to the four sections and principles of the EYFS:

- a unique child;
- positive relationships;
- enabling environments;
- learning and development.

At the end of each section I reflect on my practice as:

- a practitioner and childminder (others could be playing other roles including):
- a team;
- a SENCO;
- a leader or manager.

In my case I play all these.

In my setting I ensure inclusion of all children including those with disabilities and specific needs. One of my own children has a disability – autism and learning difficulties. Therefore, the legal entitlement of disabled children and young people for equality of treatment and the principles of working inclusively, placing the child/young person in the centre, is very important and I outline it in accordance to the government code of practice; as follows.

Relevant regulations that place the child at the centre

The following regulations are relevant to matters covered in the code of practice of SEN:

- The Education (Special Educational Needs) (England) (Consolidation) Regulations 2001;
- The Special Educational Needs (Provision of Information by Local Education Authorities) (England) Regulations 2001;
- The Education (Special Educational Needs) (Information) (England) Regulations 1999.

I am also aware of other guidance that place the child at the centre.

Guidance on inclusion

- Section 316A of the Education Act 1996 requires maintained schools and local education authorities to have regard to guidance on the statutory framework for inclusion. The separate guidance, *Inclusive Childcare/Schooling – Children with Special Educational Needs*, provides advice on the practical operation of the framework of the legal entitlement of disabled children and young people for equality of treatment and the principles of working inclusively, placing the child/young person in the centre. It gives examples of the reasonable steps that maintained schools and LEAs could consider taking to ensure that the inclusion of a child with a statement of special educational needs in a mainstream school is not incompatible with the efficient education of other children.

The Disability Rights Code of Practice for Schools/Settings (placing the child at the centre)

- Part 2 of the Special Educational Needs and Disability Act 2001 amends the Disability Discrimination Act 1995 to prohibit all schools from discriminating against disabled children in their admissions arrangements, in the education and associated services provided by the setting/school in relation to exclusions from the setting/school. The reasonable adjustments duty on schools does not require the provision of auxiliary aids and services or the removal or alteration of physical features. Decisions about the provision of educational aids and services for children with SEN will continue to be taken within the SEN framework.

- From September 2002, settings/schools are required not to treat disabled pupils less favourably for a reason relating to their disability and to take reasonable steps to ensure that they are not placed at a substantial disadvantage to those who are not disabled.

- LEAs and relevant schools are also required since September 2002 to plan strategically and make progress in improving accessibility for disabled pupils to schools' premises and to the curriculum, and to improve the delivery of written information in an accessible way to disabled children or pupils.

Defining Specific Education Needs (Section 312, Education Act 1996).

Specific education needs are usually referred to as 'special needs'. Children have special educational needs if they have a learning difficulty that calls for special educational provision to be made for them.

Children have a learning difficulty if they:

(a) have a significantly greater difficulty in learning than the majority of children of the same age; or

(b) have a disability which prevents or hinders them from making use of educational facilities of a kind generally provided for children of the same age in schools within the area of the local education authority; or

(c) are under compulsory school age and fall within the definition of (a) or (b) above or would so do if special educational provision was not made for them.

Children must not be regarded as having a learning difficulty solely because the language or form of language of their home is different from the language in which they will be taught.

Special educational provision means:

(a) for children of two or over, educational provision which is additional to, or otherwise different from, the educational provision made generally for children of their age in schools maintained by the LEA, other than special schools, in the area;

(b) for children under two, educational provision of any kind.

In my setting, I implement my policies of equality, inclusion and anti-discriminatory practices as follows: 'A child is disabled if he is blind, deaf or dumb or suffers from a mental disorder of any kind or is substantially and permanently handicapped by illness, injury or congenital deformity or such other disability as may be prescribed.' This is Section 17 (11), Children Act 1989. Therefore, the definitions enable my setting to work within the above legal entitlement of disabled children and young people for equality of treatment and the principles of working inclusively, placing the child/young person in the centre.

In summary

I am aware that each setting or school must produce a range of policies that formally set out the guidelines and procedures for ensuring equality. These must take account of the rights of all individuals and groups (with children at the centre) within the setting/school.

When considering the way policies work to ensure equality and inclusion, as practitioners we do not just think of the teaching and learning that is happening in the setting/classroom. Policies must also pay regard to the values and practices that are part of all aspects of childcare/school life.

Before exploring the policies in my own setting, it is helpful to gain an understanding of relevant legislation and its purpose as I have set out above. A practitioner may not need detailed knowledge of each one, but it is important to understand the legal duties of the practice/setting/school. This will help the understanding of one's own role and responsibility to adhere to legislation and policy.

Therefore, the main laws relating to disability discrimination and to special educational needs in education are:

- Equality Act 2006;
- Disability Discrimination Act 2005;
- Disability Discrimination (Public Authorities) (Statutory Duties) Regulations 2005,

SI No. 2966;

- Special Educational Needs and Disability Act 2001;
- Education Act 1996;
- Disability Discrimination Act 1995.

That is how I outline the legal entitlement of disabled children and young people for equality of treatment and the principles of working inclusively, placing the child/young person in the centre.

1.2 Compare service-led and child- and young person-led models of provision for disabled children and young people.

My setting is a child- and young person-led model. I allow the views and ideas of children and young people in my care to influence my services and overall practice. I therefore compare service-led and child- and young person-led models of provision for disabled children and young people as follows:

A service-led model of provision is where children and young people are not consulted about the outcomes and strategies and how these are delivered and created. For example, with good reason to do so, the school curriculum is dictated to by the government. Especially for disabled children, in some cases service-led provisions are not useful or effective in offering the correct support to children, young people and their families because decisions have been made about services without them being involved.

A child- or young person-led model of provision is where the people the service and support is designed for will have had some influence on the provisions provided. For example, the children and young people will have decided what type of activities and equipment they need, they will help make decisions whilst also being supported by others. This empowers the children and young people by allowing them to have a say in what happens to them and the type of support they need and allows them a sense of responsibility. I allow the voices of children to be heard. The views and ideas of young people have to influence what I have to provide. I notice the children's and young people's contributions, especially through listening and or observation as they interact with me and their peers. Play is what children and young people do in their own time, for their own reasons. I learn lessons from children and adapt equipment to their liking or needs, such as if a child has a disability I ensure activity for them with and among others for inclusivity. When playing, children choose what to do, how to do it and who to do it with. Play takes many forms: doing nothing in particular; doing lots; being boisterous; showing off; being contemplative; being alone; being social; being challenged; being thwarted; overcoming difficulties. Through play, children explore the world and learn to take responsibility for their own choices. This is how I compare service-led and child- and young person-led models of provision for disabled children and young people.

1.3 Critically analysing the difference between the social model and medical model of disability and how each model affects provision.

In my setting I critically analyse the difference between the social model and medical model of disability and how each model affects provision. I do this by adjusting the environment to suit the needs of the child and appropriate resources and facilities are provided to allow the child to be confident. This also helps me and my assistant or other people who are working with the children and should focus on what the child can do instead of on what s/he cannot do. For instance, if I had a child in my setting who has a hearing impairment I would provide visual aids and I would, or get my assistant to, be trained using the Makaton system to enable the child to feel positive and confident about making progress. I do not think of children as special needs, but I think of them as children with specific or additional needs. In my setting we aim to give all children the same opportunities and children are not singled out because they have different needs. For example, although some children require one-on-one support we don't remove them from their peers; the child will still work in his/her group but they will get extra support. Low expectations about the potential of a disabled child, or being over protective can limit what they achieve. It is important that I as a practitioner have positive attitudes about what requirements I provide so children can have opportunities for making developmental progress.

Social models and medical models of disability

Labelling a child because of their disability can prevent us from seeing the child as a whole person. Like their gender, culture and social background, the medical model is a traditional view of disability and that through medical intervention the person can be cured, where in fact in most cases there is no cure. They expect disabled people to change to fit into society.

The social model of disability looks at ways to address issues to enable people to achieve their potential, by looking at ways to adapt the environment so the child can feel included; this is very important. The social model has been constructed by disabled people and by listening to what disabled people want and to remove any barriers that may be in their way. By removing barriers and adapting the environment you are allowing children and young people chances to achieve and learn, which promotes confidence and self-esteem.

My setting has removed potential barriers by providing wheelchair ramps around the house and having hygiene labels in toilets. I also have height adjustable chairs for a child to be included in different activities at different height levels if a baby or shorter. We also use visual symbols around the setting. IEPS (Individual Education Programmes/Individual Care Programmes) are reviewed three times a year and are set according to the needs of the child. I would involve my assistant and different agencies if required and hold meetings to work together for the child's targets. The children are aware of their targets and in childcare setting we would use pictures for them to use to see what their targets are. When planning is being done it will be done so certain activities will be adapted, for example a lower ability child would need to sequence the pictures and write the first sound of a word whereas the higher ability group would need to sequence and write a whole sentence. I have worked in school reception classes during my NVQ2 training and we have had a child in class who had her phonics adapted due to her disability and she would take part at the same time as the whole class but was requiring one-on-one support; this makes the activity different to suit her needs and ability.

One type of support available is speech and language therapy. These therapists will usually work in partnership with parents, childminders/teachers and support staff and anyone else who has regular contact with the child, and provide training and coaching sessions and provide them with ideas and strategies to put into place to help promote the child's speech. I myself have sat in on a session with a child in school when the speech therapist came to have a meeting with the child and she gave me advice sheets on how best to help him with his speech, including picture cards with words on with either two, three and even four syllables and the child was encouraged to clap the amount of syllables while saying the word. My own child has had speech therapy also using similar learning aides.

Medical Model: Support from health professionals offers additional learning support – a child who has a disability like Down Syndrome may need extra support in the classroom to help them learn. There are children who can come into a setting for social skills and may be provided with their own teaching assistant to support specific needs. A child with epilepsy is likely to require regular monitoring from health professionals and medication, which needs to be adjusted appropriately.

Assistive technology

This would be anything that will help someone, for example wheelchairs, hearing aids, walking frames. In my setting we use large computer keyboards for some children and for a child who is blind you could use software that reads text from a screen. There are many different aids available for children and adults to help them with everyday tasks.

Specialised services

In the school where my child with learning disability and autism goes we have a Special Educational Needs Coordinator (SENCO). Therefore in all settings, and in particular my own setting, I use other services such as physiotherapists, speech therapists, school nurses and social services. We use these services in order to provide the right care for the child.

In my setting that is how I critically analyse the difference between the social model and medical model of disability and how each model affects provision.

1.4   Explaining the importance of:

- advocacy;
- facilitated advocacy for children and young people who require it;
- the personal assistant role.

Advocacy – It is important that I am aware that some children or young people may require an adult to represent their point of view putting forward ideas, thoughts and views on behalf of them. It is important you appreciate their views, as this makes them feel involved and can help everyone make better decisions. It is not just good practice, it is a legal requirement under the Children Act. It's about giving children a voice and they must be listened to and you must also let the child or young person know what is happening. An advocate will listen, interpret, liaise and negotiate to secure children's rights. They can help parents gain information and support, and advocacy promotes social inclusion, equality and social justice.

Facilitated advocacy – This is important because it allows groups to work alongside decision makers to change the way that local services are run. They will put forward their ideas on what needs to be in place to benefit them. It allows them a voice to be heard and to make the decision makers aware of what is actually needed to ensure they get a better service.

The personal assistant role – The person in this role offers support and care to help them achieve things that would be difficult for them, but to also to allow them to make decisions so they feel empowered and allow them to be as independent as possible. It is important to respect their views and personal space and not rush them or put them under any pressure. It's also important that as a care assistant you don't do the things that the child or young person is able to do just because you can get it done quicker. You must always allow them to do what they are capable of doing.

In summary therefore, advocacy/facilitated advocacy is a means to support children with disabilities.

Disabled children are very vulnerable because they have learning difficulties or communication difficulties of some form. This is where an adult becomes important for a child; the adult will represent the disabled person's point of view. Advocates are often volunteers, however some are paid or appointed by courts so that the child's views can be heard. This is important for the child and is law for a child to have their views heard. The advocate should represent the child's views rather than their own (advocate's) views. When there is a case conference children will not be present, so the advocate will put the child's views across. Providing that there is no significant harm involved the child's wishes should be respected and facilitated, but at other times an advocate will work with the child to get to understand what they want and they will facilitate for them. Facilitate means that the advocate will put the child's views across. Therefore, the personal assistant role is where we help children/young people to care for themselves with some guidance, help and support. A child with learning difficulties can still decide on what they want to do or where they want to go, but they may need our assistance to help them achieve this. This will also stop them getting angry or frustrated because they are making choices. A personal assistant will help the child/young person to be independent but give support where it is needed. This will help them not to get frustrated. The children/young people may use different forms of communicating such as Makaton so they need help to communicate with others so when they are out and about the personal assistant will help with this and other aspects of the child's life.

1.4 Explaining the importance of encouraging the participation of disabled children and young people.

In my setting I recognise and implement the policies that demonstrate that it is important to encourage the participation of disabled children and young people. In childcare practice, opportunities for children and young people to participate in decisions and issues that affect them have increased significantly. However, it is said by Participation Works, a charity that works for children that, "…this is not the case for disabled children and young people, particularly those with complex needs and communication impairments, despite them being disproportionate users of support services in health, social care and education settings." Therefore, the importance of encouraging the participation of disabled children and young people is critical for practitioners due to the following reasons:

- To comply with UN convention: Disabled children and young people have the same rights as non-disabled children and young people to participate in decisions and issues that affect them. This is outlined in both the UN Convention on the Rights of the Child (CRC) and in the UN Convention on the Rights of Persons with Disabilities (CRPD). Despite this, disabled children and young people continue to face significant barriers and challenges to participation.

- To include or imbed disabled children: In order to effectively embed disabled children's participation, it needs to be fully accessible and inclusive. The social model of disability provides a framework for inclusive participation by focusing on changing attitudes and removing or minimising barriers that prevent disabled children accessing the same opportunities as other children and young people.

- To be professional in good practice: The social model of disability defines disability as arising from the interaction between someone with an impairment and the barriers that exist in the environment, these being physical, attitudinal and the policies, practices and procedures of organisations.

- To overcome barriers: Barriers and challenges to disabled children and young people's participation sit within three broad areas – training, support and resources; knowledge, understanding and attitudes; process, systems and structures. Identifying and recognising the barriers and challenges provides a good basis for planning to further disabled children's participation.

- To recognise that: Whilst participation of disabled children and young people is not yet embedded, clear examples of their involvement in decisions at individual, service and strategic levels have been identified, and a number of tools to support disabled children's and young people's participation are available. These include mechanisms for making complaint procedures accessible to disabled children, practical tool kits such as communication passports, practice guidance, training materials and multi-media approaches.

- Ensuring that: The participation of disabled children and young people should be an ongoing and flexible process, not an end in itself. Settings should routinely and actively seek disabled children's views about individual, service and strategic level decisions as well as local and national issues.

In my setting or any other practice, by building this into participation work undertaken with all children and young people, disabled children's voices are equally represented and will meaningfully influence the agenda rather than just be 'added on'. The question is not whether disabled children and young people can participate, but rather how we as professionals ensure that it happens. I have found the following tools to be useful in helping disabled children to participate in all programmes in a childcare setting:

Making Ourselves Heard: Exploring Disabled Children's Participation. Based on a series of eight seminars with local authorities, this book sets out the current policy context for disabled children and young people's participation. It also outlines the barriers and challenges to effective participation and highlights what is working well.

Top Tips for Participation. Developed in partnership with disabled young people, this poster highlights, in young people's own words, what adults can do to better involve them in decisions.

Young Campaigners Guide. A guide for disabled young people explaining what campaigning is and how to campaign in your local area.

Disabled Children's Manifesto for Change. This is a booklet and film that sets out what disabled children and young people want the government to do to make life better.

Going Places! This guide sets out what disabled children and young people think about the play and leisure opportunities available to them and what needs to change to improve them.

If I Could Change One Thing... Children, young people and their parents were asked 'If you were Prime Minister for the day, and could change one thing, what would it be?' Their answers are set out in a number of booklets.

CDC Inclusion Policy. This is a policy and a set of principles from the Council for Disabled Children, which are crucial to the development of inclusion.

Inclusion Posters. These are a series of A3 posters showcasing each of the six principles of the Inclusion Policy.

Pushing for Change. This report from the Alliance for Inclusive Education (ALLFIE) looks at some of the ways different organisations are including young disabled people and encouraging their leadership and includes the voices and experiences of young disabled people on leadership matters.

Two Way Street. This is a training video and handbook from Triangle about communicating with disabled children and young people. The video is aimed at all professionals whose role includes communicating with children, it was developed in consultation with disabled children and young people.

Our Play – Our Choice. This good practice briefing outlines the findings of a play consultation carried out by KIDS with disabled children, and includes signposts to useful organisations and resources on participation and inclusion

Communication Passports. Personal Communication Passports are a practical and person-centred way of supporting children, young people and adults who do not use speech to communicate.

Include Me Too. Championing the rights of disabled children and young people, this website supports the National Charter of Rights for Disabled Children and Young People.

Listening to Young Disabled Children. A series of six leaflets that provide a guide to finding out more information to help practitioners design ways of listening to children and to each other.

See Me, Hear Me. A guide to using the UN Convention on the Rights of Person with Disabilities to promote the rights of children. The first book to look at how two UN conventions can be used to support disabled children.

LEARNING OUTCOME 2

BE ABLE TO WORK IN PARTNERSHIP WITH FAMILIES WITH DISABLED CHILDREN OR YOUNG PEOPLE AND THOSE WITH SPECIFIC REQUIREMENTS

2.1 Explain the concept and principles of partnership with carers of disabled children and young people and those with specific requirements.

In my setting this means that I have to understand and draw from the concepts and principles of partnerships with carers of disabled children and young people and those with specific requirements. It means involvement at all stages of assessment, delivery and review, concept of parents as experts on their own child, parent partnership services, shared goals, parental rights and responsibilities, supporting informed choice, improved outcomes for children and young people, involvement in shaping services and policy development. Therefore in my setting I always seek good practice and use available resources to meet the needs of children in my care so as to be able to work in partnership with families with disabled children or young people and those with specific requirements. In England, the Department of Health draws from public policy and guidance to explain the concept and principles of partnership with carers of disabled children and young people and those with specific requirements as follows. When working, I use a standard approach of child-, young person- and family-centred services. I draw good practice from the *National Service Framework for Children, Young People and Maternity Services*, which establishes clear standards for promoting the health and well-being of children and young people and for providing high quality services that meet their needs. As a child minder I have a vision to work in partnership with families with disabled children or young people and those with specific requirements. I aim to see that:

- my communication is directly with children and young people, listening to them and attempting to see the world through their eyes;
- children, young people and their families have equitable access to high quality, child-centred health promotion, prevention and care services, which are responsive to their individual developing needs and preferences;
- the views of children, young people and families are valued and taken into account in the planning, delivery and evaluation of services;
- children and young people and families receive high quality services, which are co-ordinated around their individual and family needs and take account of their views.

Every childcare provision should adapt the following Principles of Good Practice:

i. Every child, young person and parent is actively involved in decisions about the child's health and well-being, based on appropriate information.

ii. Confidentiality and consent policies are developed and made explicit to children, young people and their parents.

iii. Children and young people and their families have opportunities to access health and local authority primary care services in a range of settings such as early years settings, especially children's centres, extended schools or drop-in centres.

iv. There is an agreed process to plan local service provision in partnership and provide co-ordinated care.

v. Primary care trusts and local authorities work together with other agencies to develop a system so that information derived from an assessment of a child or young person and their family, can follow them and be accessible through their journey.

vi. The views of children, young people and their parents inform the needs-based commissioning strategies, developed by local authorities and primary care trusts and children's trusts.

vii. Every organisation or service identifies a senior lead for children and young people to ensure that children's and young people's needs are at the forefront of local planning and service delivery.

viii. All staff working with children and young people receive training and are skilled in the common core of skills, knowledge and competencies set out in this standard, which enable them to communicate with children and young people and their parents, and assist them to achieve their full potential.

Further, to explain the concept and principles of partnership with carers of disabled children and young people and those with specific requirements I have found the following rationale useful:

- Each child or young person needs to be seen as a 'whole', in the context of their family, carers, school, friends and local community. This should involve an understanding that, as children and young people grow up, their needs change.

- For services to be effective, they need to respond to children's and young people's individuality, developmental age and social circumstances, and be co-ordinated around the child and family.

- Children and young people and their families need to participate actively in designing services and in providing feedback on the care they receive.

- Services value diversity and plan to be inclusive for all groups of children, young people and their families who may be in the minority as a result of their culture, faith, race, ethnicity, sexual orientation, disability, geographical disadvantage such as living in rural areas, their social or family situation. To promote equity and reduce inequalities, professionals and services need to respect these differences and ensure equity of access to services which are appropriate for each individual.

- Integrate and co-ordinate services around the child's and families' identified needs.

- Graduate smoothly into adult services at the right time.

- Work in partnership with children, young people and their parents to plan and shape services and to develop the workforce.

- Follow best practice in obtaining consent and respecting confidentiality.

- Ensure the child is seen and communicated with using their preferred communication method or language.

To further explain the concept and principles of partnership with carers of disabled children and young people and those with specific requirements I have found the following interventions useful:

- Listening and responding to children, young people and parents.

- Ensuring that the views of individual service users and the local population are sought and responded to is an increasingly important requirement of national and local government policy. In childcare, a good service should be designed and deliver services around the needs of the person using them, with an emphasis on developing partnerships between patients and professionals. This means seeing services through the eyes of the child and family, and planning and delivering services according to their needs.

- Children have a right to be involved in decisions about their care (UN Convention for the Rights of the Child, Article 123). The need to secure sustained national improvements in NHS patient experience by 2008 is a target in *National Standards, Local Action*, which specifies the need to ensure that individuals are fully involved in decisions about their care. I have found out that whilst providing childcare the local authority has a duty to monitor or scrutinise what providers do.

- Overview and scrutiny is a fundamental way for local councillors, as democratically elected community leaders, to voice the views of their constituents to decision makers and require them to listen and respond. This is particularly the case in relation to the power of health scrutiny that allows local councillors to scrutinise matters relating to public health and the NHS. Non-executive councillors are encouraged to look at both the services provided by their own authorities and issues of wider concern.

- Particular efforts should be made to ensure that children and young people who are often excluded from participation activities are supported in giving their views, e.g. disabled children or looked-after children. *The Healthy Care Programme* (NCB 2002) promotes participation by children, young people and their carers in decisions about service development for looked-after children.

- Parents' views are important in determining local service provision and should be considered in planning and service development. The views and opinions of very young children should also be sought in appropriate ways.

- Inclusiveness can be promoted by providing a welcoming and responsive environment for discussions with children, young people and their families, and ensuring that meeting times and locations are sensitive to providing local access, travel, childcare and other personal needs.

- Professionals from all agencies adopt a systematic approach, which enables children and young people to contribute to discussions about their needs, care or treatment during consultations or meetings and to express their views. This includes children with communication needs or who use non-verbal communication.

- Local authorities use their overview and scrutiny role to scrutinise local childcare, health and social care issues of concern to children and their parents in accordance with the *Overview and Scrutiny of Health* (DH 2003).

- Children, young people and their parents participate in planning, evaluating and improving the quality of childcare services. User participation follows the principles set out in *Learning to Listen: Core Principles for the Involvement of Children and Young People*. Findings from user participation consultation, in all settings, are reviewed by care providers including childminders or at management/board level, reflected in improvements in services and are available to children, young people and their families. So Ofsted reports are available for children, young people and parents.

- In healthcare for disabled children NHS Patient Advice and Liaison Service (PALS) provide confidential assistance to children, young people and families in resolving problems and concerns quickly, as well as explanations of complaints procedures and how to get in touch with someone who can help. PALS act as a focal point for feedback from children, young people and families and provide valuable information to trusts to inform service improvements.

- Formal working arrangements are in place for the provision of link workers, advocates to support children and young people, interpreters and/or support workers for children in special circumstances or from minority groups, to represent their needs during individual consultations and on multi-disciplinary review and development groups.

In explaining the concept and principles of partnership with carers of disabled children and young people and those with specific requirements I have learnt that it is important to respect children, young people and parents.

- Children and young people and their parents are not always treated with respect, sensitivity, or courtesy. They have rights that are not always understood or respected. There are many children and young people whose needs may differ from the majority by reason of their race, culture, faith, ethnicity, sexual orientation, disability, social or family situation.

- All children and young people require care and support, which meets their developmental needs and provides them with the opportunity to achieve, or maintain, their optimal standard of health, development and well-being, regardless of their individual circumstances or those of their families and communities.

- Respecting the role of parents is a significant part of providing services for children and young people. It is important to ensure that the views of parents are sought and their concerns responded to. As children mature, their changing needs are sometimes ignored. For example, their increasing concern for privacy and autonomy.

- Childminders must ensure that a wide range of communication strategies are used to obtain the views of children, young people and their parents and to respond to their needs.

- Children and young people are offered choices wherever possible, for example, in the location of care or treatment, treatment options or the gender of the professional that they see. Play techniques can help children understand the options and exercise choice.

- Children, young people and their families are informed about children's rights and are able to make a complaint where necessary, supported by an advocate where appropriate.

2.2 Explaining the types of support and information carers may require.

In my setting I ensure to use the types of support and information carers may require which are:

- impartial advice;
- signposting to available support and information, e.g. resources;
- financial support and/or benefits;
- services, transport;
- support during statutory assessments;
- provision of respite care;
- short breaks or overnight care;
- palliative care, end of life care;
- bereavement support;
- mediation or advocacy services, education, training and work opportunities;

- work;
- support with childcare;
- online support.

Therefore, as a childcare provider I am aware of the types of support and information that carers require as already outlined, but I also ensure that I meet any additional types of support as follows:

- learning to use sign language, Makaton;
- speech board;
- social and emotional issues, such as coming to terms with the impact of disability on own family;
- financial support;
- information about services and availability;
- information about children's and families' rights.

In my setting I usually gather information leaflets to pass on to parents and carers. These are available from local libraries or CABs. As a childcare provider I am a carer too and in view of the fact that I have a child of my own with autism and learning difficulties, I also need the information for myself.

- Information about Support and Treatment for Children and Young People and their Parents: In order for children, young people and their families to participate actively in their own health and social care, they need the following appropriate information about services, problems or specific health conditions and the choices which are available to them. Duties under the Disability Discrimination Act need to be taken into account when considering the provision of information in appropriate formats and language.

I have learnt that information provision is a 'process', which will vary during the child's or young person's journey. Information needs to vary at different stages/parts or ages of the child or young person's life journey.

I have found out that:

- Commissioners and providers of services for children work with other agencies to provide comprehensive information about all relevant local services for children, young people and their parents, including specialist and voluntary services. The material signposts all relevant local and national resources.
- As part of the Information Sharing and Assessment Programme, all local authorities have an electronic 'service directory' covering all service providers in the area, which is accessible to practitioners, parents or carers, children and young people. Information is accessible in a range of community settings, e.g. youth clubs, community centres, pharmacies.
- All information resources (both written and oral) for children and their families are sensitive to developmental, cultural, social and language differences and are available to the child or young person, as well as to the parent or carer. Specific provision is made for disabled children with high communication needs or who use non-verbal communication. Processes are in place to ensure that the information remains up-to-date.
- Information about treatment and care is based on the best available evidence, and tailored to the needs, circumstances and wishes of the individual and family to allow for shared decision making and development of self-management.

2.3 Demonstrate in one's own practice partnership working with families.

Observation

Here you will be required to show in practice how you work with parents, e.g. invite some mothers/fathers into your setting, and/or on outings, consultations on ideas using questionnaires, etc. So you will show or demonstrate in your own practice partnership working with families.

LEARNING OUTCOME 3

BE ABLE TO SUPPORT AGE AND DEVELOPMENTALLY APPROPRIATE LEARNING, PLAY OR LEISURE OPPORTUNITIES FOR DISABLED CHILDREN OR YOUNG PEOPLE AND THOSE WITH SPECIFIC REQUIREMENTS

3.1 Demonstrate in one's own practice engagement with disabled children or young people.

Observation

This simply means that you have to be observed by a tutor or an assessor whilst practising/implementing by doing. Here you will have to show or demonstrate in your own practice engagement with disabled children or young people.

3.2 Encourage children or young people to express their preferences and aspirations in their chosen way of communication.

Observation

This simply means that you have to be observed by a tutor or an assessor whilst practising/implementing by doing. So here you will encourage children or young people to express their preferences and aspirations in their chosen way of communication.

3.3 Demonstrate in one's own practice how you work with children or young people and their families to assess a child's or young person's learning, play or leisure needs, identifying solutions to any barriers according to the principles of inclusions.

Observation

This simply means that you have to be observed by a tutor or an assessor whilst practising/implementing by doing, which is the means of demonstrating in your own practice how you work with children or young people and their families to assess a child's or young person's learning, play or leisure needs, identifying solutions to any barriers according to the principles of inclusions.

3.4 Develop a plan with an individual child or young person to support learning, play or leisure needs.

Observation

This simply means that you have to be observed by a tutor or an assessor whilst practising/implementing to develop a plan with an individual child or young person to support learning, play or leisure needs.

3.5 Implement the learning, play or leisure plan according to one's own role and responsibility explaining and evaluating its effectiveness and suggesting changes for the future.

Observation

This simply means that you have to be observed by a tutor or an assessor whilst practising/implementing the learning, play or leisure plan according to your own role and responsibility, explaining and evaluating its effectiveness and suggesting changes for the future. They want to see you plan for the future, immediate, medium and long-term.

LEARNING OUTCOME 4

BE ABLE TO EVALUATE, SUPPORT AND DEVELOP EXISTING PRACTICE WITH DISABLED CHILDREN AND YOUNG PEOPLE AND THOSE WITH SPECIFIC REQUIREMENTS

4.1 Demonstrating in one's own practice how barriers which restrict children and young people's access are overcome.

In my setting, overcoming barriers which restrict children's and young people's access is a practical and demonstrable procedure. I ensure access to, e.g. learning, play, leisure activities, work and training. I ensure independent living, overcoming barriers such as physical access, resources and equipment. I ensure that inappropriate methods of communication are not used; I ensure that financial and organisational barriers (policies, procedures; attitudinal) are overcome; I ensure overcoming barriers, e.g. adapting the environment and resources, knowledge of the child's or young person's needs, stage of development and abilities. I ensure identifying financial support using a child- or young person-led model. I ensure the use and adaptation of materials and resources. I ensure the use of specialist aids and equipment and mobility aids.

In order to demonstrate in my own practice how barriers that restrict children's and young people's access are overcome I ensure that I have all my safeguarding policies in place and implement them at all levels. I ensure that the equalities and inclusion policies are implemented, monitored and reviewed. I pay particular attention to the specific needs of a child from admission and through their stay in my setting. If and when I or my assistant have concerns on any kind of abuse that was taking place then the safeguarding policy would be used and followed. If any abusive behaviour was noticed then this will be reported to me as key worker/the manager of the setting. I would then take the appropriate action.

To demonstrate in my own practice how barriers that restrict children's and young people's access are overcome, I ensure that I abide by The Disability Discrimination Act (DDA) 1995 and the Special Educational Needs and Disability Act (SENDA) 2001. All childcare settings have a duty and it is the law not to treat disabled children less favourably than non-disabled children. Childcare settings should make reasonable adjustments to ensure that disabled children have access to all six areas of the EYFS. The new Disability Discrimination Act 2005 strengthens the Disability Discrimination Act 1995 and SENDA 2001 by broadening the definition of a disabled child/adult and imposing on settings a duty to promote inclusion and equality of opportunity for disabled children/adults.

To demonstrate in my own practice how barriers that restrict children's and young people's access are overcome, I ensure that I abide by new regulations and guidelines such as. in England, in October 2010, there was a new law brought in called The Equality Act 2010. This act has replaced a lot of the previous Disability Discrimination Act. However, the disability equality in the Disability Discrimination Act still applies.

In my setting I am aware that The Equality Act 2010 has been put in place to protect people and prevent disability discrimination. It gives disabled people legal rights in employment, education and many more areas. This means that disabled people will be treated fairly with no discrimination. The act provides rights for people not to be discriminated against because they are associated with a disabled person.

In my setting I would ensure that I am able to demonstrate in my own practice how barriers that restrict children's and young people's access are overcome. I ensure that I abide by my policies. The Inclusion Policy and Equality Policy would be used if there were any signs of a child being discriminated against. For example, if a child cannot take part in an activity because they cannot access another room, the setting would be responsible for moving the barriers that are in place, because the Equal Opportunities Policy (valuing diversity and promoting equality) states that we make inclusion a thread that runs through all of the activities of the setting. Therefore, my setting is committed to providing an environment that allows disabled children full access to all the areas – we have doors that are wide enough for wheelchair access and I have adapted the ground floor of my home to be wheelchair accessible, as it is the main provision and provides a welcome environment into the setting.

4.2 Explaining the importance of evaluating and challenging existing practice and becoming an agent of change.

In my setting it is important to evaluate and challenge existing practice and to become an agent of change, so that lessons are learned and improvements made as change, e.g. routines, practice, and attitudes in order that there may be improving outcomes for children, young people and families. This helps to bring about working more effectively, developing and/or strengthening partnerships. Through this I am able to develop better application of my skills through observation and assessment, so that my actions become innovative practice, which results in problem solving, allowing me to manage change, so that I can work towards participation and involvement in the design and delivery of services for children and young people, families and colleagues (staff). I always ensure that I work towards making myself a role model. Therefore, I have to be dealing with resistance to change. In order to explain the importance of evaluating and challenging existing practice and becoming an agent of change I follow a systematic procedure as follows:

I ensure that through my previous training, learning and knowledge I would be able to evaluate my own performance. I therefore evaluate my own knowledge, performance and understanding against relevant standards.

In the UK I would evaluate my knowledge and performance by compliance with the standards and requirements of EYFS and Ofsted. In Scotland I would base my evaluation on SCSWIS in order to meet welfare requirements, making sure that I am following and doing everything that is expected of me as a child carer (safeguarding the child). I use observation, so I observe. I carry out a safety check in my setting, I complete a checklist and ask myself, "Is the setting safe for children?" I look at the building and its maintenance or condition. I look at the cleanliness of the general environment. I look at food preparation areas, safe storage and use of equipment/toys, outdoor areas, outdoor play, my working practices that promote health and safety.

Demonstrating how I use feedback to evaluate one's own performances and inform development.

I use my own devised questionnaires. The following scenario is useful. Let us imagine I have a mentor because I am new to the practice of childcare. (In the UK such a mentor could be either a local authority officer or a long term practitioner of childcare.) Therefore, I bounce ideas with a mentor who has been to see my setting, advising of any changes or things that need to be made to improve my setting. I find the feedback from the questionnaires filled by parents very useful. It is through bouncing ideas that my mentor advised me on taking this course to improve my practice and understanding the development, care and safety of children. I also use regular tick-charts, checklists and conversations to gauge the feelings of parents and children. Therefore, conversations, questionnaire feedback and my own checklists enable me to evaluate my performance and inform development for my setting.

Be able to agree personal development plan. Identifying sources of support for planning and reviewing own development.

I find that in my setting I am a self-motivated person. I have to identify sources of support for planning and reviewing my personal development. I have made links with a local authority officer who provides me with information about training and courses or legislation. I then enrol on courses that will better me and my setting. I also make sure I am working within Ofsted's guidelines and regulations.

HIGHLY RECOMMENDED

As I practise in the UK I have put in place a subscription with the Pre-School and Learning Alliance, a professional association for childcare and early years services providers, who provide monthly and periodical magazines and information on new trends and changes within the industry of childcare. I enrich my personal knowledge by reading various information articles on the EYFS and Ofsted websites.

Demonstrating how to work with others.

I work with others to review and prioritise my own learning needs, professional interests and development opportunities. For instance, working with my mentor, parents, my assistant, and other childminders. There are cases where a contract is shared between myself and another childminder (job-share) this helps me to develop myself.

Demonstrating how to work with others to agree personal development.

I reflect on working with others or colleagues. This helps me to create better relationships and teams, enabling me to enjoy my work more. The people I liaise with are mainly my mentors that I acquired when I first started training as a childminder. This has helped me very much in view of working independently. Regular communication with them enables me to maintain up-to-date information and up-skill my qualifications in such areas as first aid and safeguarding children. The courses/training also become a point of networking and meeting up with other childminders and sharing information and experiences. Through my mentor I am enabled and directed to various resources. I am also able to enrich my work, drawing from working directly with children's out of school play schemes, libraries, or cinemas where I take children in my setting to enjoy play and events as appropriate. Through my contracts I work with parents to ensure permission for any outings. I also work with teachers at the school that I collect children from.

In the UK I have to be DBS (Disclosure and Barring Service, formerly CRB) checked before working with children. With DBS check certification I am also on the volunteer list to support local schools with outings when I am not working. This helps schools meet the ratio of adults to children when walking on streets or in parks. The ways in which I interact with others in the community and work with colleagues makes a difference to the services I provide for children and their families. For instance, simple acknowledgements of teachers when I collect the children from school enhances a rapport and communication. Asking whether the child has been alright during the school day enables the teacher to recognise my role.

Using learning opportunities and reflective practice to contribute to personal development. Evaluating how learning activities have affected practice.

In my setting, I create a scenario that I have been on various useful training opportunities since completing my NVQ Level 2 in Childcare. I have found the courses an opportunity of reflection on my practice and a major contribution to my work with children and parents. I have found myself more equipped and confident to deal with situations that arise. I am more confident with using visual signs and supporting children, even those with challenging behaviour, using appropriate strategies. I have had to be my own challenger, developing and improving the quality of the practice/setting. I determine the focus of the setting's work and dedicate some of my time to training. However, I also bounce ideas with my assistant, sharing my thoughts, and I seek second opinions for support in making any changes. Therefore, through reflective practice, I also review and evaluate the changes I make so that their effect may be smooth. I ensure sensitivity especially where the change may affect the children or parents.

Demonstrating how reflective practice has led to improved ways of working.

Training courses are a good source or motivator of reflection. The courses give me new ideas and thoughts about practice. I normally take advantage of provisions from early years advisors from the local authority to get information on training courses. When I first started my practice I had to think of standards and guidelines, legislation and then practice. I had to reflect on the setting, the building and how I keep it clean (e.g. I had to change the flooring in my setting so I could clean it properly with disinfectants). I also had to think about the equipment, in reflective practice with health and safety. After training, for example, I have had to practise fire drills every week with children. I go through this practice as I get new children, using behaviour strategies. I have developed listening skills and patience to be able to listen to others and secure information that helps me reflect on my practice/setting. I have learnt to listen to feedback, especially from parents without being defensive. This helps me to improve performance. Usually parents give a honest view in their feedback, enabling me to evaluate activities affecting my setting.

Recording progress in relation to personal development.

I have found that it is important for me to be sensible and develop my own skills and be aware of my own strengths, weaknesses and training requirements. I have devised my own unwritten personal development plan. Firstly, this helps me to take responsibility of my own career and development. Secondly, my own plan means that I can specifically set aside timescales and goals. Setting my own plan motivates me more than if someone were to tell me what I need to do next. I also find that this planning enables me to examine what is out there for childminders and how else I can improve the setting for both children and parents. In order to be able to use learning opportunities and reflective practice to contribute to my personal development, I record progress. I have devised a personal profile file wherein I file my certification and qualification documents. I then add these into self-evaluation forms as appropriate annually in the Ofsted evaluation requirement.

4.3 Explain how and when to use policies and procedures to challenge discriminatory, abusive or oppressive behaviour.

For me, to explain how and when to use policies and procedures to challenge discriminatory, abusive or oppressive behaviour I use the following:

In the UK, I follow the guidelines outlined in The Disability Discrimination Act (DDA) 1995 and the Special Educational Needs and Disability Act (SENDA) 2001. Childcare settings have a duty and it is the law not to treat disabled children less favourably than non-disabled children. Childcare settings should make reasonable adjustments to ensure that disabled children have access to all six areas of the EYFS. The new Disability Discrimination Act 2005 strengthens the Disability Discrimination Act 1995 and SENDA 2001 by broadening the definition of a disabled child/adult and imposing on settings a duty to promote inclusion and equality of opportunity for disabled children/adults.

I am aware that in October 2010 there was a new law bought in called The Equality Act 2010, which has replaced a lot of the Disability Discrimination Act. However, the disability equality in the Disability Discrimination Act still applies.

I have through this training learnt that The Equality Act 2010 has been put in place to protect people and prevent disability discrimination. It gives disabled people legal rights in employment, education and many more areas. This means that disabled people will be treated fairly with no discrimination. The act provides rights for people not to be discriminated against because they are associated with a disabled person.

The Inclusion Policy and Equality Policy would be used if there were any signs of a child being discriminated against. For example, if a child cannot take part in an activity because they cannot access another room, the setting would be responsible for moving the barriers that are in place, because the Equal Opportunities Policy (valuing diversity and promoting equality) states that we make inclusion a thread that runs through all of the activities of the setting. Therefore, my setting is committed to providing an environment that allows disabled children full access to all the areas. We have doors that are wide enough for wheelchair access and I have adapted the ground floor of my home to be wheelchair accessible as it is the main provision and provides a welcome environment into the setting. If and when myself or my assistant find concerns on any kind of abuse that was taking place then the Safeguarding Policy would be used and followed. If any abusive behaviour was noticed then this will be reported to me as key worker/the manager of the setting. I would then take the appropriate action.

4.4 Describing the impact of differences which many prefer to call disability within different cultures and the importance of culturally sensitive practice.

My view is that everyone has a difference, even the most identical of twins. I recognise the influence of difference or disability on different cultures, e.g. level of acceptance and integration, effects of stigmatisation or exclusion, effects of stereotyping, understanding values and context, attitudes (positive or negative), notion of attitudes to different types of disability, sensitivity to language and religious beliefs. Different cultures usually have different approaches to life/beliefs and the upbringing of their child. I know from personal experience of a child who attended a school where I volunteer; in this setting she needed help.

There was not only a language barrier but a cultural one as well. The child and parents did not speak English. We had a multi-agency team including a translator but the mother was very reluctant to accept any help from 'outsiders', even though the translator was from her country. The translator was from a different part of the country with a different dialect and caste. This was not brought to the mother's attention by anyone – she knew all this herself from the translator's accent and dialect. She also knew her caste would be different. Of course, with patience and trust built up we were able to help her child (and the family) but there was a lot of mistrust on her part (at first) and it took very much longer to sort things out, yet all the time her child was in need of help.

There has also been something in the press just recently about a high proportion of Asians' arranged marriages to first cousins. Although it is legal in the UK to marry a first cousin, it was suggesting many of the brides and grooms in arranged marriages are now intertwined in close family relationships (with first cousins marrying, then their children marrying first cousins and so on) that there are many infants with severe learning and physical disabilities. In other countries such as Uganda it is illegal to marry relatives as it is seen as incestuous. Very often mothers from some cultures will not seek help and keep themselves very much to themselves (away from the community) and children may not attend an early years setting.

Apart from that, if any child is in need of help (in any way) if one operates a nursery, or childcare facility or even a play club we have to ensure we are sensitive towards the parents feelings – even for those parents that are from the same country and culture and speak the same language, we would never dream of saying, "Oh by the way, did you know your child is deaf as a post?" We build up a good professional and trusting relationship and get to know them, so we know how to approach them. In my setting I might chat to them casually and ask them how they think their child is progressing – sometimes a parent has a doubt/concern that their child needs help and this allows them to take charge and feel better, knowing they have picked up on it. Sometimes they haven't, and as practitioner you have to remember to be sensitive so as not to upset them – it's very often a shock for them to be told their child has special needs. All the expectations or hope you have for your child and the possibility may be that they aren't able to do what the parent hoped for depending on the severity of the child's needs. (I know from personal experience that the process of having to have a child diagnosed with special needs is extremely traumatic, as my own child took me through it.) Therefore, also, if a parent asks you if a child has this/that or has a condition such as... remember it is not our place (as childminders/carers/teachers) to diagnose. There are other professionals for that, and sometimes even then a parent may not want their child 'labelled'. Children are given time to develop, allowing professionals to observe, set Individualised Education Programme (IEP) targets and monitor them before they are 'labelled'. It is very easy to label, but very hard to undo, so we must always think carefully as we strive to help children with special needs. Therefore, in answering this question I have given an example about dealing with parents of the same culture whose child may have special needs/disability, etc. and how hard it is to suggest to parents that their child would benefit from outside help. Therefore it would possibly be doubly difficult if a parent's language/culture and beliefs are very different from yours (the practitioner).

4.5 Explaining the importance of systems of monitoring, reviewing and evaluating services for disabled children and young people.

In my setting the importance of systems of monitoring, reviewing and evaluating services for disabled children and young people is in my knowledge, my skills and how I work as a practitioner. I am aware that there are some communities that attach stigma to people's differences (usually referred to as disabilities). Therefore, as my practice is in my community, I place particular importance on my systems by monitoring, reviewing and evaluating services for disabled children and young people. I do this through focus on outcomes for children and young people, transparency of policies, procedures and processes for participation and feedback. I ask my service users to let me know what good, if any, the service has done for them. I seek information on excellence and poor performance using a service feedback form with ratings or scales from one to five. I, on a daily basis, review my activity plans, inspect my equipment, and make risk assessments. I work whilst monitoring, bearing in mind that I have to be recognising the influence of disability on different cultures, e.g. level of acceptance and integration, effects of stigmatisation or exclusion, effects of stereotyping. I work to understand the values and context of the children and young people in my care. I monitor the attitudes of parents and the children and young people in my care (positive or negative), the notion of attitudes to other people's physical, learning, social differences and the different types of disability (difference) and sensitivity to language and religious beliefs.

My methods of monitoring development may include:

- assessment framework/s;
- observation;
- standard measurements;
- information from carers and colleagues.

My reasons for monitoring may include:

- disability;
- emotional;
- physical;
- environmental;
- cultural
- social;
- learning needs;
- communication.

This exercise helps me in observations, information from others, preferences of the child or young person, findings and solutions to obstacles, looking at how to overcome barriers. I use my systems to record observations and/or outcomes of the child's learning, expectations and outcomes of their development/learning plan. This informs my monitoring and information for parents and other professionals/agencies. Therefore, in my setting the importance of systems of recording enable monitoring, through reviewing and evaluating outcomes, and enable services improvement for the children and young people and their families/carers. Using monitoring, reviewing and evaluating services I am able to evaluate support and develop my existing practice with disabled children and young people and those with specific requirements.

My view is that differences are not disabilities; disabilities are labels given by a negative and discriminative society – a society that assumes a perfection that is unrealistic. In my thinking everyone is different, everyone is beautiful in their way; disability is in the eye of the beholder. Society disables us, instead of enabling us. They build steps instead of ramps for wheelchair users and thereby fail those who do not walk on two feet.

LEARNING OUTCOME 5

UNDERSTAND HOW TO WORK IN PARTNERSHIP WITH OTHER AGENCIES AND PROFESSIONALS TO SUPPORT PROVISION FOR DISABLED CHILDREN AND YOUNG PEOPLE AND THOSE WITH SPECIFIC REQUIREMENTS

5.1 Explain the roles and responsibilities of partners that are typically involved with disabled children and young people and those with specific requirements.

In my setting I know the roles and responsibilities of partners that are typically involved with disabled children and young people. They include the following services (which may be statutory, third sector or private): specialist health services; sensory services; palliative care services; youth and play workers; children's social services; special educational needs co-ordinator; portage services; advocacy services; role of family centres; physiotherapists; physiotherapists; mentors. I would be having and developing partnerships with them in order to improve outcomes for young people and children. The partnership would be on a mutual exchange of information. The process of communication demands confidentiality to safeguard the children and young people. In some instances I may have to seek the permission of parents to share information, but if there is a child at risk of abuse or neglect, I would have to act in the interest of the child. My working in partnership may include support for children's and young people's needs such as:

- disability;
- emotional;
- physical;
- environmental;
- cultural;
- social;
- learning needs;
- communication.

By the above explanation of the roles and responsibilities of partners that are typically involved with disabled children and young people and those with specific requirements, I understand how to work in partnership with other agencies and professionals to support provision for disabled children and young people and those with specific requirements.

5.2 Analysing examples of multi-agency and partnership working from one's own practice.

In my setting the examples of multi-agency and partnership working could be in the following situations if I required support for children:

- those with complex needs and their families;
- from partnerships;
- from commissioning services;
- from multi-agency programmes that support children;
- from young people and families, e.g. early support programmes;
- transition support programme, independent living support.

141

There are important stages when children and families require such support, for instance:

- Emotional – affected by personal experience, e.g. bereavement, entering/leaving care;
- Physical – e.g. moving to a new educational establishment, a new home/locality, from one activity to another;
- Physiological – e.g. puberty, long-term medical conditions;
- Intellectual – e.g. moving from pre-school to primary to post-primary.

In my setting, I have had to seek partnership for the special needs of my own child who suffers from Autism Spectrum Disorder and learning difficulties. These have included a whole range of statutory, private and community services. This is how I understand how to work in partnership with other agencies and professionals to support provision for disabled children and young people and those with specific requirements.

The differences of children's needs vary; your task is to identify them and rise to the challenge. The children have no difficulty and no disability, they just have differences. Disability, if any, is the eye of the beholder. Rise to the challenge.

CHAPTER 8
PROMOTING POSITIVE BEHAVIOUR

In my setting I have addressed issues relating to how to

PROMOTE POSITIVE BEHAVIOUR

UNIT AIM: I have found that the purpose of this unit is to provide the learner with the knowledge, understanding and skills required to promote positive behaviour and respond appropriately to incidents of challenging behaviour.

LEARNING OUTCOME 1

UNDERSTAND HOW LEGISLATION, FRAMEWORKS, CODES OF PRACTICE AND POLICIES RELATE TO POSITIVE BEHAVIOUR SUPPORT

1.1 Explain how legislation, frameworks, codes of practice and policies relating to positive behaviour support are applied to one's own working practices.

In my setting this is how legislation, frameworks, codes of practice and policies relating to positive behaviour support are applied to my own working practices. As a childminder I ensure that children's behaviour must be managed effectively and in a manner appropriate for their stage of development and particular needs. I manage behaviour using specific legal requirements. The specific legal requirements are:

Behaviour management: As a childcare provider I must not give corporal punishment to a child for whom I provide early years provision and, so far as it is reasonably practical, shall ensure that corporal punishment is not given to any such child by:

a) any person who cares for, or who is in regular contact with children;

b) any person living or working on the premises.

I am aware that an early years provider who, without reasonable excuse, fails to comply with this requirement, commits an offence.

A person shall not be taken to have given corporal punishment in breach of the above if the action was taken for reasons that include averting an immediate danger of personal injury to, or an immediate danger of death, of any person (including the child). Providers must not threaten corporal punishment, nor use or threaten any form of punishment that could have an adverse impact on the child's well-being. Providers must have an effective Behaviour Management Policy that is adhered to by all members of staff.

1.2 Define what is meant by Restrictive Intervention.

I define what is meant by restrictive intervention as follows, in accordance with statutory guidance to which providers should have regard. Physical intervention should only be used to manage a child's behaviour if it is necessary to prevent personal injury to the child or other children or an adult, to prevent serious damage to property or in what would reasonably be regarded as exceptional circumstances. Any occasion where physical intervention is used to manage a child's behaviour should be recorded and parents should be informed about it the same day. Through this course I have learnt that all adults who work within a childcare environment have a responsibility to themselves and the setting to model a high standard of behaviour, both in their dealings with the children and with every other adult within their practice, as their example of behaviour has a significant influence on the children's behaviour. Good, strong teamwork between adults will encourage good behaviour in children. Each childcare setting or school has a behaviour policy that staff should be aware of and adhere to. All new staff follow an induction programme to guarantee a dependable approach to behaviour management within childcare settings or schools.

I have learnt through this course that classroom organisation and teaching methods have a major influence on children's behaviour, as in classroom environments children are aware of the level to which they and their efforts are valued. A relationship between a teacher/teaching assistant and the children, the positive strategies that are used, together with group/classroom displays that the children have done by themselves all have a bearing on a child's behaviour. The whole ethos at my own setting is built around our emphasis on rewards that strengthen good behaviour and by showing children that they are highly valued as a pupil. By giving children praise, whether it is informal or formal, in groups or individually will reinforce their feeling of belonging to the school, which in return produces good behaviour. I ensure that my setting rewards system consists of:

- positive and the appropriate praise;
- writing constructive and positive comments on children's work;
- using the suitable stickers when needed;
- nominating 'Star of the Week' for each class;
- awarding a 'Star of the Day'.

These types of rewards are intended to increase the motivation in a child and by recognising their success will lead to their good behaviour and a positive work ethic. However, where there is praise there must also be sanctions; this will teach children that unacceptable behaviour will not be accepted. Behaviour that may include bullying, disrespect to adults, disruptive behaviour and racism, the use of sanctions in these instances are:

- It is made clear to the child why the sanction has been used in order for them to understand.
- That change in their behaviour is required in order for further sanctions not to be used.
- Group sanctions are avoided whenever possible as they can breed dislike amongst children.
- There is a clear difference made between minor and major offences.
- The focus is on the behaviour rather than the pupil as an individual.

Although instances of poor behaviour are fairly minor at my setting and can be dealt with through simple responses and communication, it is also important to remember that when using sanctions the sanction does not outweigh the actual offence.

In my setting we also have a set of 'golden rules'. These are our codes of conduct and are designed to show children how they can achieve acceptable standards of behaviour. Rules encourage children to behave in a thoughtful and considerate manner, which will produce a positive learning environment. These rules are displayed throughout the setting and are referred to continuously by myself and my assistant and children equally. We also have group rules that have been developed by the children themselves and are a positive device for encouraging good behaviour. The children can then monitor their own behaviour as well as the behaviour of other children in the class. I am aware that attendance at school will also have an adverse affect on behaviour as children need the stability that a school offers. Not only do children learn and educate themselves at school but they also learn to develop their social skills, which are extremely important for making friends. If a child does not attend school for long periods of time then both of these key attributes will suffer, leading to bad behaviour both in and out of the classroom. In order to attain attendance at school, or in my setting, I allocate stickers to the children with the largest amount of days of presence each week along with a present/card/certificate (trophy). This inspires the children and their parents or carers to strive for better attendance throughout that week, resulting in good behaviour from the children. For children who find it difficult to cope socially in the playground and who often display signs of bad behaviour at a school, the school could introduce a 'nurture club'. The club may be run by support staff and could provide a range of quality activities for the children. This club, whilst restrictive, would be planned to meet the needs of children who would misbehave in the playground by fighting and causing distress to other children. That is how I define restrictive intervention.

1.3 Explain when restrictive interventions may and may not be used.

When a verbal warning can be given and when the risk of injury or damage is very little, it is best not to use intervention. In my setting I adhere to the explanation for physical intervention given in England's EYFS, 2008, page 27, which states that, 'Physical intervention should only be used to manage a child's behaviour if it is necessary to prevent personal injury to the child, other children or an adult, to prevent serious damage to property, or in what would reasonably be regarded as exceptional circumstances. Any occasion where physical intervention is used to manage a child's behaviour should be recorded and parents should be informed about it on the same day.'

Restrictive Intervention is the act of any intervention which restricts a person's right and freedom of movement. Restrictive intervention can be used or not used in forms such as:

- Social intervention – where harmful or destructive behaviour can be contained and moderated with the use of language, including facial expressions and words. This intervention may be and should be used as a primary action.

- Mechanical intervention – the use of devices to prevent or contain a person's movement such as highchairs, stair gates, barrier erection, locked doors.

- Physical intervention – using actual bodily contact, which should only be used with clear justification and in guidance of the settings, policies and procedures and staff training. Physical intervention may only be used upon ensuring safeguards are in place for the member of staff and also the person involved and when social and mechanical intervention is not sufficient. Moderate risk to prevent danger to others should be expected but physical intervention may not be used if there is a substantial risk of injury or it conflicts with any individual care plans in place.

- Planned Intervention – using evidence from observations, assessments, care plans and risk assessments. A planned intervention may be ensuring that a member of staff sits with a child at group times to support, facilitate and moderate their behaviour towards the other children.

- Emergency intervention – actions taken to diffuse/deflect unpredicted events.

I have learnt that restrictive intervention can only be used when appropriate and as the only course of action in view of the behaviour of the child, in light of the following understanding.

I understand that the meanings for antecedent, behaviour and consequences are:

- antecedent is what happens before the behaviour;

- behaviour is the actions that are perceived as challenging behaviour or unwanted behaviour;
- consequences are what happened as a result of the behaviour.

Instead of restrictive interventions, it is always bet to use least restrictive principle. This is an approach or policy title that reflects the ethos of a setting in wanting to provide as many unrestricted opportunities as possible. Least restrictive principle will have set procedures/proactive strategies for helping children deal with their behaviour in an ongoing way and reactively for helping them to understand what happened preceding an incident/display of less appropriate behaviour.

In my setting I promote child and young person development to be able to support children's and young people's positive behaviour. Supporting positive behaviour may include:

- least restrictive principle;
- reinforcing positive behaviour;
- modelling/positive culture;
- looking for reasons for inappropriate behaviour and adapting responses;
- individual behaviour planning;
- phased stages;
- planning interventions to reduce inappropriate behaviour;
- de-escalate and diversion;
- containment;
- following management plans;
- boundary setting and negotiation;
- supporting children's and young people's reflection on and management of their own behaviour;
- anti-bullying strategies;
- time out (following up-to-date guidance);
- use of physical intervention (following up-to-date guidance).

In my setting I strive to ensure that least restrictive interventions are used. I therefore support children and young people to make positive changes in their lives. Therefore, I am able to support children and young people to make positive changes in their lives. Interventions may include:

- learning and development support;
- anger management;
- behaviour support classes;
- restorative justice;
- support to address substance misuse;
- support to address mental health issues.

An action plan may include:

- identify the positive changes the child/young person needs to achieve;
- identify the barriers to achievement;
- identify achievable and realistic goals for the child/young person to achieve;
- identify the interventions required.

1.4 Explain who needs to be informed of any incidents where restrictive interventions have been used.

Who I would inform if I had to restrict a child in my setting as a childminder would immediately be the parents. In a school environment I would follow the following procedure. I would inform:

- Head/deputy head teacher.

They will interview the member of staff and the child involved and record all details.

- Parents/carers.

The child's parents/carers must be informed as soon as possible.

- Social services.

If a child is in care their social worker must be informed immediately.

- Inclusion manager.

If the child has a behaviour management plan in place, or has been involved in a number of challenging behaviour situations or is having their behaviour monitored, the inclusion manager must be informed so that all appropriate paperwork and records can be completed and updated to ensure the child receives maximum targeted support.

- School governors.

The head teacher will report incidents to the governors as they have a responsibility in terms of reviewing school policy and behaviours.

1.5 Explaining why the least restrictive interventions should always be used when dealing with incidents of challenging behaviour.

In my setting there are alternatives to restrictive intervention that I would use, and only resort to restrictive intervention as little as possible. I apply the least restrictive principle – this shows that interventions should always be used when dealing with challenging behaviour to try and promote positive behaviour and inclusion. At my setting whenever any challenging behaviour occurs we act as appropriate to the incident. An example is if a child hits, smacks or bites another child then they are removed from the activity immediately. My assistant will check the child who has been injured and apply first aid as necessary. I will remove the child who has acted inappropriately, speak to them about the incident, explaining our golden rules again. The child is then directed to a different activity. If the behaviour occurrs again in a short space of time the child will be reminded again of the rules and directed to another activity. If there was a third incident then detailed observations would be carried out to see if there is any pattern or common trigger. The child's parents would also be approached to see if they could share any information from home. In my setting, the following are some of the challenging behaviours we may see and what interventions we use to try and sort out the problem and stop it escalating into a situation where physical interventions may be needed.

Repetitive/Obsessive

- Give responsibilities to the child for them to engage in (this helps build up self-esteem);
- Side-step any confrontations;

147

- Agree a response plan if any confrontations develop;
- Give choices to the child.

Withdrawn

- Ensure the child is included in all activities;
- Encourage the child to try new situations with support from an adult;
- Develop a circle of friends.

Aggressive

- Try to calm the child by talking with them, explaining it is not nice to be aggressive;
- Remove the child from the situation using distraction techniques;
- Provide support.

Self-injurious

- Remove the child from the situation;
- Provide support.

Disruptive

- Remove the child from the situation by encouraging them to choose another activity;
- Reward positive behaviour.

Anti-social or illegal

- Remove the child from the situation;
- Give the child support.

Verbally abusive

- Explain that verbal abuse is not acceptable;
- Remove the child from the situation.

Why I take the above actions is to ensure that I use less restrictive intervention. This helps and:

- will prevent the child or young person from getting hurt;
- will help to promote positive behaviour;
- a child's human dignity should be respected;
- will help to avoid the situation escalating and prevent further aggressive behaviour;
- can help to prevent a breakdown of relationships;
- restrictive interventions may be inappropriate for some children, for example those who have been sexually abused;
- has a higher risk of negative side effects, such as becoming more aggressive or disruptive;
- its potential to provoke more anger, opposition and hostility;
- often takes two members of staff for restrictive interventions, which may cause staffing shortages

In my setting, 'least restrictive principle' helps to:

- prevent a child from getting injured;
- help to promote positive behaviour;
- if the behaviour is aggressive it will help to calm it down and prevent it from escalating.

With the least restrictive principle, interventions should always be used when dealing with challenging behaviour to try and promote positive behaviour and inclusion.

1.6 What safeguards have to be in place if I had to restrain.

In my setting, safeguarding is foremost for children, myself, my assistant and all who come in the setting. The key to the effective use of proactive and reactive strategies is a good understanding of the children's individual behaviour patterns and any possible triggers to their behaviour. This is important so you can establish proactive strategies that will prevent these triggers or patterns of behaviour occurring. However, if their challenging behaviour does get triggered, understanding the child as an individual will mean you will be able to spot early signs of behavioural agitation so you can then react to these and defuse the situation before it can turn into an incident of challenging behaviour. If this does not happen and an incident occurs it will also be useful to understand the child, as this could help in defusing the situation. Staff using restrictive physical interventions must ensure safeguards are in place for both themselves and the child involved. If there is an incident either of biting, scratching, head banging against wall/floor then there is a danger of bleeding as well as cuts and lacerations. There is a risk of contamination from bodily fluids because of injury. Due to this, all staff must be familiar with the guidance of infection control. Staff should always be careful when using a physical intervention not to hold the child too tightly so as to cause injury. They should always have the child's back to their front to avoid being bitten by the child. If possible they need their arms around the child's arms to avoid being hit. When holding the child they should always keep a check on the child to ensure they are breathing correctly and there are no other health problems indicated. Staff should always ensure there is another member of staff present when using physical restrictions as a witness to what has occurred. Staff should have some training in how to use physical restraints correctly to protect both themselves and the child. Staff should avoid wearing unnecessary jewellery as this can be pulled and cause injury or bleeding.

After an incident there needs to be a calm environment where the child can be helped to relax and calm down as necessary. The child may need to talk to and be reassured by someone who was not involved in the incident. After an incident has occurred then the child and staff member will be checked for injuries and, if necessary, first aid given.

LEARNING OUTCOME 2

UNDERSTANDING THE CONTEXT AND USE OF PROACTIVE AND REACTIVE STRATEGIES

2.1 Explanation of the difference between proactive and reactive strategies.

In my setting the key to the effective use of proactive and reactive strategies is a good understanding of the children's individual behaviour patterns and any possible triggers to their behaviour. This is important so you can establish proactive strategies that will prevent these triggers or patterns of behaviour occurring. However, if their challenging behaviour does get triggered, understanding the child as an individual will mean you will be able to spot early signs of behavioural agitation so you can then react to these and defuse the situation before it can turn into an incident of challenging behaviour. If this does not happen and an incident occurs it will also be useful to understand the child as this could help in defusing the situation.

In my setting I use proactive and reactive strategies, which I explain as follows:

Proactive strategies are the strategies that are already in place to deal with behavioural problems. Proactive behaviour management is basically 'training' the children in what is expected of them. Reasons children behave as expected could be that they simply 'know' what is expected of them or they 'know' the consequences for not behaving appropriately. Praise is the best way of promoting a proactive behaviour management plan. We need to give lots of praise for positive behaviour and logical consequences for inappropriate behaviour. The best way to let children know what you expect of them is to remind them every day, tell them the rules of the setting, discuss choices with them and don't forget to praise them when they are behaving appropriately. The strategies I would use include:

- rule making and boundary setting;
- know how to undertake observations that identify events and triggers;
- know policies and procedures;
- celebrate and praise all children's accomplishments.

Reactive Strategies are how you deal with an incidence of inappropriate behaviour at the time it occurs. We respond to the child's choice and implement a consequence for inappropriate behaviour. No matter how good our proactive strategies are we will at some time need to use a reactive strategy. Consequences that are reinforced to children on a daily basis as part of proactive strategies will be carried out in reactive strategies. If a child makes an inappropriate choice then we must redirect their behaviour.

The strategies I would use include:

- using knowledge to manage an incident of conflict;
- supporting children to achieve a positive resolution and agree ways to avoid conflict in the future.

2.2 Identifying the proactive and reactive strategies that are used within one's own work role.

In my setting I understand that the meanings are as follows:

Reactive – how you react/respond to something that has happened.

Proactive – how you plan to prevent something from happening.

Strategy – A plan of action or policy designed to achieve a major or overall aim.

Policies and Procedures

Following the above mentioned, if I were thinking of reactive strategies and behaviour, how am I expected to respond to times/incidents of aggressive, inappropriate, explosive, vocal, distressing behaviour? In school environments maybe – chatting, nose picking, fidgeting, unwillingness to stay seated, inability to wait for a length of time, instigating conflict, e.g. hair pulling and retaliation. I am expected to model behaviour and maybe remain calm, patient, listen and hear what's being said – verbally and non-verbally, remain unbiased, be fair, support with praise, encouragement, understanding, use facial expressions and eye contact that conveys meaning, remain consistent, know how not to judge, discriminate or show prejudice, provide activities that help to explore feelings, expression and language, provide a range/level of responsibility – self care, tidy up.

I ensure this in my setting by asking myself: What proactive strategies take place to protect everyone? What policies are in place, regular/planned meetings do I hold with my assistant? Which assessments do I use – for individual needs and for risk, reporting, updating, feedback systems, planned occasions that help set rules and boundaries, and discussing a group's expectations ahead of events?

In my own work setting my role involves:

- diversion strategy;
- negotiation – that de-escalates a situation, restore calms, resolves conflict and disputes;
- mediation;
- containment;
- physical and verbal intervention;
- challenging inappropriate behaviour;
- anti-bullying strategies;
- practitioner's knowledge of how to avoid escalating a situation;
- explaining the potential outcomes of children's chosen actions;
- time out or breather, calm down strategy;
- behaviour management training;
- monitoring buddy systems or other peer support strategy;
- organising the environment;
- naming the unwanted behaviour versus labelling the child;
- using non-confrontational language that avoids blaming – YOU did that!;
- whole setting approach, room approach, indoor, outdoor approach;
- strategies that examine how home setting partnerships support, include and can alienate a child;
- planning activities that will instil a sense of importance, e.g. providing hi-visibility jackets when going on walks, alongside adult to child ratios. Doing these ahead of a trip out helps to promote road safety and responsible roadside behaviour;
- utilising planned circle times to explore issues;
- first aid procedures and training;
- I am aware that I may have to remove resources/equipment that are considered a threat, implement reward/gift type strategies and consequence/sanction punishments, which aim to evoke a reinforced behaviour;
- I have both the Behaviour Policy and the Health and Safety Policy, which I adhere to.

2.3 Explanation of the importance of identifying patterns of behaviour or triggers to challenging behaviour when establishing proactive and reactive strategies to be used.

In my setting I find that it is important that we try to identify patterns of behaviour or triggers because:

- It can reveal what the child or young person gets (what need is being met) through their behaviour.
- It allows you to learn about the child before you intervene.
- It can identify the reasons behind their change in behaviour.
- It can reveal whether the same trigger is being experienced by more than one child.
- It can help identify the situations where challenging or negative behaviour doesn't occur and provide possible areas of solution.

2.4 Explaining the importance of maintaining a person- or child-centred approach when establishing proactive strategies.

In my setting, the importance of maintaining a person- or child-centred approach when establishing proactive strategies is key to achieving positive results for the child. I know from my own child who has special needs, and often displays challenging behaviour, that challenging behaviour is a very individual thing; the causes and triggers differ according to each individual, as do the reactions and their degrees of severity. It is therefore important that when planning strategies for dealing with challenging behaviour we ensure that they are just as individual as the triggers.

Over the years, I have learnt that no two people will respond in the same way to established strategies. Rather than attempting a 'one size fits all' approach you are showing an ability to adapt and respond. This shows that you can identify and recognise each individual's strengths, incorporate them into your planning and build on them. It tells the child or young person you are supporting that they have recognisable value and worth and that no matter how challenging their behaviour may be there is always something positive to build on. Therefore, every plan, approach or strategy has to be child-centred. This is how I would explain the importance of maintaining a person- or child-centred approach when establishing proactive strategies

2.5 Explaining the importance of reinforcing positive behaviour with individuals.

I explain the importance of reinforcing positive behaviour with individuals as follows. In my setting I have developed to appreciate that children have an inborn desire to please people and gain approval. If they don't get this through the acknowledgement of positive behaviour they are more likely to use negative or challenging behaviour. By reinforcing positive behaviour you are encouraging children to seek attention as a result of appropriate rather than inappropriate behaviour. Focusing on negative behaviour will only trigger your own frustrations and aggression, causing you to exhibit exactly the behaviour you are striving to avoid. By focusing on reinforcing positive behaviour you are therefore modelling the kind of behaviour you feel is appropriate because you are calm, focused and feeling positive.

2.6 Evaluation of the impact on an individual's well-being of using reactive rather than proactive strategies.

In my setting I evaluate the impact on an individual's well-being of using reactive rather than proactive strategies as follows. If you use proactive strategies then you can stop the behaviour before it starts. Therefore the child feels calm and relaxed and everyone is happy. If reactive strategies are used then the behaviour has already happened and the child may be experiencing remorse, be ashamed, confused, humiliated about the incident/outburst. Whereas proactive strategies identify triggers and early indicators that help to stop the behaviour before it starts, reactive strategies deal with the behaviour once it's done. If house rules or boundaries aren't known then the child won't know what is expected from them.

LEARNING OUTCOME 3

BEING ABLE TO PROMOTE POSITIVE BEHAVIOUR

3.1 Explaining how a range of factors may be associated with challenging behaviours.

I would explain how a range of factors may be associated with challenging behaviours as follows. A practitioner childcare provider may look at the behavioural factors of a child, who having witnessed domestic abuse, the child or young person might feel that this is the right way because of what they are constantly seeing and this can cause them to behave aggressively. Additionally, the following factors may cause or contribute to challenging behaviour:

- communication;
- environment;
- power imbalance;
- excessive demands;
- boredom;
- inconsistent approaches;
- lack of boundaries or goals;
- emotional expression;
- sensory needs;
- physical health;
- mental health;
- an individual's past experiences;
- age and gender.

3.2 Evaluating the effectiveness of proactive strategies on mitigating challenging behaviours.

To reduce challenging behaviour in my setting, proactive strategies are tools, ways or methods that I already have in place to deal with behaviour. I am aware that challenging behaviour can be hitting, kicking, spitting, hair pulling or anything that is aggressive, confrontational and also children that don't want to take part where a carer or a teacher thinks they should. The question, "Evaluate the effectiveness of proactive strategies on mitigating challenging behaviours" asks me to look at whether those strategies work or not, how well that might be or how bad. Mitigate means to make less severe, serious or painful, spreading out the challenging behaviour so staff can deal with what's going on. In my setting, when supporting positive behaviour, it very much depends on the child, their age and existing knowledge of their behaviour as to which method you use. I have learnt that **reinforcing positive behaviour** is following B.F. Skinner's theories of positive enforcement. This works as children respond more to positive enforcement than to punishment. Children need not be given a reward each time so making the child strive for a reward, but with this approach there needs to be a threat of punishment to keep the child from reverting to their old behaviour.

Modelling follows Bandura's theories that a child will model or copy behaviour. This works if the child has a good role model but if the child sees bad behaviour they will copy that too.

Speech, language and communication is by improving the child's ability to communicate we can help the child's behaviour. Following management plans that have preventative practice, trying to redirect the child's attention elsewhere. Specific instructions can make it easier for the child to understand the language used. Complex or ambiguous instructions might not be understood, meaning communication needs to be at the age and ability of the child.

Ignoring – giving positive attention to those who do well can get a child to notice, 'If I behave like that I can get more attention'.

In my setting I notice that the children help make their own pre-school rules and boundaries, which helps the children remember their behaviour. If this is not done then sanctions can happen using the 3 steps or strikes method. This gives children a chance to process what can happen if they don't think about and change what they are doing wrong and make choices based on that information. Older children can draw up contracts with teachers. This helps the child want to improve their behaviour, especially if backed up with positive reinforcement. Children are encouraged to reflect on their own behaviour, which encourages them to take responsibility for their behaviour. It can be useful to focus on positive behaviour rather than just on negative behaviour as this can help children think about what they need to do in the future and about other people's feelings.

In my setting I ensure that when children start to bully other children or exclude them from playing, these incidents need to be handled quickly. Children need to understand this is not acceptable behaviour. This can be done with the children then and there, explaining to the child how they think the other child feels. Then I have a discussion over circle time so all the children can learn positive behaviour and not to bully other children. Older children need more in-depth material and may need to have specialist support. This can help a child overcome the problem, which has made the child feel they have to bully others.

In my setting, the use of **physical intervention** is a last resort and should only be used if the child is in danger of hurting themselves or others. If in immediate danger staff can react and explain once they are safe. This can upset the child but then the children and staff are safe and no injuries have occurred. These occasions have to be recorded on paper and parents informed on the same day. **Diversion** is another approach for young children to distract them from the behaviour they are displaying or about to display. In my setting I also use **proactive strategies,** which are actions that are put into place to prevent behaviours from happening, e.g. setting boundaries and rules together, for everyone to work within. I always undertake **event observations** to help understand why behaviours are happening or what resources are being accessed in the setting. I ensure that I am **adapting the environment** if it's found that any aspect triggers challenging behaviour. I take action to ensure that I am **changing routines** if any aspect is found to trigger challenging behaviour. I have **policies and procedures in place** that help my assistant/colleagues deal reactively with incidents of conflict and reporting causes/triggers.

I organise to have **training information** that helps my assistant/staff identify triggers, mitigate/minimise risks and manage challenging behaviour appropriately. I always reflect and would be **evaluating the effectiveness** of these or the strategies that you have in place at your setting to see if they work, if not why and how can they be improved. If yes, why and how they do.

Proactive strategies are very useful in mitigating challenging behaviour in my setting. I ensure that children must always be treated with dignity and respect. I know that this may be difficult when their behaviour is threatening to their peers or members of staff, but it underlines the need for planning and adopting well thought-out strategies where members of staff are enabled to intervene positively.

As part of proactive intervention in any setting therefore, following an incident in which restrictive physical interventions are used, both children and staff should be given separate opportunities to talk about what happened in a safe and calm environment, when everyone involved has regained their composure. These interviews should be designed to discover exactly what happened and the effects on those involved, and should be carried out by the line manger of the staff involved. There must also be an interview with those with parental responsibility. The interview should not be used to apportion blame or punish those involved (if however there is clear evidence that a member of staff used force that was excessive and against agreed guidelines the line manager needs to record carefully the views of everyone concerned for possible disciplinary action). Prompt medical attention should be given to any child or member of staff involved if significant injury or distress has been experienced. Carers and/or family members of a child should be informed of any incident and invited to contribute their views. The line manager of the staff involved should ensure that all paperwork, including any necessary assault/incident reporting documentation, is completed accurately and in a timely manner and a de-briefing given to all those involved and other relevant individuals. Staff must be encouraged to report truthfully and accurately all information they have in relation to an incident where physical intervention has taken place. It is their responsibility to share any concerns they have about actions taken with their line manager, and to raise with line managers and other professionals and carers if a child's behaviour is changing so as to require increasing interventions. I am aware that when you support a child through an incident of challenging behaviour you may go through a 'fight or flight' response (a release of adrenaline and other chemicals) and experience some other emotions (fear, anger). After the incident you may feel tired and upset. It is important to talk to someone else about what has happened. The child should be checked over by a member of staff who was not involved in the incident of challenging behaviour. Immediate action should be taken to ensure medical help is sought if there are any injuries that require more than basic first aid. At my setting or any school all injuries should be reported and recorded using the schools' systems.

3.3 Highlight, praise and support positive aspects of an individual's behaviour in order to reinforce positive behaviour.

Observation

This is to be done in the practice you do. You will show how you do it, by highlighting, praising and supporting positive aspects of an individual's behaviour in order to reinforce positive behaviour, so you have real children in the setting and encourage them, praise them, and reward them. Rewards are the things you use to reinforce results.

3.4 Demonstrate how to model to others best practice in promoting positive behaviour.

Observation

Remember observation alludes to you being seen to do what is required of you. Implement and practice. (I think it can be that what do you do that promotes positive behaviour, like... if I was talking to my assistant (a member of staff), I would not shout, especially near children as they mimic what teachers/carers do. Because I won't shout, I would be modelling to children the correct manner of speaking and that should prevent the children from shouting at each other.)

LEARNING OUTCOME 4

BEING ABLE TO RESPOND APPROPRIATELY TO INCIDENTS OF CHALLENGING BEHAVIOUR

4.1 Identifying types of challenging behaviour.

This may include tantrums, hitting or kicking other people, throwing things or hurting themselves. Living with challenging behaviour can be a stressful and exhausting time – parents have told Mencap, the mental health agency in England, that even everyday activities, such as going to school or to the park, can become complicated when they are worried their child may get angry or upset with those around them. I have witnessed this with my own child who has autism. Challenging behaviour is not just a 'stage' that someone with a learning disability will grow out of. It often appears in people who have difficulty communicating their needs and wishes in other ways. If a child suddenly starts to act in a challenging way, it may also be an indication that something new is wrong – for example, that they are in pain or something has upset them.

Challenging behaviour includes biting, fighting/physical aggression, temper tantrums, self-harm, abusive language, unacceptable language, truancy, name calling, refusal to heed instructions or guidance, refusal to eat, disruptive behaviour, attention seeking.

4.2 Demonstrating how to respond to incidents of challenging behaviour following behaviour support plans, agreed ways of working or organisational guidelines.

In some cases of challenging behaviour a plan or a statement has to be agreed and produced by the local education authority of early years for children. This may constitute a planned manner of providing childcare services and guide the practitioner. This is how I respond to incidents of challenging behaviour following behaviour support plans, agreed ways of working or organisational guidelines. I base my response on having a proactive response plan. I have always organised and taken training information that helps my assistant/staff identify triggers, mitigate/minimise risks and manage challenging behaviour appropriately. I always reflect and would be evaluating the effectiveness of these or other strategies that you have in place at your setting means to see if they work, if not why and how can they be improved. If yes, why and how they do. I have learnt through my practice that the environment in which an individual spends his/her formative years has a profound effect on his/her personality, one that will last him/her a lifetime. This is a widely-known and accepted fact. An individual who has spent his childhood in a violent or aggressive environment will have an aggressive or violent streak to his personality. On the other hand, individuals who belong to a quiet, peaceful and secure environment turn out to be confident, secure and balanced adults.

One way of responding to incidents of challenging behaviour following behaviour support plans, agreed ways of working or organisational guidelines is through positive reinforcements. Positive reinforcement is the process whereby desirable behaviour is encouraged by presenting a reward at the time of occurrence of such behaviour. Positive reinforcement is a tried and tested method in what is known in psychology as 'operant' conditioning. It is widely studied and used in behaviour analysis. Some of the advantages of using positive reinforcement are that it can be successfully used to increase the frequency of a wide range of behaviours (positive and negative). It can be used to produce new behaviours. It can be effectively used in the classroom to help students identify their strengths and to put them to optimum use to accomplish tasks allotted to them.

Another way to respond to incidents of challenging behaviour following behaviour support plans, agreed ways of working or organisational guidelines is positive communication. Positive communication is an important tool of positive reinforcement. Using positive communication helps build self-esteem, which, in turn, is the basis of self-confidence and independence. At this point, it may be useful to know that an individual's self-esteem is greatly influenced by the quality of interaction and the kind of relationship they share at home and in the workplace.

Motivation is another factor that highly impacts the use of positive reinforcement. Motivation affects all aspects of living. Being positively motivated in life is essential for growth, success and the overall well-being of a person. It can also be successfully used for motivating people.

Timing is critical to achieve the best results by using positive reinforcement. The desired behaviour needs to be rewarded immediately. A delay in rewarding the positive behaviour will have no effect in reinforcing the desirable behaviour since the time gap between the desirable behaviour and recognition of the same can make or break the behaviour.

Consistency is of utmost importance. A particular behaviour that may be considered positive or desirable and which has been rewarded should stay in that category. Something that is considered 'good' behaviour today should not be labelled otherwise tomorrow. Such inconsistency can be counterproductive, lead to confusion in the child's mind and indecisiveness about acceptable behaviour in future. If implemented properly, positive reinforcement is a simple technique that can help change an individual's behaviour around – usually very quickly.

I respond to incidents of challenging behaviour following behaviour support plans, agreed ways of working or organisational guidelines. Proactive strategies are very useful in mitigating challenging behaviour in my setting. I ensure that children must always be treated with dignity and respect. I know that this may be difficult when their behaviour is threatening to their peers or members of staff but it underlines the need for planning and adopting well thought-out strategies where members of staff are enabled to intervene positively.

As part of proactive intervention I respond to incidents of challenging behaviour following behaviour support plans, agreed ways of working or organisational guidelines. In any setting therefore, following an incident in which restrictive physical interventions are used, both children and staff should be given separate opportunities to talk about what happened in a safe and calm environment, when everyone involved has regained their composure. These interviews should be designed to discover exactly what happened and the effects on those involved, and should be carried out by the line manger of the staff involved. There must also be an interview with those with parental responsibility. The interview should not be used to apportion blame or punish those involved (if, however, there is clear evidence that a member of staff used force, which was excessive and against agreed guidelines the line manager needs to record carefully the views of everyone concerned for possible disciplinary action). Prompt medical attention should be given to any child or member of staff involved if significant injury or distress has been experienced. Carers and/or family members of a child should be informed of any incident and invited to contribute their views.

I respond to incidents of challenging behaviour following behaviour support plans, agreed ways of working or organisational guidelines because I am the key worker (the line manager) of my assistant (the staff) and when they are involved in an incident I should ensure that all paperwork, including any necessary assault/incident reporting documentation, is completed accurately and in a timely manner and a de-briefing given to all those involved and other relevant individuals. Staff must be encouraged to report truthfully and accurately all information they have in relation to an incident where physical intervention has taken place. It is their responsibility to share any concerns they have about actions taken with their line manager, and to raise with line managers and other professionals and carers if a child's behaviour is changing so as to require increasing interventions.

I am aware that when you support a child through an incident of challenging behaviour you may go through a 'fight or flight' response (a release of adrenaline and other chemicals) and experience some other emotions (fear, anger). After the incident you may feel tired and upset. It is important to talk to someone else about what has happened. The child should be checked over by a member of staff who was not involved in the incident of challenging behaviour. Immediate action should be taken to ensure medical help is sought if there are any injuries that require more than basic first aid. At our school all injuries should be reported and recorded using the school's systems. That is how I respond to incidents of challenging behaviour following behaviour support plans, agreed ways of working or organisational guidelines.

4.3 Explaining the steps that are taken to maintain the dignity of and respect for an individual when responding to an incident of challenging behaviour.

Here explain the steps that I take in my setting that are taken to maintain the dignity of and respect for an individual when responding to an incident of challenging behaviour. Therefore I think about providing privacy, e.g. remove other individuals, speak with respect, don't shout, ask them to co-operate, don't tell them, inform them about what you are doing and why, etc. Children must always be treated with dignity and respect. This may be difficult when their behaviour is threatening to their peers or members of staff but it underlines the need for planning and adopting well thought-out strategies where members of staff are enabled to intervene positively. Following an incident in which restrictive physical interventions are employed, both children and staff should be given separate opportunities to talk about what happened in a safe and calm environment, when everyone involved has regained their composure. These interviews should be designed to discover exactly what happened and the effects on those involved, and should be carried out by the line manger of the staff involved. There must also be an interview with those with parental responsibility. The interview should not be used to apportion blame or punish those involved (if, however, there is clear evidence that a member of staff used force, which was excessive and against agreed guidelines the line manager needs to record carefully the views of everyone concerned for possible disciplinary action). Prompt medical attention should be given to any child or member of staff involved if significant injury or distress has been experienced. Carers and/or family members of a child should be informed of any incident and invited to contribute their views.

In my setting I am the key person functioning as the line manager of my assistant (the staff) who may be involved in an incident. I encourage my assistant that s/he should ensure that all paperwork, including any necessary assault/incident reporting documentation, is completed accurately and in a timely manner and a de-briefing given to all those involved and other relevant individuals. My assistant (staff) must be encouraged to report truthfully and accurately all information they have in relation to an incident where physical intervention has taken place. It is their responsibility to share any concerns they have about actions taken with their line manager, and to raise such issues with line managers and other professionals and carers if a child's behaviour is changing so as to require increasing interventions.

When I support a child through an incident of challenging behaviour I may go through a 'fight or flight' response (a release of adrenaline and other chemicals) and experience some other emotions (fear, anger). After the incident the carer may feel tired and upset. It is important to talk to someone else about what has happened. I have a mentor who I always contact to bounce ideas with and also share concerns for appropriate guidance.

In order to follow the steps that are taken to maintain the dignity of and respect for an individual when responding to an incident of challenging behaviour, after an incident the child should be checked over by a member of staff who was not involved in the incident of challenging behaviour. Immediate action should be taken to ensure medical help is sought if there are any injuries that require more than basic first aid. At my setting or in the school I volunteer in, all injuries should be reported and recorded using the setting's or school's systems. This is how I explain the steps that are taken to maintain the dignity of and respect for an individual when responding to an incident of challenging behaviour.

4.4 Demonstration of how to complete records accurately and objectively in line with work setting requirements following an incident of challenging behaviour.

In my setting I demonstrate how to complete records accurately and objectively in line with work setting requirements following an incident of challenging behaviour, as follows.

When recording the incident it is essential to:

- describe what happened;
- report who was present;
- describe who did what;
- confirm whether help was called (e.g. the police) and how long it took for assistance to arrive;
- report any injuries sustained by anyone involved in the incident;
- list damage to property;
- evaluate the situation – Why did it happen? How could it be prevented in the future?

Those are the ways in which I can demonstrate how to complete records accurately and objectively in line with work setting requirements following an incident of challenging behaviour.

LEARNING OUTCOME 5

BEING ABLE TO SUPPORT INDIVIDUALS AND OTHERS FOLLOWING AN INCIDENT OF CHALLENGING BEHAVIOUR

5.1 Demonstrating methods to support an individual to return to a calm state following an incident of challenging behaviour.

In my setting I can demonstrate methods to support an individual to return to a calm state following an incident of challenging behaviour as follows. My own child with autism and sensory issues has a phobia of rumbling noises such as a motor bike raving, a vacuum cleaner, a lawn mower, etc. She can become very agitated, scream and be traumatised whilst kicking or hitting anything or anyone close by. I have learnt that to bring her to calm includes preparation when we are to encounter any of these situations. We are also able to hold in a comfort manner until the situation passes. I am therefore able to demonstrate methods to support an individual to return to a calm state following an incident of challenging behaviour through taking corrective action, appropriate actions such as advance warning.

I also remove the stressor (the reason for the incident) or remove the individual to a calm, private area, use person-centred strategies (e.g. music that you know calms them) to distract attention, use a calm voice and positive body language etc.

There are numerous examples such as a particular child who gets upset when the bin men come. I may have to show him that if he goes into a back room he can't see or hear them (a proactive strategy). The next time they come he doesn't start an incident, he just goes straight to the back room. I praise him for his actions. This reinforces his positive behaviour and he is more likely to repeat it next time.

I would do this with others who know the individual well. I discuss the things that cause the incidents and the consequences of the incidents.

5.2 Describing how an individual can be supported to reflect on an incident including:

- how they were feeling at the time prior to and directly before the incident;
- their behaviour;
- the consequence of their behaviour;
- how they were feeling after the incident.

In my setting I am able to support an individual to reflect on an incident including:

- how they were feeling at the time prior to and directly before the incident.

I looked after Child 'K' on one occasion when I took him to a summer play club. At first all seemed well as he was interacting well with the other children. Then he became very angry at a particular point. Prior to the incident, K felt angered, frustrated and denied the item he requested to have.

- Their behaviour:

K asked to have a particular chair to sit on, but the child that was asked told K that he was already using the chair, and that would K wait a bit. K became angry and aggressive and began to hit other children close to him. Other children withdrew from him, but he continued his rage and had to be restrained.

- The consequence of their behaviour:

Restriction through isolation was the consequence of his behaviour. He could not continue to play with others that he was hitting. K had to be restrained by isolating him, withdrawing him from the group. He had disrupted the calm of peaceful, friendly play. He understood that his isolation was a way of telling him that what he had done was unacceptable

- How they were feeling after the incident:

K was isolated. This was to ensure that he is given respect and dignity, through privately tending to him. I was able to talk to him to find out how he felt after being isolated. K stated that he was sorry, and that he was embarrassed.

In order to help K as an individual so he can be supported to reflect on an incident includes how they were feeling at the time prior to and directly before the incident, their behaviour, the consequence of their behaviour and how they were feeling after the incident.

I took the matter further and informed his mother and, on discussing the issue further, I learnt that K had witnessed domestic violence, wherein it seemed alright to hit others if demands made were not met. I was therefore able to structure a plan of support to K to help him to learn to not hit other children, not to be angry just because someone told him to wait, etc.

5.3 Describing the complex feelings that may be experienced by others involved in or witnessing an incident of challenging behaviour.

I have learnt through training and experience that when you support a child through an incident of challenging behaviour you may go through a 'fight or flight' response (a release of adrenaline and other chemicals) and experience some other emotions (fear, anger). After the incident you may feel tired and upset, judgemental, shocked, surprised, angry, sad, glad it is over. It is important to talk to someone else about what has happened.

Therefore, challenging behaviour can create confusion and mixed feelings to those who witness it. In a childcare setting some of the children can become scared if a child throws tantrums, becomes abusive or aggressive. It is important to calm the children down and talk to them, enabling to deal with their feelings. Younger children would always say things such as, "K was naughty... he scared me... that was not very nice..." and so on. It is important to debrief the child with challenging behaviour, just as it is to debrief those present or witnessing the incident, to enable positive outcomes or lessons to be learned and overcome any traumatic experiences as a result.

That is how I would describe the complex feelings that may be experienced by others involved in or witnessing an incident of challenging behaviour.

5.4 Demonstrating how to debrief others involved in an incident of challenging behaviour.

In my learning I have been made aware that it is important to be able to debrief others involved in an incident of challenging behaviour. Those involved will include the child with challenging behaviour, the carer or teacher, and other children in the setting.

Debriefing children

Immediately following any incident the child will be supported with dialogue, consistent with their age and understanding. This may be with the carer(s) involved in the incident, or with another person designated by the child's social worker. This must be constructive and designed to help the child understand the causes and consequences of their actions, and how to avoid similar situations arising in the future. If a young person does not have speech, or has communication difficulties, all efforts must be made to use a communication specialist who is able to meaningfully consult with the child. Immediately following any incident the child will be assessed for any signs of injury or psychological distress by such person as is designated by the manager on site, or the carer. To protect both the child and carer, it is imperative that a contemporaneous written record is made of this, which will form part of the full report of the incident. A body chart must be completed to record injuries. If they are of sufficient age and understanding, the permission of the child or young person must be sought before any assessment of injury is undertaken. If a child or young person refuses to remove an item of clothing and a carer is concerned that there may be a hidden injury, they must seek immediate medical advice. On no occasion will any assessment of injury by a carer involve invasive exploration.

Debriefing carers/staff/volunteers

As soon as is practicable following any incident involving physical intervention, an appropriate supervisor will arrange a de-briefing session with the carer(s) involved. This will provide valuable support to carer(s) who may be feeling vulnerable and/or shocked. This may also need to include children and adults who witnessed the incident. This practice will enable managers and supervisors to ascertain the carer(s) attitude towards physical interventions and the possibility that they may be becoming habituated to its use.

5.5 Describing the steps that should be taken to check for injuries following an incident of challenging behaviour.

I describe the steps that should be taken to check for injuries following an incident of challenging behaviour as follows:

1. The child should be checked over by a member of staff who was not involved in the incident of challenging behaviour.

2. Immediate action should be taken to check the child for injuries.

3. First aid must be administered immediately if there are any injuries to the child and/or adult involved.

4. Ensure medical help is sought if there are any injuries which require more than basic first aid.

5. In my setting and at the school I volunteer in, all injuries should be reported and recorded using the school's systems.

6. When the incident is over and the child has calmed, carers should:

   - check again and treat any accidental injury;
   - reassure and calm those present;
   - talk through the incident with those present/involved;
   - reassure others and seek reassurance;
   - write down an account of the incident using the prescribed form;
   - inform a senior manager, other relevant professionals and the child's parent(s);
   - reflect upon the incident and learn from the experience;
   - arrange to review the Behaviour Management Plan (BMP).

That is how I describe the steps that should be taken to check for injuries following an incident of challenging behaviour.

LEARNING OUTCOME 6

BEING ABLE TO REVIEW AND REVISE APPROACHES TO PROMOTING POSITIVE BEHAVIOUR

6.1 Working with others to analyse the antecedent, behaviour and consequences of an incident of challenging behaviour.

In order to work with others to analyse the antecedent, behaviour and consequences of an incident of challenging behaviour I can say that this has been directly impacting on me as a childminder and as a parent. My child who has learning disabilities, sensory issues and autism exhibits a lot of challenging behaviour. Therefore I am being self-reflective, working as part of a team to promote a child's positive behaviour. I have worked with neurologists, general practitioners, social workers, speech therapists, respite carers, nursery teachers, reception teachers and the local authority. I have carried out research to establish the following:

The A B C of behaviour:

A is what happened before the behaviour, what caused the behaviour;

B is the behaviour;

C is the consequence.

The analysis will often conclude that there is an A which is causing behaviour.

The most basic tenet of behavioural analysis is to view behaviours as a function of a person and their environment. That is, something happens to precede behaviour (the antecedent), which in effect causes or influences the behaviour, resulting in a consequence. We can't change a person, but we can influence the way they behave by shaping the environment they function within it.

In my setting I understand that others may include parents or carers of the child. Others may include social workers, personal doctor or GP, class teacher, language therapist, behavioural therapist and others who may have close links to the child. This would help to draw a pattern of common observations. That is how I would identify others with whom to work to analyse the antecedent, behaviour and consequences of an incident of challenging behaviour.

6.2 Work with others to review the approaches to promoting positive behaviour using information from records, debriefing and support activities.

To work with others to review the approaches to promoting positive behaviour using information from records, debriefing and support activities. In my setting, if we hope to design behavioural change, we would need to focus beyond what is happening right now. One way to ensure we are looking ahead is to be mindful of the behaviour we want to observe in the future. Set behavioural goals, just as you would set design goals, and let this guide your strategy and design process.

I consider the following points when designing solutions that need to drive behaviour change:

- Define the desired behaviour change you want to observe.

- Feed this into the business strategy and design process and let it guide these processes.

- Define your target audience, then go a bit outside the norm. You often learn more from those who do not meet your assumed or expected specifications.

- Conduct research and understand the behavioural predictors of the population (attitudes, norms, control, stages of change). Qualitative and quantitative data are needed here.

- Monitor, measure and modify. Remember, changing behaviour can take time, so I have to be patient!

I have been impressed by an assistant teacher in reception class who was giving one-on-one guidance and support to my daughter as part of her learning plan. While working in reception class the assistant teacher was asked by the class teacher to support my child who has behavioural difficulties.

The assistant teacher used rewards to help my child improve her behaviour. She got a chart with stickers. That was similar to when I was doing my NVQ Level 2 and was placed to work in a reception class in a school and went through the following experience. I am familiar with child 'M' as I have seen him in the playground and have often sat with him, but I have never supported him in class with his work, am aware that he has speech and language problems and he becomes frustrated when he is told he needs to do his work. Subsequently his work is poor and academically he is falling behind the other children in his class. Miss P asked me how I would like to work with M. I informed her that I thought it would be a good idea if we worked together in a one-to-one situation. Then, that way, M would have no distractions and he could have my full attention rather than being nervous about other children in the class. I decided that I would work with him in the cookery room as it was quiet in there and there would be no interruptions. His work consisted of writing a Mother's Day card and all he was asked to do was write a few lines about his Mum. When we were seated I told M that I was really looking forward to seeing his beautiful work and that I was also glad I was working with him. This made him feel a little confident and I could visibly see him start to relax. I told him that I would write the words down on the white board but he needed to help me with the sounds. I was very surprised at how confident M seemed when he was not with other children and realised that it was because he had no other distractions and obviously felt comfortable with me. We worked on his card for 20 minutes and during that time M told me the words he wanted to write about his Mum. I wrote down the words while he used his sounds and eventually produced a beautiful card. When we went back to class, Miss P was very surprised at how well M had done. I told her that I thought in my opinion that M should have a sticker chart, which would increase his confidence and therefore his work would improve. As I have done this many times with other children who I have supported I know the benefits that it can bring. Although Miss P is quite strict in her ways and has a set programme for her class, she was unsure about the idea so I told her that maybe she could try it for a week and if she was not happy about singling M out for the chart then she could stop using it She said she would try.

That is how I work with others to review the approaches to promoting positive behaviour using information from records, debriefing and support activities.

6.3 Demonstrating how reflection on one's own role in an incident of challenging behaviour can improve the promotion of positive behaviour.

In my setting I use reflection on my own role in an incident of challenging behaviour, which can improve the promotion of positive behaviour. Reflection works in a way that enables me to critically analyse what happened, what I did, what effect that had, what might have happened if I had responded in a different way, what I might have been able to do, what could happen in the future. This has the potential to speed up a resolution, help children negotiate more effectively with each other through the use of language, explanation, choice or avoid a situation altogether maybe by having identified triggers and re-designing the play environment or activities on offer. I also work with colleagues to identify specific aspects of my role and who takes responsibility for what, deployment of known figures that children have a positive relationships with, support a child individually in times of conflict or upset, and work with the the children as a group as they witness challenging behaviour or conflict and colleagues to more effectively cope as situations occur. Therefore, in my setting, reflection helps identify proactive and reactive strategies that form a natural and planned part of daily practice, and gaps where training, professional confidence, practising responses for difficult times may be useful. In my setting I may find that talking with parents/carers more frequently helps you keep up with what's new in a child's world and how that might be impacting on behaviour. I use the experience of the real incidents of my everyday work to reflect on. This demonstrates my true reaction and role within my setting or the team in any childcare setting, as that particular situation and behaviour occured, which provides reliable evidence to base an account of professional, self-evaluation on.

t is how I demonstrate how reflection on my own role in an incident of challenging viour can improve the promotion of positive behaviour. This is what enables me to and revise approaches to promoting positive behaviour.

CHAPTER 9

SUPPORTING CHILDREN'S SPEECH, LANGUAGE AND COMMUNICATION

In my setting I have dealt with

SUPPORTING CHILDREN'S SPEECH, LANGUAGE AND COMMUNICATION

UNIT AIM: To prepare learners to work as home-based child carers/childminders. As well as learning relevant aspects of childcare, this knowledge-based unit supports the development of policies and procedures relevant to registration and the basic business skills to set up a home-based childcare service.

LEARNING OUTCOME 1

UNDERSTANDING HOW TO SET UP A HOME-BASED CHILDCARE SERVICE

1.1 Outlining the current legislation covering home-based childcare, and the role of regulatory bodies.

In my setting, I have had to put in place a number of measures to ensure compliance with the requirements of legislation covering home-based childcare, and the role of regulatory bodies. These measures had to be in place in order for me to start my practice as a childminder.

Where I am here in England, Ofsted inspect and regulate services that care for children and young people. Their role and aim as a regulatory body is to promote and improve the services they inspect and regulate, to benefit children, young people, parents and carers. I have discovered through my work and learning that if one wished to become a childminder or care for children under the age of 8 years, one will have to register with one of the UK's regulatory bodies by law. There is also a voluntary register for those that wish to work with children over 8 years. The body to register with will depend on what part of the UK you live and wish to work in. Therefore, if you live/work in:

England – The Office for Standards in Education (Ofsted).

Northern Ireland – The Local Health and Social Services Trust.

Scotland – The Scottish Commission for Regulation of Care (the Care Commission).

Wales – The Care and Social Services Inspectorate for Wales (CSSIW).

In my setting I have implemented the following measures after learning that here in England Ofsted inspect and regulate services that care for children and young people. Their aim is to promote and improve the services they inspect and regulate, to benefit children, young people, parents and carers. I am aware that by law Ofsted are allowed to carry out inspections to insure childcare practitioners are complying with the requirements. Anyone wishing to be on either part of the register must meet with requirements at all time when providing childcare. To register and work I or any practitioner must have the following in place at all times while providing childcare:

Certificate of registration

In England this will be issued by Ofsted (other countries use departments affiliated to education and children) and the practitioner must inform them of any changes that may affect it within 14 days, e.g. if you have a baby or move home.

Public Liability Insurance

A legal requirement for anyone providing home-based childcare is the holding of valid Public Liability Insurance from an approved supplier that will ensure an individual has legal security against accidents and incidents that may occur in line with working with children. This can be provided (and I recommend) by the Pre-School and Learning Alliance and is renewable yearly.

An introduction to child care

This is based on England. This must be completed before or within 6 months of registration.

Department of Education, or in England the Ofsted complaints procedure

This poster must be displayed at all times while providing childcare. Additionally, I am aware through my experience when I was starting my practice that to register, a number of legal criteria must be in place.

Valid paediatric first aid certificate

This must be provided by a recognised body and is renewable every 3 years. It is a legal requirement for registration that the child carer holds a current first aid certificate from an approved provider recognised by the local authority and focusing on paediatric care.

Security Checks: Enhanced DBS (Disclosure and Barring Service, formerly CRB)

This will be carried out by Ofsted and must be renewed every 3 years. Part of the registration includes security checks on both the childcare provider and any other adults that live or work on the premises where the childcare will be carried out. Checks are carried out through a Disclosure and Barring Service disclosure and the vetting and barring schemes of the Independent Safeguarding Authority (ISA). These check the history of the individuals and ensure there is no record of any issues that would prevent the safe working with children.

Pre-registration visit from Ofsted to inspect the premises

Ofsted, before giving registration, will give each applicant a pre-registration visit. The pre-registration visit checks all policies and procedures set up by the childcare provider, and inspects the equipment and premises against the required minimum standards for childcare provision. It is a registration requirement that a pre-registration inspection has occurred before registration is completed.

Appropriate training

Registration conditions include that childcare providers must already have an appropriate childcare qualification or, at a minimum, complete an introductory childcare course that covers the required aspects of learning and development criteria set in the Early Years Framework. This must be completed within 6 months of registration.

Health check

A requirement of registration is also that all childcare providers undergo a health check carried out through a health declaration form and completed by a doctor to ensure that the health of the childcare provider is also at the required standards for the safe care of children.

ICO

Legal requirement for all childcare providers that are storing information for their work in an electronic form (i.e. photos on a digital camera or personal information such as names and addresses on a computer) should register with the Information Commissioners Office (ICO) in line with the Data Protection Act.

Ofsted

The registration conditions that are set out and enforced by Ofsted are to ensure all home-based childcare meets the same required standards and meets the guidelines set out in the Childcare Act of 2006, Early Years Framework.

Their aim is to promote high quality childcare provision. This includes an aim to protect children, while I promote environments that ensure children are safe, well cared for, and actively learning and developing. Ofsted performs a number of checks on the childcare provider and the childcare premises during the registration process to ensure registration conditions have been met. They then regulate childcare providers post-registration, through regular inspection (three years currently for home childcare providers) and the use of self-evaluation forms. Ofsted publishes theses inspection reports, making them available for parents and guardians to see, and therefore allowing comparison and review of childcare provision.

Local authority

In Sheffield we have a section of Sheffield City Council known as 'Pathways to Registration'. This is the first point of call for those wishing to register as practitioners. The route to registration involves initial contact with the local authority, to attend a pre-registration course, which outlines the requirements for Ofsted registration. The local authority has a legal duty to ensure that there is sufficient childcare for parents or guardians that are working (set by the 2006 Childcare Act) and therefore their role is to monitor and maintain childcare requirements and promote the registration of home-based childcare in their area.

1.2   Develop policies and procedures for:

- accidents, illness and emergencies;
- behaviour;
- safeguarding;
- equal opportunities;

and explain how these will be implemented.

In my setting I have all relevant policies and procedures required to operate a registered home-based childcare service.

Accidents, Illnesses and Emergency Policy

Accident/incident:

- The safety of the children in my care is of major importance and I will act in a responsible and safe way at all times.
- My premises have been equipped with fire guards, stair gates, and cupboard locks.
- A risk assessment of all the rooms in my premises has been carried out and is reviewed regularly.
- Risk assessment checklists are performed on a daily basis to remove hazards and ensure safety features are in place and functional.
- I hold a valid paediatric first aid certificate.
- I keep a fully stocked first aid kit in my house and my car.
- I carry parent contact details and emergency contact numbers with me at all times when caring for each child.
- I keep record of all accidents and incidents however minor.

Fire:

- My home is equipped with a smoke alarm on each floor and these are checked on a monthly basis.
- My kitchen is equipped with a fire blanket and fire extinguisher.
- My fire exits are clearly labelled/signposted.
- Fire exits will be kept clear and accessible at all times.
- My fire procedure is displayed on my notice board.
- My fire evacuation process is practised with the children and recorded on a monthly basis.
- There is a no smoking policy on my premises.

Illness:

- I cannot accept to my setting any child that is suffering from, or has suffered from a contagious illness such as diarrhoea, sickness or conjunctivitis in the last 24 hours.
- I have a valid first aid certificate.
- I can only administer medication to a child with prior written consent.
- All medication (i.e. children's paracetamol) must be provided by the parent/guardian, and clearly labelled and within expiry date.

Missing/lost child:

- When on outings I will teach children about acting responsibly and safely at all times.
- The safety of the children in my care is paramount and doors are kept locked at all times when not in use.
- Visitor are recorded and supervised at all times and children are not left unattended with visitors.
- Children must be collected from designated individuals specified by the parent or guardian with sole legal responsibility for the child. In the event that children are picked up by a new or unfamiliar individual, ID or family designated code words will be used to ensure security.

Accidents, Illnesses and Emergency Procedure

Accident/incident:

- If there is an accident I will comfort and reassure the child initially.
- I will ensure the safety of other children in my care if required while I attend to the incident /accident.
- I will assess the level of injury from the accident based on my first aid training.
- If necessary I will then call for medical assistance/ambulance (999), and then administer any first aid treatment required.
- If the injury is minor and no medical assistance is needed I will administer first aid treatment in line with my first aid training.
- I will then contact the parent/carer as soon as possible to inform them of the accident.
- I will then record all details of the accident/incident in my Accidents Records Folder.
- I will ask the parent or guardian to read and sign the Accident Records Folder and receive a copy.

Fire:

- In the event or discovery of fire, or on hearing the smoke alarm, all children will be informed and gathered in a calm manner.
- The children will be evacuated through the nearest safe exit to a safe location outside the premises.
- The fire service (999) will be called.
- Parents/guardians will be contacted and informed of the situation.
- We will then stay in the dedicated fire evacuation place until it is safe to return.
- I will then record all details of the incident in my Accidents/Incidents Records Folder.
- I will ask the parent or guardian to read and sign the Accidents/Incident Folder and receive a copy.

Illness:

- In the event of a child becoming ill when in my care, parents will be contacted and a decision will be made whether it is appropriate for the child to be collected.
- I will isolate the child from other children in my care if it is safe to do so while waiting for parents to collect them.
- If required I will administer first aid in line with my training.
- If written parental permission is given I will administer a child's provided medicine to the child in the stated dose on the bottle (e.g. paracetamol).
- All records of medicines administered will be recorded and signed by the parents. Parents will then receive a copy.

Missing/lost child:

- In the event of a missing child I will make a search of the premises.
- I will locate and check the attendance of all children in my care.
- I will locate any potential breaches of security (e.g. open doors).
- I will notify the police (999).
- I will then notify the parent/guardian.

My setting's Behaviour Policy

In order to promote a safe and happy environment, all children will be treated with respect and care. To achieve this I need to set boundaries and limits to certain behaviours and promote positive social interactions. I never use corporal punishments that cause pain, discomfort or humiliation to a child. In my setting, negative behaviours are discouraged through clear explanations of boundaries, positive reinforcement and by setting good examples to the children through being a positive role model. This is how I implement behaviour policy. I use a behaviour procedure as the implementation:

- I reward good behaviour and respond positively.
- I use distraction to redirect unwanted behaviour in young children.
- I act as a good role model.
- I encourage self-discipline and respect for others.
- I set realistic limits according to the child's age and development.
- I encourage children and give clear explanations and choices.
- I am consistent and firm with my rules and boundaries.
- I give praise and attention to maintain self-esteem.
- I may use physical restraint, but only in the event of preventing injury or harm.

Safeguarding Policy

If I have any cause for concern for the children in my care I will report it, following the local Safeguarding Children Board procedures. The relevant local procedures that are held by me are available on request. I understand that child abuse can be physical, sexual, emotional, neglect or a mixture of these, and I ensure I have regular safeguarding training in order to aid me in recognising possible signs of child abuse. To support this it is very important that parents communicate fully any details about a child and their home circumstances, for example any injuries sustained or emotional upset (e.g. death in the family, or parent separation). A copy of *Worcestershire Early Years and Childcare Service – Guidelines for Childcare Providers for Safeguarding* booklet is available for you to read if required (www.worcestershire.gov.uk/eycs). This sets out the guidelines for how I will record any incidents and disclosures and the procedures I will follow.

Safeguarding Procedure

I may become concerned about a child's welfare if I recognise one or more of the following:

- Significant changes in a child's normal behaviour or well-being without reasonable explanation from the parent/guardian.
- Unexpected or suspiciously located bruising or marks where there is no reasonable explanation from the parent/guardian.
- Comments from the child that give me cause for concern.
- I will keep detailed written records of conversations and observations made about the child. Conversations held with the child will be carried out carefully, with non-leading questions, and the exact words that the child uses will be noted.
- I will report all concerns to the Worcestershire Children's Services Access Team. Under these circumstances the information relating to the child will no longer be confidential, but will be shared with Ofsted, children's services and the police if requested.

Equal Opportunities Policy

I aim to promote equality of opportunity and anti-discriminatory practices for all children, and work to include all children in my setting. I follow legislation and practice set by the Equal Opportunities Commission.

I use the following means to implement Equal Opportunities Procedure:

- Children are treated with equal concern and respect at all times no matter their race, religion, culture, language, gender, ability, sexual orientation, class/status, health or age.
- I recognise that each child is a unique individual with different needs.
- I provide equal chances for each child to learn and develop to their full potential.
- I arrange access to a range of toys and resources that provide positive images and examples of the diversity of life in our society.
- I act as a positive role model and challenge racist and discriminatory remarks, attitudes and behaviour from the children in my care.

1.3 Explain the importance of confidentiality and data protection.

In my setting, confidentiality for me as a practitioner of a home-based childcare setting is essential to create and maintain a trusting and respectful relationship with children and their families. Child carers should respect the privacy of the children and the families at all times, and information both written and verbal should be considered confidential at all times.

Disclosure of information can be done with specific permission of the parent or guardian, for example if you wish to display a photo of the child for visitors in your home. There may also be incidences where some confidential information is required to be shared if you are working with colleagues or assistants, on a need-to-know basis. For example, health information regarding allergies for staff that are making a meal for the child.

In my setting I recognise that there are exceptional circumstances where personal information may be disclosed without parental permission, for example in a safeguarding issue where the child's health and well-being means that information needs to be disclosed to the appropriate agencies such as the children's services or the police.

In my setting I have to ensure that notes and records about children should be or are written with care and attention to ensure confidentiality. Although parents have the right to inspect the records about their child at any time, it is important to protect the confidentiality of other children at the setting. For example, an accident or incident report shown to one parent should not have the names of other children involved in the accident in the report. Child carers should not discuss details about children in public places and photos or comments regarding children should not be loaded onto social networking sites.

I keep records because child carers are required to keep a number of records as part of their job. This includes personal data such as addresses, names, and telephone numbers, and also more sensitive information regarding a child or child's family, such as race, religion, or health. It is essential that child carers comply with the Data Protection Act (1998). The act lays out the principles for recording, storing, and preserving confidential data effectively.

To comply with the act, written or electronic records should be stored correctly and securely, where they cannot be viewed or accessed by visitors or other children.

In my practice I ensure that I comply with ICO because if child carers keep any electronic data or information (e.g. digital photos or computer spreadsheets) they are also required by law to register with the Information Commissioners Office (ICO).

1.4 Develop a marketing plan for your own home-based childcare service.

In my home-based childcare service I have developed a marketing plan as follows:

(a) Ofsted: through Ofsted's registration and inspection my details are placed on the Ofsted website. Many parents when looking for childcare always go straight to the Ofsted website.

(b) Local authority: The children's services department working in conjunction with the education directorate, both advertise registered childcare providers. I have through Ofsted ensured that my home-based childcare service is listed and contact details are available, showing my unique services to attract parents who wish to buy my services of childcare.

(c) 'Pre-School and Learning Alliance' an Association for Childcare and Early Years providers. I am a member of this association to ensure professional support when required. This provides me with several additions to the credibility I need to show to my potential customers and attract them to buy services from me. I get insurance that comprehensively covers my home-based childcare services. I get a national network that I can use for marketing.

(d) Mentor: I have a childcare qualified mentor from the local authority's children's services, with whom I meet regularly and maintain links with Sheffield City Council, as most potential childcare services customers are directed or referred from enquiries they make at Sheffield City Council's information desk.

(e) Personal advertising: I use personally designed business cards, leaflets and a poster that I circulate widely within my catchment area including schools, community centres, supermarkets, libraries and faith communities.

(f) Childminders and carer's network meetings: I have developed a partnership working with another childminder. This helps to meet the needs of customers, for instance where there is a need for pick up or taking children to school, I or my colleague could provide the service depending on convenience. This enables me to market niche elements of a home-based childcare service.

This is how I have successfully developed a workable marketing plan for my own home-based childcare service.

1.5 Demonstrating financial planning for your own home-based service.

In my setting I have demonstrable financial planning as follows. I have to plan and work diligently to ensure financial planning for my home-based childcare service.

(a) Perimeters: I draw two financial perimeters to ensure that I separate what is business and what is for my home.

(b) Pricing: I ensure that I carry out market analyses, to compare prices with competitors and match quality with cost, so my pricing is commensurate with these factors.

(c) Bookkeeping: I use basic bookkeeping to record financial income and expenditure to ensure that I am accountable for the necessary tax returns

(d) Tax returns: I keep in contact with HMR who advise on various aspects of making tax returns.

(e) Bank account: I operate a bank account where income is banked and expenditure drawn. I set up direct debits for parents to pay me, and ones for me to pay e.g. Pre-School and Learning Alliance subscriptions, insurances and various other necessities, such as; rents, staff, services of gas, electricity and water.

(f)   Accountant: I am aware that if necessary I can engage an accountant. However, I have not had to as I have previous administrative training.

(g)   Financial records: I keep financial records such as receipts and invoices for purchasing items for my home-based childcare service. I keep a record of all the payments made to me and bank the money.

(h)   Petty cash: I keep a small amount of petty cash for emergency or immediate expenditures not exceeding £30, and I remember to replace it if it is expended. Petty cash helps for instance where a parent requests that a child is to be collected from school by a taxi and that I pay the driver when they drop off the child to me.

1.6   Identify sources of support and information for the setting up and running of your home-based childcare business.

In my setting, I have learned through my previous training to identify sources of support and information for the setting up and running of my home-based childcare business including the following:

- Networking: I have built a strong network starting with engaging an assistant. I have ensured that s/he acquires training relevant to childcare and gets first aid training and police checks so that s/he can be a source of support. Additionally, the local authority has a forum of childminders at which I am able to meet and share concerns and ideas.

- Mentor: I have a mentor who is on hand to support me in complex situations that I may encounter, or just to bounce ideas with. My mentor is a children's services officer within the local authority.

- Colleagues and community groups: I have a job-share colleague who is also a registered childminder with whom I can refer clients. I also refer children to community agencies such as UK KIDZ who support children and parents in out of school activities.

- Pre-School and Learning Alliance: I am a member of the Pre-School and Learning Alliance This Association is invaluable they provide a lot of legal and practical advice as and when needed or appropriate.

- Schools: I work closely with local schools as I have a role of volunteer in accompanying on school outings. I am able to secure support from schools as appropriate to ensure a valuable and appropriate service for my business. Many parents come to buy my services resulting from schools contacts.

- Professional services/external agencies: Amongst others I ensure good contact with local surgeries of doctors/GPs in the area so as to ensure positive support when I contact them. I keep a list of useful telephone contacts for fire and emergencies, police, doctor, NHS Direct, social services and children's services.

- Parents: I find that the most important source of support for my home-based childcare business is parents.

- Ofsted: There many practical and operational aspects that I find guidance provided from Ofsted.

- Community: I have to keep good community relations, knowing neighbours and keeping abreast of news and events. This way the support of community becomes an invaluable source of support for my home-based childcare business.

LEARNING OUTCOME 2

UNDERSTANDING HOW TO ESTABLISH A SAFE AND HEALTHY HOME-BASED ENVIRONMENT FOR CHILDREN

2.1 Explaining the key components of a healthy and safe home-based environment.

In my setting the key components of a healthy and safe home-based environment are based on safeguarding of children and all that come into the setting. As a childminder my aim is to provide a safe environment. In my home I provide the following:

General: Age-related toys to avoid choking etc., ensuring they are not broken or have any sharp edges or things hanging off. A stair gate, smoke alarms, first aid kit, radiator guards, plug socket covers. I do a risk assessment each morning in the home and garden to make sure that everything is safe for the children to come into. I make sure all main doors are kept locked and the key put on a hook near the door out of reach from the children. Alcohol is not allowed on my premises, if it were it would be put away and out of sight from the children. I have no pets, but if I had, pet food would be put out of children's reach. All highchairs/booster seats have 5 point harnesses.

Kitchen: All household cleaners are locked away. Plastic bags are out of reach. I have a fire blanket. I make sure all sharp objects are out of sight and reach of children. I use short coiled flexes on electrical equipment.

Bathroom/toilet: I have a toilet downstairs dedicated for the children's use. I keep all cleaning materials out of reach. I make sure all air fresheners are kept out of reach. I make sure the floor is kept dry and clean. I make sure toilet seats are regularly cleaned using disinfectant.

Outside: I make sure all shed/garage doors are kept locked. Any items containing water are covered. I make sure all gates are secure and locked. I make sure all fences are secure. I make sure all toys are safe and have safety marks and are not broken. I make sure all large play equipment is safely secured in place.

Outings: I make sure prams/buggies are safe, e.g. I use or ensure harnesses and brakes are in good repair or working order. I ensure child(ren) walking under 5 has reins or hand strap. I ensure child number ratios to accompanying adults. I ensure the children cross the road in a safe place. I always practise road safety with the children. If travelling by car I make sure that I have children in the right car seats/harness for their age. I assess any play area and do a risk assessment on it before letting the children go and play. I check to ensure that the area is clean and safe, assuring that any play equipment is safe to play on.

Medicines: All medicines are stored safely away and out of the reach of children and are properly labelled. I never give medicines without having written permission from the parents, keeping a record of when the medicine was administrated and how much was given.

Healthy home environment: I ensure to maintain a clean, safe, healthy setting at all times. Whilst I generally do not allow smoking in my setting I am always ensuring that all bins are regularly emptied and cleaned, all floors are clean and I ensure that if a baby's dummy drops onto the floor to wash /sterilize it.

My personal hygiene: I am always using gloves when changing nappies and cleaning up bodily fluid. I ensure that I always wash hands before feeding babies or children, before handling baby's bottles, before I eat, before handling raw or cooked food and before dealing with any cuts or grazes. I always wash hands after using the toilet, changing nappies, wiping noses, touching pets or cleaning up after pets, after handling money and after being outside.

Children's personal hygiene: I am concerned about safeguarding. I always make sure they wash their hands before eating. I always help children to wash hands after using the toilet, coughing and sneezing, touching pets or playing outside.

Nappies/toilet hygiene: I always wrap disposable nappies in a bag and put it in an outside dustbin as soon as possible. I never change babies or use a potty in a kitchen. I always change individual hand towels regularly. I ensure I wash out potties with disinfectant and wash down changing mats after each nappy change.

I regularly update my information on health and safety by obtaining the current guidance on health and safety risk assessment of the home-based setting from the websites ROSPA, Brake, Pre-School and Learning Alliance and HSE.

This is how I list the key components of a healthy and safe environment for my home-based childcare practice.

2.2 Explain the principles of safe supervision of children in home-based setting and off site.

In my setting every activity has to be planned. This means that I plan for the unexpected or unusual to happen. So my foremost plan is to be alert. Therefore, I am alert when planning an activity, making sure the location or setting of what I plan to do with the children is the right environment for the activity. For example, if I was using bikes and scooters in the play area outside my house, firstly I would ensure that the equipment, i.e. bikes and scooters are in safe and good working condition. Secondly, I would ensure the bikes and scooters are used in the proper manner and with plenty of space so in my setting we would not use them indoors as there is not enough space – they would be used outside. I would also ensure that the main gates to the setting are closed so that no child or young person could wander out without my knowledge. My assistant helps me to support those children who are only still learning to ride a tricycle and I have at the ready a helmet that they have to wear.

When I am using the environment it is important the children have the space required for the planned activity. When using outdoor environments I make sure the plants around do not pose a threat. Sometimes I may plan an activity of going to a park so I ensure that there is no dog or cat mess around. I also ensure I go to areas of the park where the hard ground is even and rubbish is removed on a daily basis. I am aware that a varied environment supports children's and young people's learning and development; it gives them confidence to explore and learn in safe and secure yet challenging indoor or outdoor space. In my setting risk assessments are carried out for all activities and regular checks are carried out around the setting daily. I, on a daily basis, check that the toilet area is clean and has toilet paper and soap available for the children to wash their hands. In my risk assessment I also make sure that children and young people are individuals, each with different needs. I am a member of the Pre-School and Learning Alliance, which provides my setting with insurance risk cover for unexpected professional occurrences.

The principles of safe supervision are as follows. They are five steps to risk assessment:

- I Identify the hazards;
- I decide who might be harmed and how;
- I evaluate the risks and decide on precaution;
- I record my findings and implement them;
- I review my assessment and make updates if necessary.

It is important that I do not overcomplicate the process. In my settings, the risks are well known and the necessary control measures are easy to apply. I already know for example, where people are most likely to slip or trip. So, I check that I have taken reasonable precautions to avoid injury. The above information is for me, the factors to take into account when planning healthy and safe indoor and outdoor environments and services.

Off-site and on outings: I monitor and teach the children the importance of safety, for instance not to go outside the setting gates, and I ensure they are supervised at all times. Off-site, or on outings such as walks, we hold hands and walk close to one another. I make sure prams/buggies are safe – for example I use or ensure harnesses, brakes are in good repair or working order. I ensure child(ren) walking under 5 have reins or a hand strap. I ensure child number ratios to accompanying adults. I ensure the children cross the road in a safe place. I always practise road safety with the children. If travelling by car I make sure that I have children in the right car seats/harnesses for their age. I assess any play area and do a risk assessment on it before letting the children go and play. I check to ensure that the area is clean and safe assuring that any play equipment is safe to play on. I pay regard to the following. Children must be kept safe whilst on outings. For each type of outing, I must carry out a full risk assessment, which includes an assessment of required adult-child ratios. This assessment must take account of the nature of the outing, and consider whether it is appropriate to exceed the normal ratio requirements (as set out in this document), in accordance with providers' procedures for supervision of children on outings. I ensure that the assessment is reviewed before embarking on each specific outing. I ensure that I obtain written parental permission for children to take part in outings. I take essential records and equipment on outings, for example, contact telephone numbers for the parents of children on the outing, first aid kit, a mobile phone.

Records are kept about vehicles in which children are transported, including insurance details and a list of named drivers. Drivers using their own transport should have adequate insurance cover.

That is how I explain the principles of safe supervision of children in home-based setting and off-site.

2.3 Identifying ways of ensuring that equipment is suitable for children and meets safety requirements.

In my setting I identify the following ways of ensuring that equipment is suitable for children and ensure equipment meets safety requirements. I always ensure that play equipment is suitable, age appropriate and takes account of the physical abilities of the children. I always check equipment manufacturer signs and markings, plus instructions to ensure that equipment meets safety standards and the suitability of the purpose of child development. For instance, electrical items and toys, swings and climbing apparatus must meet the safety standards and on a daily basis checked, maintained and/or repaired and if necessary replaced if I have found them unsuitable, in disrepair, damaged or dangerous. I always carry out a risk assessment on a daily basis as a major way of ensuring that equipment is suitable and meets safety standards or requirements. When children are using the equipment, they are monitored and supervised at all times to ensure that no risks are taken unnecessarily. That is how I identify ways of ensuring that equipment is suitable for children and meets safety requirements.

2.4 Knowing where to obtain current information on health and safety risk assessment of the home-based work setting.

In my setting I know where to obtain current information on health and safety risk assessment of my home-based work setting. I work to update my practice with current information for safeguarding, especially in health and safety risk assessment. Therefore I liaise with the central fire prevention centres who provide current information on fire prevention. I find out current information from the health authority on any current health issues such as infectious disease. I work and consult with the local authority information services who disseminate information on current information on health and safety risk assessment of my home-based work setting. I also regularly receive information and magazines' updates on current issues affecting childminder practice from the Pre-School and Learning Alliance, of which I am a member. I regularly study the website of EYFS (the statutory framework foundation stage). I also keep myself informed and abreast with news of the practice through the local authority. I look at what my policies state, what health and safety legislation states and how I match what is required. Therefore, in my setting, current health and safety legislation, policies and procedures are implemented as follows:

My Health and Safety Policy

I update my policies regularly.

Specific Responsibilities: The overall and ultimate responsibility for health and safety within the setting rests with me, the main childminder.

I will generally advise the staff in the implementation of my policies and practices. Members of staff, e.g. my assistant, will be responsible for areas/activities in which they are involved:

- by ensuring that the Health and Safety Policy is satisfactorily implemented;
- by ensuring that all new employees, whether paid or voluntary, are aware of and observe the policy;
- by conducting a full investigation of any accidents or incidents that result in injury.

My assistant or any employees, whether paid or voluntary, have a responsibility for health and safety including the safety of others that may be affected by their acts or omissions. As such, they should familiarise themselves with the Health and Safety Policy of the provision and the safe practices appropriate to their place of work.

Staff Responsibilities: These would apply both to myself and my assistant.

- Ensuring all electrical appliances are checked on a daily basis by me, but also an annual basis by a competent person;
- Checking and keeping stocked the first aid box;
- Routinely checking that all electrical appliances in my setting/provision are usable and reporting any defects to the Management Committee.

I check what current information is available through the Health Executive on their website. If I was not sure of anything I would always ask through the various networks of childcare provisions including Ofsted, childcare departments and memberships I have. That is how I know where to obtain current information on health and safety risk assessment of the home-based work setting.

2.5   Explaining how to store and administer medicines.

Storage of medicine: I keep medicines out of reach of children. Medicines are stored according to the manufacturer's guidance, some in a cool dry place, others in a fridge.

Administering medicine: I have a policy for medicine in my setting. At all times the administration of medication must be compliant with the Welfare Requirements of the Early

Years Foundation Stage and follow procedures based on advice given in *Managing Medicines in Schools and Early Years Settings* (DfES 2005).

Oral medication: Asthma inhalers are now regarded as 'oral medication' by insurers and so documents do not need to be forwarded to my insurance provider.

- Oral medications must be prescribed by a GP or have manufacturer's instructions clearly written on them.

- My setting must be provided with clear written instructions on how to administer such medication.

- All risk assessment procedures need to be adhered to for the correct storage and administration of the medication.

- I must have the parents' or guardians' prior written consent. This consent must be kept on file. It is not necessary to forward a copy of documents to your insurance provider.

Life saving medication and invasive treatments: In all case of medicines, I ensure written consents. Adrenaline injections (Epipens) for anaphylactic shock reactions (caused by allergies to nuts, eggs, etc.) or invasive treatments such as rectal administration of Diazepam (for epilepsy).

- My setting must have a letter from the child's GP/consultant stating the child's condition and what medication if any is to be administered. Written consent from the parent or guardian allowing staff to administer medication and proof of training in the administration of such medication by the child's GP, a district nurse, children's nurse specialist or a community paediatric nurse, must also be secured.

- Copies of all three letters relating to these children may first be sent to the Pre-School and Learning Alliance for appraisal and advice to me. Confirmation will then be issued in writing, confirming that the insurance has been extended.

That is my explanation of how to store and administer medicines.

LEARNING OUTCOME 3

UNDERSTANDING THE IMPORTANCE OF PARTNERSHIP WITH PARENTS FOR ALL ASPECTS OF THE HOME-BASED CHILDCARE SERVICE

3.1 Explaining the importance of partnership with parents for all aspects of the home-based childcare service.

In my setting the importance of partnership with parents for all aspects of the childcare service is based on the daily routines of my setting which are based on:

a) **Meeting a child's needs:** I have to visit the parents once they express interest in their child joining my home-based childcare provision. Through this I meet the child and the parents and invite them to visit my setting in order to build a constructive partnership. I get information on the child's name, age and identify any special needs, e.g. communication, dietary, health, etc.

b) **Agreements with parents:** Following on from the exchange of visits, parents may want to place the child in my setting, this entails an agreement. As part of a good relationship my contract would spell out the terms and conditions including payments and methods, e.g. direct debits. The contract also sets out times of the child being brought to me and when collected and by whom. The partnership of parents ensures that I am able to implement my safeguarding policies, as parents have to comply with my policies for the welfare and development of the child. Part of my partnership development is for the parent to understand that I also care for other children and that this demands that the child will participate in activities I provide, engaging other children.

c) **Participation of children:** The partnership with parents helps them to give their consents to activities such as off-site visits where the child would participate in learning, e.g. going to the library, swimming pool, or even a walk and play in the local park.

In my setting, the partnership with parents demands of me and the parents to adhere to the contract or agreement as a mechanism by which they (the parents) would adapt routines for me to meet the needs of children at different ages and stages of development.

In my setting, the importance of partnership with parents for all aspects of the childcare service is that it becomes a means of how I ensure that each child is welcomed and valued in the home-based work setting. The routines in my setting include:

- **Arrivals and departures:** For my safeguarding purposes parents have to agree on the terms of who will bring the child to and collect them from my setting.

- **Taking children to and from school/playgroup/pre-school:** This routine has to be maintained, and if there are any changes they have to be notified, so I always seek an alternative or a relative's telephone number and/or address, which can be used in emergency when the parent may not be available.

- **Meal and snack times:** Children like routines to know simple things like when to eat, or even when to lay the table. I get any information on dietary needs if I have a good partnership with parents. The partnership with parents helps messages to be understood and actions reinforced at home.

- **Sleep and rest:** With a good partnership I am able to plan better when children can rest or sleep, which helps them to be healthy and not be overtired with activity. Parents know their children better, so a good partnership reinforces my service's quality for children.

- **Play and activities:** It is important in my setting that a partnership with parents is in place to guarantee that the children participate in play and activities. This happens when the parent signs an agreement with me. It also enables the safety of children, especially when they have special needs and cannot participate in certain activities. I always seek where possible for parents to join in play and activities. Parents' consents are important for certain activities.

- **Off-site visits:** When I arrange off-site visits I seek parents' permissions. Some parents like to come along, but also consents are sought as part of good practice. Whether suitable action such as sun cream and waterproof clothing may be necessary. Thereby necessitating the partnership I have with parents.

- **Outdoor activities:** I work diligently to consult parents as I plan and carry out some outdoor activities. I ensure that the partnership I have is positive to generate information about children who for one reason or another are unable to be part of any outdoor activity due to health, safety or disability reasons. In many instances I can ask the parent to come and join in the outdoor activity so that their child does not miss out.

- **Homework and evening activities for school age children:** In some cases I look after children after school and the contract between myself and the parent entails support with homework for the child. The partnership I have with the parent must therefore be one in the interest, learning, welfare and personal development of the child.

Therefore there is of great importance a partnership with parents for all aspects of the childcare service.

3.2 Describing how partnerships with parents are set up and maintained.

In my setting I have learnt that a partnership model works around a theory of collaboration, understanding and communication. It is a way that helps to recognise how the best outcomes can happen for children when care, development and learning provision/setting, a child, their parent/family/carers, other settings and agencies all work co-operatively together. Identifying needs via a partnership/multi-agency document can happen though the Pre Common Assessment Framework (PCAF) assessment check list and Common Assessment Framework (CAF), which is shared with appropriate agencies.

Alongside the aims of the Early Years Framework (EYFS), children's progress is seen to be greater when a partnership model of working together is supported. Evidence based on *The Effective Provision of Pre-School Education* (EPPE project), which states that, 'This finding indicates that what parents do is more important for the academic and social behavioural development of their children than what parents are.' (Source: Abstract of EPPE Technical 7 Paper.) This supports a joint or joined up approach. This enables me to check how my setting promotes an open door policy and involves, actively invites and works towards engaging parents/carers in the setting's planning and decision-making processes.

I maintain partnerships with parents through how I share observations – daily happenings, how parents/carers contribute and are part of all assessments and updates by letting settings know about development, interests, medical and dietary needs, whilst I ensure data protection, observing confidentiality and freedom of information. In my setting I take into account for a partnership model the potential barriers that could be involved:

- Communication and how to overcome those barriers – language, use and access to technology, e.g. phone, email, literacy skills.
- Confidence and self-esteem – anyone with less confidence, sense of worth and value may feel uncomfortable/incapable of imparting their ideas, views and opinions.
- Obligations of work – time and income have a bearing on how active a parent/carer can be in a partnership model.
- Learning disabilities and culture can impact on relationships with care providers as an expectation to work together may be unexpected, unfamiliar, cause suspicion and be unwelcome. It is also possible an appearance of professionalism creates a barrier, anxiety and withdrawal.
- Understanding equal opportunity, equality and inclusion in participation. Whilst this is a practice approach that may be extended to all, it may not be taken up by individuals in the same way.

To set up and maintain parental partnerships can be done through evaluation methods, e.g. feedback, survey and sensitive questionnaires can help identify areas a setting does well in, those for further investigation and aspects of provision that individuals enjoy being part of or can see a way to suggest improvement in. I am aware and careful knowing that breaking/breaching confidentiality in a partnership model can cause mistrust and impact negatively on the effectiveness of future engagement. Therefore, oral, paper & electronically kept information following the Data Protection Act must be adhered to. Scholars have helped strengthen the view to maintain parental partnerships, e.g. one such scholar is Howard Gardner: He argues that there is a multi-intelligence theory. Supporting parent partnerships he says in his *Frames of Mind* publication that there must be recognition of the role of the parent as a child's first educator, providing physical and emotional influence. Another scholar called Reggio Emilia has argued for a development of a philosophy and educational approach which emphasises the cooperation of parents with childcarers. Alongside these scholars in emphasising the cooperation between practioners of childcare settings and parents I found that there is also the Parent Co-operative Model for Provision, the Committee Run Pre-School (www.bernardvanleer.org), which uses the attachment theory – linked through psychoanalysis supported by the following scholars: Sigmund Freud 1856-1939, Melanie Klein 1882-1960, John Bowlby 1907-1990, Mary Ainsworth 1913-1999, and Donald Winnicott 1896-1971, including Transitional Object. All of these scholarly pieces of work support partnerships between childcare settings with parents. I am aware in my practice that the limit of children's resilience is in repeated disruption to attachments, when people leave or let them down. When a child leaves home for a school or a nursery, the attachment of a parent is left behind. Yet if the teacher or carer has a partnership with the parent, the child will feel secure in school knowing it is as if s/he has gone from one friend to another. To emphasis more on the importance of partnership between childcarers and parents Barbara Tizard suggests roles for children's well-being. Physical and emotional development exist in significant others with a genuine commitment and continuity of interest in remaining present in a child's life – carers, adoption, looked after settings, foster parents, guardians, sibling care and parenting responsibilities carried out by other immediate and extended family members. Therefore I have to maintain partnerships with parents.

To set up and maintain parental partnerships I use the key worker/person system as set out by Peter Elfer, where he refers to partnership with parents as 'Working Together'. This shows that every childcare practitioner must have partnerships with parents using England's EYFS framework theme of positive relationships, using the principle of parents as partners. Parents/carers are stakeholders in their children's education providers in that they are the ones who retain a continued presence after a setting has been left/provision ended.

LEARNING OUTCOME 4

UNDERSTANDING THE PRINCIPLES OF DEVELOPMENT OF ROUTINES FOR HOME-BASED CHILD CARE

4.1 Explaining how routines are based on:

- meeting a child's needs;
- agreement with parents;
- participation of children.

Routines are based on meeting a child's needs. I, as practitioner, provide the service that meets the need, in agreement with the parent, and help ensure that the children participate in the service provisions. This is realised as follows. The routines in my setting include:

- **Arrivals and departures:** For my safeguarding purposes parents have to agree on the terms of who will bring the child to and collect them from my setting, the child has to arrive or depart, i.e. participate.

- **Taking children to and from school/playgroup/pre-school:** This routine has to be maintained, and if there are any changes they have to notified, I always seek an alternative or a relative's telephone number and/or address, which can be used in an emergency when the parent may not be available. The routine in my case is for the child to be taken to my setting.

- **Meal and snack times:** Children like routines to know simple things like when to eat, or even when to play outside. I get any information on dietary needs if I have a good partnership with parents. So the basis of routine is when the child expects to eat and what to eat, agreement is what sort of food the parent has requested the child should be fed or whether a packed lunch been provided.

- **Sleep and rest:** This routine addresses the child's need to rest. I am able to plan better when children can rest or sleep, which helps them to be healthy and not be overtired with activity. Parents know their children better, so a good partnership reinforces my service's quality for children.

- **Play and activities:** This routine meets the need for development and learning coupled with social skills or interaction with other children. It is important in my setting that partnership with parents is in place to guarantee the children's participation in play and activities. This happens when the parent signs an agreement with me. It also enables for the safety of children, especially when they have special needs and cannot participate in certain activities. I always seek where possible for parents to join in play and activities. Parents' consents are important for certain activities.

- **Off-site visits:** When I arrange off-site visits I seek parents' permissions. Some parents like to come along, but also consents are sought as part of good practice. Whether suitable action such as sun cream and waterproof clothing may be necessary. Thereby necessitating the partnership I have with parents.

- **Outdoor activities:** I make it a routine to take children outdoors so they can enjoy fresh air. This helps the children to learn, yet it may be a routine, but a visit to the garden or park helps knowledge about plants and develops the horizons of children. I work diligently to consult parents as I plan and carry out some outdoor activities. I ensure that the partnership I have is positive to generate information about children who for one reason or another are unable to be part of any outdoor activity due to health, safety or disability reasons. In many instances I can ask the parent to come and join in the outdoor activity so that their child does not miss out.

- **Homework and evening activities for school age children:** When the child participates in doing homework, the need for learning is addressed by the routine. In some cases I look after children after school and the contract between me and the parent entails support with homework for the child. The partnership I have with the parent must therefore be one in the interest, learning, welfare and personal development of the child.

That is how meeting a child's needs, agreements with parents and participation of the children are the basis of routines.

4.2 Explaining how they would adapt routines to meet the needs of children at different ages and stages of development.

In my setting the ideal daily schedule is one that meets the needs of each of the children, my own family and myself – a challenging goal at the best of times. Planning helps me. I ensure remembering the many activities, from cooking to imaginative play to taking a walk in the park or the neighbourhood, which can meet a variety of developmental needs at the same time. Children of different ages and stages don't always have to be involved in different activities. As a practitioner I just have to be creative to find ways to make activities easier for the little ones and more challenging for the older children. Here are some suggestions:

1. I keep my plans simple. The best schedule is the one that allows the most flexibility.
2. I plan my day as a whole. I schedule my usual activities so that they fit together well. For example, quiet, relaxing activities like story time help children move from play time to nap.
3. I allow sufficient time between activities for preparation and clean-up.
4. I think, plan and do ahead. If I am attending play group in the morning, I prepare lunch before I go, so that it can be ready in a few minutes when we all return hungry and tired from the morning out. Better still, I prepare and freeze several days' worth of snacks and lunches for hectic days.

5. I develop consistent routines so that children know what to expect. Children feel more comfortable knowing what comes next and are usually more agreeable about routines like nap time or clean-up time if they are part of the regular day.

Therefore, I would adapt routines to meet the needs of children at different ages and stages of development as follows:

Babies' routines: naps, feeding, changing, etc.

1-year olds: less naps, change of diet, learning to walk, more interaction, small activities.

2-year olds: potty training, more challenging activities, etc.

3-year olds: major change in routines due to starting nursery, may need naps.

4-year olds: starting full time school.

Older children activities to suit varied or all age groups. Interaction with younger children. I help and teach them patience and understanding while helping younger children count and take turns.

This is how I explain how I would adapt routines to meet the needs of children at different ages and stages of development.

4.3 Explaining how they ensure that each child is welcomed and valued in the home-based work setting.

In my setting I ensure that each child is welcomed and valued in the home-based work setting using inclusive methods:

- I implement practice and polices of treating children as individuals who are respected, valued and accepted regardless of social or ethnic background or abilities or health status. I implement my equal opportunities and inclusion policies, ensuring equal treatment and access to provisions.

- I ensure that in all my behaviour and actions around the children I am a role model. I am the one to say, "Good morning X" to the child when s/he is arriving in the setting. I am the one to say, "Thank you" to any good act from the children – this way children copy what I say and do.

- I ensure that I challenge any stereotypes and offensive remarks and attitudes appropriately. I do not allow children to be abusive amongst themselves. I show that I treat each one properly regardless of disability, race, culture, etc. I encourage sharing amongst children.

- I ensure that I acknowledge children have rights and responsibilities. I ensure that everything that I do is done in the interest of developing routines that meet the needs of each child.

In my setting that is how I ensure that each child is welcomed and valued in the home-based work setting using inclusive methods.

LEARNING OUTCOME 5

UNDERSTANDING HOW TO PROVIDE PLAY AND OTHER ACTIVITIES FOR CHILDREN IN HOME-BASED SETTINGS THAT WILL SUPPORT EQUALITY AND INCLUSION

5.1 Explaining the importance of play to children's learning and development and the need for an inclusive approach.

My setting upholds the importance of play to children's learning and development and the need for an inclusive approach is to understand how to provide play and other activities for children in home-based settings that will support equality and inclusion.

The importance of play is designed to introduce children in their early years to the benefits of creativity, development and skills for their future adult life. The importance of physical activity with an emphasis on gross motor and movement skills is evident in my setting and takes centre stage to convey messages to children in a manner they enjoy and can develop into their routines. The importance of play provides for assessing my setting's competence in my planning and implementing inclusion through engaging children to play together and enjoy learning through physical activities and routines, whilst it encourages evaluation of the effectiveness of equal opportunities in my practice.

Play gets children to interact with one another, to share and appreciate one another, enhancing their social skills as well as their overall development. In my setting there are five important outcomes to the use of play and inclusion in learning.

As a practitioner I am able to:

1. use and understand the importance of play, physical activity and the development of movement skills for young children's development, health and well-being;

2. prepare and support a safe and challenging environment for young children that encourages play, inclusion and physical activity and the development of movement skills;

3. plan and implement play and physical activities as a means for inclusion and social interaction for young children;

4. build opportunities for play, inclusion, physical activity into everyday routines for young children;

5. evaluate the effectiveness of learning and play provision in supporting young children's inclusion and physical activity and movement skills. I observe to see what effect is made to the child by particular inclusion or play.

In my setting, inclusive teaching means recognising, accommodating and meeting the play and learning needs of all the children in my home-based childcare provision. It means acknowledging that the children in my setting have a range of individual learning needs and are members of diverse families or communities. A student with a disabling medical condition may also have English as an additional language and be from a single parent family. Inclusive approaches in my setting help me to avoid pigeonholing children into specific groups with predictable and fixed approaches to play, development and learning.

Inclusive approaches to play:

- takes a coherent approach which is anticipatory and proactive, i.e. when I put two children to play I expect them to learn to share or strike a conversation of sorts;

- has a strategy for delivering equal opportunities and diversity policies. In play, children of different backgrounds usually do not notice one another's differences, they strive to play together;

- involves the whole setting – everyone becomes involved;

- matches provision to the children's needs;

- incorporates regular reflection, review and refinement of strategies and methods that actively involve children with disabilities.

This is how my setting upholds the importance of play to children's learning and development and the need for an inclusive approach is taken through understanding how to provide play and other activities for children in home-based settings that will support equality and inclusion.

5.2 Planning a challenging and enjoyable learning environment in the home that includes using everyday domestic routines and household items.

In order to make my setting a well-planned, challenging and enjoyable learning environment in the home that includes using everyday domestic routines and household items, I have had to put in place a number of measures to ensure compliance with the requirements of legislation covering home-based childcare, and the role of regulatory bodies. These measures had to be in place in order for me to start my practice as a childminder. Where I am based in Sheffield, which is in England, Ofsted inspect and regulate services that care for children and young people. Their role and aim as a regulatory body is to promote and improve the services they inspect and regulate, to benefit children, young people, parents and carers. To plan a challenging and enjoyable learning environment in the home, which includes using everyday domestic routines and household items, would be appropriate if one wished to become a childminder or carer for children under the age of 8 years. One will have to register with one of the UK's regulatory bodies by law. There is also a voluntary register for those that wish to work with children over 8 years.

Where I practice here in England, Ofsted inspect and regulate services that care for children and young people. Their aim is to promote and improve the services they inspect and regulate, to benefit children, young people, parents and carers. In order for me to plan a challenging and enjoyable learning environment in the home that includes using everyday routines and household items, I base my plan on my understanding and skills of upholding the importance of play to children's learning and development and the need for an inclusive approach is taken through my understanding of how to provide play and other activities for children in home-based settings that will support equality and inclusion. I do this because I know that by law Ofsted are allowed to carry out inspections to insure that childcare practitioners are complying with the requirements. Anyone wishing to be on the register must meet with the requirements at all times when providing childcare. So I look at the routines such as arrival in the setting, snack time or napping. I plan, e.g. for snack time to be a challenging and enjoyable learning activity in my home environment using everyday domestic routines. I ask and support the children to lay the table. I help with finding our plastic utensils, the cups, the knives, the spoons and the plates. We learn where to place each item together in a group. The challenges are where we place the spoons or forks. We count the spoons, we count the forks, we count our cups. The children enjoy finding the correct spot to place these items and these are routines using household items.

Within the parameters of good practice that is how I would plan a challenging and enjoyable learning environment in the home that includes using everyday domestic routines and household items.

5.3 Explaining what can be learned about children by observing them at play.

In my setting I find that observation of children's play provides important insights into children's ideas and feelings. This helps me to be able to plan future activities as I need to adopt a participant observer role. Observing children's play offers an important way in which adults can monitor and assess children's progress. I am aware that this view is set out in the Qualifications and Curriculum Authority's document *Curriculum Guidance for the Foundation Stage*.

'Logging children's use of a particular activity or play scenario helps practitioners monitor how children use their time, their particular interests and any gaps in their experiences, so that practitioners can plan a balanced curriculum that takes note of children's strengths, interests and needs.' (QCA, 2000:24)

In my setting, playtime offers a context where children's free play can be observed. I always draw on outside play observations to inform indoor thinking. In my setting I love being around the children. It's very interesting for me to see them as a childminder indoors and as their playtime supervisor outside. I can very often take back a lot of things that have happened at playtime to inform our next activity. Or maybe I've seen something in a child's character outside that I'm able to discuss with the parents that might explain what's happening in the overall picture of a child's life. So it's quite valuable to be in both situations.

I have read some information that because of their emphasis on the co-construction of knowledge, practitioners in Reggio Emilia adopt a somewhat different approach to observation. Observing children in unstructured or play activities may reveal what a child has already learnt. The suggestion is that in order to be able to plan future activities the adult needs to be a participant observer, taking part in the activity, listening to and discussing the children's ideas and engaging in self-observation in order to identify possible future paths of learning.

I have also read that Hyder (2005) argues that children can reveal a great deal through their fantasy and imaginative play, and that listening and watching is a crucial part of gaining access to children's ideas and feelings. However, we must be wary of the dangers of seeing what we want to see. Children's play is complex, and we need to be cautious about assuming that, because we have observed the observable (i.e. what the children are doing or saying), we have accessed their thoughts and ideas. We need to be careful that we see what actually happens and not what we expect or want to see. There are always different ways of interpreting situations; these may not be 'correct' from a scientific point of view, but if we are not open to what we didn't expect, if we are not open to different ways in which a topic can be approached, the different connections it is possible to make, the different premises, then it becomes difficult to discover the knowledge-building processes of the children. It is important not to over-predict what will happen. I therefore would explain what can be learned about children by observing them at play as a provider of important insights into children's ideas and feelings, which helps me to be able to plan future activities as I need to adopt a participant observer role.

5.4 Identifying how and why it is important that children receive equal treatment and access, based on their individual needs and acknowledging their rights.

In my setting it is important that children receive equal treatment and access, based on their individual needs and acknowledging their rights. I am drawing from the UN Charter to

Identify the Rights of the Child. The United Nations guiding principles identify the rights of the child as follows. The following principles, based on international legal norms and standards, should guide all justice for children interventions, from policy development to direct work with children. The children also have individual needs that entail that they are respected in order to address their needs appropriately. The children's needs range from speech disabilities, autism, physical disabilities, etc. These should be dealt with using inclusion policies. Diversity and equality issues affect everyone, so I, as a childminder in my setting, must support all children in their development as active citizens. As a practitioner I need the empathy, understanding and skills to help children achieve a positive sense of themselves and of others. My role is to protect and value all children in the setting, foster empathy and provide accurate information about differences to enable children to think critically about and challenge bias.

I also have a duty as a practitioner to address diversity and equality. In my setting a diversity and equality approach involves creating a childcare setting where each child feels a sense of belonging. Practitioners should observe and listen to children's play and adult interaction to identify any bias or discrimination, then develop methods to deal with issues that arise. Every aspect of the setting comes into play. How children relate to each other, how I and my assistant relate to minority and majority children, how language is used, how and what discussions take place, and what activities are undertaken. I apply the United Nations guiding principles identified as follows:

1. Ensuring that the best interests of the child is given primary consideration. In all actions concerning children, whether undertaken by courts of law, administrative or other authorities, including non-state, the best interests of the child must be a primary consideration.

2. Guaranteeing fair and equal treatment of every child, free from all kinds of discrimination. The principle of non-discrimination underpins the development of justice for children's programming and support programmes for all children's access to justice. A gender sensitive approach should be taken in all interventions.

3. Advancing the right of the child to express his/her views freely and to be heard. Children have a particular right to be heard in any judicial/administrative proceedings, either directly or through a representative or an appropriate body, in a manner consistent with the procedural rules of national law. It implies, for example, that the child receives adequate information about the process, the options and possible consequences of these options, and that the methodology used to question children and the context (e.g., where children are interviewed, by whom and how) be child-friendly and adapted to the particular child. In conflict and post-conflict contexts, it is also important to involve children in transitional justice processes.

4. Protecting every child from abuse, exploitation and violence. Children in contact with the law should be protected from any form of hardship while going through state and non-state justice processes and thereafter. Procedures have to be adapted, and appropriate protective measures against abuse, exploitation and violence, including sexual and gender-based violence put in place, taking into account that the risks faced by boys and girls will differ. Torture or other cruel, inhuman or degrading treatment or punishment (including corporal punishment) must be prohibited. Also, capital punishment and life imprisonment without possibility of release shall not be imposed for offences committed by children.

5. Treating every child with dignity and compassion. Every child has to be treated as a unique and valuable human being and, as such, his/her individual dignity, special needs, interests and privacy should be respected and protected.

6. Respecting legal guarantees and safeguards in all processes. Basic procedural safeguards as set forth in relevant national and international norms and standards shall

be guaranteed at all stages of proceedings in state and non-state systems, as well as in international justice. This includes, for example, the right to privacy, the right to legal aid and other types of assistance and the right to challenge decisions with a higher judicial authority.

7. Preventing conflict with the law as a crucial element of any juvenile justice policy. Within juvenile justice policies, emphasis should be placed on prevention strategies facilitating the successful socialisation and integration of all children, in particular through the family, the community, peer groups, schools, vocational training and the world of work. Prevention programmes should focus especially on support for particularly vulnerable children and families.

8. Using deprivation of liberty of children only as a measure of last resort and for the shortest appropriate period of time. Provisions should be made for restorative justice, diversion mechanisms and alternatives to deprivation of liberty. For the same reason, programming on justice for children needs to build on informal and traditional justice systems as long as they respect basic human rights principles and standards, such as gender equality.

9. Mainstreaming children's issues in all rule of law efforts. Justice for children issues should be systematically integrated in national planning processes, such as national development plans, CCA/UNDAF, justice sector wide approaches (SWAPs), poverty assessments/Poverty Reduction Strategies, and policies or plans of action developed as a follow up to the UN Global Study on Violence against Children; in national budget and international aid allocation and fundraising; and in the UN's approach to justice and security initiatives in peace operations and country teams, in particular through joint and thorough assessments, development of a comprehensive rule of law strategy based on the results of the assessment, and establishment of a joint UN rule of law programme in country.

Therefore, in my setting it is important that children receive equal treatment and access, based on their individual needs and acknowledging their rights.

5.5 Comparing how other resources available for children support their play.

In my setting, in order to compare how other resources available for children support their play I make good use of my space and other resources so that children are well cared for and supported during their time in my care. I ensure that children are involved in a broad range of activities that support their language, physical and social development. In my setting I find that children are interested in and want to play with what is available. This includes toys and heuristic material. I am able to compare how other resources available for children support their play as follows. I am always able to seek other resources in addition to what I already have – I make a comparison of how other resources are available, for instance access to parks, or materials to children in my care to support their play and complement existing provisions. For instance I can use local libraries – book loan, story sack loan, CD, DVD, craft activities, galleries, etc.

I make comparisons of the impact made to children when I bring in the additional resources. I could use mobile library services to provide resources where transport, logistics of travelling to a library building and their services may be more difficult. I could find and compare those with toy library and toy loan networks. I can use the local park, playground equipment, field and seating school, health centre or toddler groups. I could use signing up to newsletters, alert and notification services on my emails or by telephone SMS text messages. I can also use support and campaign awareness events, safety, police, fire brigade, road safety, fundraising, big toddle, nature trail areas. Museums and organised events, swimming pools, soft play and larger play items, adventure play providers, animal care and rescue centres, music and movement play providers. I can compare these with local interest groups such as African Caribbean carnivals, theatrical, gardening/horticultural, needlecraft, fanciers. I would observe and gauge what differences or impact to the play, learning and development of the children are created by using the additional resources. This is how I would compare how other resources available for children support their play.

LEARNING OUTCOME 6

UNDERSTANDING HOW HOME-BASED CHILDCARERS CAN SUPPORT THE SAFEGUARDING OF CHILDREN IN THEIR CARE

6.1 Explaining the concept of safeguarding and the duty of care that applies to all practitioners.

As part of my practice I have to have a good understanding of how home-based child carers can support the safeguarding of children in their care. The concept of safeguarding is simply that 'arrangements to take all reasonable measures to ensure that risks of harm to children's welfare are minimised'. I understand that all jurisdictions will have protective measures, which include child protection procedures for the purposes 'of providing necessary support for the child and for those who have the care of the child, as well as other forms of prevention and for the identification, reporting, referral, investigation, treatment and follow up of instances of child maltreatment.' (CRC Article 19 (2)) My practice is in England, where safeguarding and promoting the welfare of children is defined in both the Children Act, Section 11, Guidance 4 and *Working Together to Safeguard Children* (2006).

Therefore, for me, safeguarding and my duty of care includes the Children Act 2004, setting out the process for integrating services to children so that every child can achieve the five *Every Child Matters* outcomes: to be healthy; stay safe; enjoy and achieve; make a positive contribution; and achieve economic well-being. In my work I have over the years familiarised myself with the knowledge and understanding of current legislation, guidelines, policies and procedures affecting the safeguarding of children and young people. I am aware that there is no single piece of legislation that covers child protection in the UK, but rather a lot of laws and guidance that are continually being amended, updated and revoked. In my work, I am now familiar with information that legislation covering child protection can be divided into two main categories: Civil law and criminal law.

Civil law is divided into public and private law.

- **Public law** puts in place systems and processes in order to minimise the risk of children coming to harm and lays out what action should be taken if children are at risk.
- **Private law** deals with family proceedings such as divorce and contact.

Criminal law deals with people who have offended or are at risk of offending against children.

In my setting I constantly refer to notes of my training and my policies in order to make sure that I follow legislation, guidelines, policies and procedures for the safeguarding of children and young people. For instance, I ensure inter-agency co-operation, linking my work with the schools where children in my care go, their GP, social worker, etc. I am also able to relate my work with such resourceful organisations as Ofsted, and draw from the history of the establishment of NSPCC to play a key role in influencing legislation to protect children. As part of my duty of care, here I give an outline of my understanding of current legislation, guidelines, policies and procedures within the UK affecting the safeguarding of children and young people as part of the concept of safeguarding and the duty of care that applies to all practitioners. The Children and Young Persons Act 1933 is one of the older pieces of child protection legislation, which has parts that are still in force today. It includes a list of offences against children and things to guard against. The Children Act 1989, upon which current child protection system is based, reformed and clarified the existing laws affecting children. It is 'the most comprehensive and far-reaching reform of child law', covering a number of principles.

In my setting this helps me so that the most important thing is that a child's welfare is top-most when making any decisions about a child's care. I am also aware that even the law in a court must safeguard the wishes and feelings of the child and shall not make an order unless this is 'better for the child than making no order at all'. In The Children Act 1989 it is stated that every effort should be made to preserve the child's home and family links. This act introduced the matter of parental responsibility which is 'the rights, duties, powers and responsibilities which by law a parent of a child has in relation to the child and his property' (Section 3). This act sets out what local authorities and the courts should do to protect the welfare of children, giving them power and 'duty to investigate if they have reasonable cause to suspect that a child who lives, or is found, in their area is suffering, or is likely to suffer, significant harm' (Section 47). Local authorities are also charged with a duty to provide 'services for children in need, their families and others' (Section 17). It is Section 31 of the Children Act 1989 that sets out the NSPCC's 'authorised person status', which means the NSPCC has the power to apply directly for a court order if it believes a child is suffering or likely to suffer significant harm. The Children Act 1989 defines 'harm' as ill-treatment (including sexual abuse and non-physical forms of ill-treatment) or the impairment of health (physical or mental) or development (physical, intellectual, emotional, social or behavioural) (Section 31).

The Framework for the Assessment of Children in Need and their Families (DH, 2000) is non-statutory guidance providing children's carers or professionals with a systematic way of identifying children in need and deciding the best way of helping those children and their families.

The guide for anyone working with children is known as *What to do if You're Worried a Child is Being Abused* (DfES 2006). This outlines the child protection processes. The Children Act 1989 legislates for England and Wales. The current guidance for Wales is *Safeguarding Children: Working Together under the Children Act 2004.*

The United Nations Convention on the Rights of the Child 1989 (UN, 1989) was ratified by the UK on 16th December 1991. It includes the right to protection from abuse, the right to express their views and have them listened to and the right to care and services for disabled children or children living away from home.

The Human Rights Act 1998 incorporates the European Convention on Human Rights into UK law. Whilst it does not specifically mention children's rights, children are covered by this legislation as they are persons in the eyes of the law, just as adults are. The Education Act 2002 includes a provision (Section 175) requiring school governing bodies, local education authorities and further education institutions to make arrangements to safeguard and promote the welfare of children. Section 120 of the Adoption and Children Act 2002 amends the Children Act 1989 by expanding the definition of 'harm' to include witnessing domestic violence. The concept of safeguarding and the duty of care that applies to all practitioners includes the Children Act 2004. Eight-year old Victoria Climbié died in 2000, so the government needed to introduce new legislation and guidance to improve child protection

190

systems in England. This resulted in the *Keeping Children Safe* report (DfES, 2003) and the *Every Child Matters* green paper (DfES, 2003), which in turn led to the Children Act 2004. The Children Act 2004 does not replace or even amend much of the Children Act 1989. It sets out the process for integrating services to children so that every child can achieve the five *Every Child Matters* outcomes: to be healthy; stay safe; enjoy and achieve; make a positive contribution and achieve economic well-being.

I am aware as a childcare provider that local authorities and their partners (including the police, health service providers and the youth justice system) have to co-operate in promoting the well-being of children and young people and to make arrangements to safeguard and promote the welfare of children. It makes Local Safeguarding Children Boards able to investigate and review all child deaths in their area (a requirement laid out in the *Working Together to Safeguard Children* statutory guidance).

I am aware that this act revises the legislation on physical punishment by making it an offence to hit a child if it causes mental harm or leaves a lasting mark on the skin (Section 58), repealing the section of the Children and Young Persons Act 1933 which provided parents with the defence of 'reasonable chastisement'. The Children and Adoption Act 2006 gives courts more flexible powers to facilitate child contact and enforce contact orders when separated parents are in dispute. The Children and Young Persons Act 2008 legislates for the recommendations in the *Care Matters* white paper (DfES, 2007) to provide high quality care and services for children in care. It places a duty on registrars to notify the Local Safeguarding Children Board of all child deaths.

The Borders, Citizenship and Immigration Act 2009 places a duty on the UK Border Agency to safeguard and promote children's welfare (Section 55), bringing them in line with other public bodies that have contact with children. The Apprenticeships, Skills, Children and Learning Act 2009 legislates for there to be two lay members from the local community sitting on each Local Safeguarding Children Board. The Sex Offenders Act 1997 requires sex offenders convicted or cautioned on or after 1st September 1997 to notify the police of their names and addresses and of any subsequent changes (known colloquially as the Sex Offenders Register).

The Female Genital Mutilation Act 2003 extends the existing legislation criminalising female genital mutilation in the UK, by making it an offence for UK nationals or permanent UK residents to take a girl abroad, or to help others to take a girl abroad, to carry out female genital mutilation, even in countries where the practice is legal. The Domestic Violence, Crime and Victims Act 2004 closes a legal loophole (whereby defendants in murder and manslaughter cases could escape conviction by claiming each other had killed the child), by creating a new offence of causing or allowing the death of a child or vulnerable adult. The offence establishes a new criminal responsibility for members of a household where they know that a child or vulnerable adult is at significant risk of serious harm.

The Home Office published a circular (16/2005), *Guidance on Offences against Children* (Home Office, 2005), which contained a consolidated list of offences for all agencies to use in identifying 'a person identified as presenting a risk, or potential risk, to children'. It also discusses the use of the terms 'Schedule One' offenders and offences. The Serious Organised Crime and Police Act 2005 set up the framework for the UK-wide Child Exploitation and Online Protection (CEOP) Centre to be created. It also includes provisions for improving the vetting system to stop adults who pose a risk from working with children (Section 163). The Safeguarding Vulnerable Groups Act 2006, established a new centralised vetting and barring scheme for people working with children (following the 2002 murders of ten-year-olds Jessica Chapman and Holly Wells). The Forced Marriage Act (Civil Protection) 2007, gives courts the power to make orders to protect the victim or potential victim of a forced marriage and help remove them from that situation. The Criminal Justice and Immigration Act 2008 ensures that people who commit sex offences against children abroad can face prosecution in the UK, even if that offence is not illegal in the foreign country in which it was committed. This is how I explain the concept of safeguarding and the duty of care that applies to all practitioners.

6.2 Outlining the possible signs, symptoms, indicators and behaviours that may cause concern in the context of safeguarding.

In my setting, it is a primary duty to safeguard children and young people. In that context we would look for the possible signs, symptoms, indicators and behaviours that may cause concern. When working with children and young people we have a duty to protect them from harm. This could be from being physically, emotionally, sexually abused or even being neglected. If a child is suffering from abuse or neglect this may be demonstrated through what they say (direct or indirect disclosure) or changes in their appearance, behaviour, body language or the way they play.

The child could experience more than one abuse. If a child is being sexually abused they may also suffer from emotional abuse. Physical abuse is the physical injury or maltreatment of a child under the age of eighteen. This is usually carried out by a person who is responsible for the child's welfare under circumstances which indicate that the child's health or welfare is harmed or threatened. For example, types of physical abuse a child could experience include being beaten with a belt, shoe, or other object. Also being bitten, broken bones, being burned with matches or cigarettes. A child could experience being hit, kicked, and deprived of food and drink, having their hair pulled, being scalded with water that is too hot, also shaking, shoving, or slapping. When then child experiences physical abuse, this may be indicated by the child's behaviour as it may alter and become more aggressive and they may have a fear of physical contact or become clingy. They may also refuse to undress out of soiled or dirty clothes due to fear of injuries being detected. Family or those in close proximity to the child could be the cause of the harm the child endures. However, they may falsify explanations as to what really happened.

Recognising signs of child abuse

There is no clear dividing line between one type of abuse and another. Children may show symptoms from one or all of the categories given below. The following is not a comprehensive or definitive list, but gives an indication of situations, which should alert me to possible cause for concern.

Physical abuse

In my setting I would look for the following signs:

- Bruises in places not normally harmed during play, for example, back of the legs, abdomen, groin area.
- Bruising in or around the mouth area (especially in young babies) – Note: 'Bruising to immobile babies' is listed in the LSCB procedures as one of the indicators for which for a referral to children's social care should always be made.
- Grasp marks on legs and arms – or chest of a small child.
- Finger marks (for example, you may see three or four small bruises on one side of the face and none on the other).
- Symmetrical bruising, i.e. the same pattern of bruising on both sides of the body/head/legs/arms, etc. (especially on the ears or around the eyes).

- Outline bruising (for example, belt marks, hand prints).
- Linear bruising (particularly on the buttocks or back).
- Old and new bruising (especially in the same area, for example, buttocks).
- Unexplained injuries, bruises or marks.
- Fear, watchfulness, over-anxiety to please.
- Bites – these can leave clear impressions of teeth. Human bite marks are oval or crescent shaped. If the distance is more than 3cm across, it indicates that they have been caused by an adult or older child.
- Fractures – these should be suspected if there is pain, swelling and discolouration over a bone or joint. As fractures also cause pain it is difficult for a parent or carer to be unaware that a child has been hurt.
- Burns/scalds – it can be very difficult to distinguish between accidental and non-accidental burns, but as a general rule, burns or scalds with clear outlines are suspicious, as are burns of uniform depth over a larger area.

Points to note. I would note the following 2 points:

- It is very rare for a child under one year to sustain fractures accidentally.
- Bruising is very rare in babies who are not yet mobile.

Neglect

In my setting I observe children to look for warning signs which include:

- Child frequently appears hungry, asks for food.
- Consistently unkempt, dirty appearance, smelly, poor hygiene.
- Babies' nappies not being changed frequently enough.
- The child's clothes are often dirty, scruffy or unsuitable for the weather.
- Repeated failure by parents/carers to prevent accidental injury.
- Medical needs of child unmet – for example, failure to seek medical advice for illness.
- Developmental delay.
- Behaviours such as head banging or rocking.
- The child is exposed to risks and dangers, such as the home being unsafe or drugs or needles being left around.
- The child is left alone with unsuitable carers.
- The child has lots of accidents.
- No one seeks medical help when the child is ill or hurt.

Sexual abuse

In my setting I have been made aware through training that some possible signs of sexual abuse will include:

- Explicit or frequent sexual pre-occupation in talk and play.
- Hinting at sexual activity or secrets through words, play or drawing.
- Sexualised behaviour – for example, pretend sexual intercourse during play.
- Sexually provocative relationships with adults.

- Itching, redness, soreness or unexplained bleeding from vagina or anus.
- Bruising, cuts and marks in the genital area.
- Repeated urinary tract or genital infections.

Emotional abuse

In my setting I observe children and would look for signs that may include:

- The parent/carer giving the repeated message to the child that he/she is worthless, unloved or inadequate.
- The parent/carer having wildly unrealistic expectations of their child's abilities, taking into account the child's age and stage of development.
- The child showing serious difficulties in his/her emotional, social or behavioural development.
- The parent/carer frequently causing the child to feel frightened or in danger.

Some possible signs

In my setting I observe children and would look for signs that may include:

- Very low self-esteem, often with an inability to accept praise or to trust adults.
- Excessively clinging, withdrawn anxious behaviour.
- Demanding or attention-seeking behaviour.
- Over-anxious – either watchful, constantly checking or over-anxious to please.
- Withdrawn and socially isolated.
- Unwillingness to communicate.
- Sudden speech disorders.
- Repetitive, nervous behaviour such as rocking, hair twisting.

This is how I outline the above possible signs, symptoms, indicators and behaviours that may cause concern in the context of safeguarding.

6.3 Outlining regulatory requirements for safeguarding children that affect home-based childcare.

In my setting I outline regulatory requirements for safeguarding children that affect home-based childcare as follows. In my setting the wider concept of safeguarding children and young people centres on child protection. I always ensure that I know the background information of where a child comes from. As a childminder I take into account the environment, for example how I safeguard children, when my own children are at home in which I also look after the children I care for. Child protection includes keeping children safe from risk of danger or harm. This concept helps a childminder like me to be able to use the following tools to achieve and implement safeguarding; which leads to well-being:

(a) In September 2003 the Government produced the *Every Child Matters* green paper to maximise opportunities and minimise risks for all children, young people and their families, and the Children Act 2004 came into force on 1 October 2005.

(b) The *Every Child Matters* green paper identified the following five outcomes as key to the well-being of children and young people:

    i. Physical and mental health and emotional well-being ('to be healthy').

    ii. Protection from harm and neglect ('to stay safe').

iii. Education training and recreation ('to enjoy and achieve').

iv. The contribution made by them to society ('to make a positive contribution').

v. Social and economic well-being ('to achieve economic well-being').

(c)   The Children Act 2004 includes Section 10 – A duty to co-operate with the Children's Services Authority (in my case Sheffield City Council) to improve the well-being of children and young people. This is through what care I provide in my setting.

(d)   The concept of safeguarding duties relates to children and young people from pre-birth to the age of 19, or 25 if the young person has learning or other disability. The fact that a child has become 16 years of age and is living independently, working, is in further education, is a member of the armed forces, is in hospital or prison does not change their status or entitlement to services or protection under the Children Act 2004.

(e)   The concept of safeguarding is to provide a framework for the safeguarding of children and young people and is consistent with and complements the policies and procedures of my setting. My policies cover all activities and services provided by the setting including my assistant and anyone who come into contact with children and young people whilst going about their everyday duties. It is also considered that the policy could act as an appropriate reference guide for use by those councillors whose particular role may involve them coming into contact with children and young people.

6.4   Explaining the procedures that need to be followed by lone workers in home-based settings when harm or abuse is suspected or alleged, either against them or third parties.

The following procedures are what need to be followed by lone workers in home-based settings when harm or abuse is suspected or alleged, either against them or third parties.

In my setting, I have the awareness that:

1.   A child or young person has a right not to be subjected to repeated medical examinations following any allegations of abuse, whether of a physical or sexual nature. A child has the right to be protected against significant harm (Children Act 1989, *Every Child Matters* 2004, United Nations Convention on the Rights of the Child, etc.). Children should contribute their own account of their own views, they should be listened to and within certain circumstances these should be applied, but when a child is in significant harm then you would look at the child's best interest to make them safe. They should be fully informed of everything that is happening to them, they should be consulted sensitively

2.   Carers and/or family members normally have the right to know what is being said about them and to respond or contribute to important decisions. The carers/parents of the child have the right to seek legal advice and be kept informed of any allegations against them and all that is going on.

3.   Children should be kept fully informed of processes involving them. If the child/young person is able to, they should be allowed to say what they wish to see resulting from the issues surrounding incidents of abuse, e.g. young people will often want to leave the environment of their abuse/neglect.

Supporting a child who tells about abuse

In my setting I have a written plan of action, should a child or young person in my care tell about abuse, I put in action the following plan:

*   I stay calm.
*   I ensure that the child is, and feels safe.

- I seek necessary medical treatment without delay.
- I tell the child they are not to blame – it's not their fault.
- I tell and show the child that they are being taken seriously – do not express disbelief.
- I explain to the child that they have done the right thing to tell you.
- I do not promise that I will be able to keep secret the things the child has told you – be honest and explain that it will be necessary to tell someone else.
- I keep questions to a minimum and ask only open questions. For example, after noticing a mark on a child, I ask, "How did that happen?" and NOT, "Did Daddy do that?", which is a 'leading' question.
- I use the child's own words but check out with the child what they mean if this is unclear (for example, the child may have particular words for parts of the body).
- I repeat back to the child (as accurately as possible) what I have heard to check my understanding of what the child has told me.
- I ask the child if s/he has told their mum/dad/other person these things.
- Any child old enough to communicate directly should be asked how s/he hurt himself/herself. In younger children it is perfectly normal to ask the parent/carer what happened where an injury is clearly visible.
- I tell the child what will happen next and what I intend to do.
- I write down what the child has told me as soon as possible after the event, ensuring that records are recorded factually and signed and dated. They should be countersigned by the designated person for child protection in my setting.

I don't:

- put it off;
- press the child for explanations;
- leave it to someone else to help the child;
- be afraid to voice my concerns, the child may need urgent protection and help.

I remember!

- Any child anywhere can be abused at any time.
- Children with disabilities are especially vulnerable.
- Child abuse can be committed by anyone – adults or children.

My responsibility as a childcare provider

I implement the Childcare Act 2006. The Childcare Act, which requires that group care providers must:

- have a written safeguarding children policy and procedure in place, in line with the Local Safeguarding Children Board (LSCB) local guidance and procedures, and implement it effectively;
- ensure through induction that all members of staff (including volunteers) understand the policy and procedure;
- ensure the policy and procedures have been explained to and are accessible to all parents;
- have a designated member of staff, with appropriate child protection training, to take lead responsibility for safeguarding children within the setting and to liaise with local statutory children's services agencies, as appropriate;

- have procedures in place to be followed in the event of an allegation being made against a member of staff and that all staff are aware of these procedures.

School-run provision

Whilst schools that directly manage childcare may use the school's safeguarding policies and procedures for their childcare provision, as long as it meets Childcare Act requirements, as a childminder I also provide a school-run service as part of my work.

Childminders

Childmindesr must have a thorough understanding of safeguarding policy and procedure. Therefore, I must always ensure that my assistant is aware of and understands the policy and procedure. As a childminder I am able to clearly define the policy and procedure for parents and take the lead responsibility for safeguarding children in my setting. I am the designated person (DP) for child protection and I attend refresher training every three years. I am aware that a setting should have more than one trained DP, if the DP works part-time or is absent from the setting for long periods. So my assistant has also received appropriate training including first aid.

My responsibility as a childcare provider – Recording concerns about children

In my setting, if I have concerns then I must:

- Write down everything that has given cause for concern and why. I do this as soon as possible.

- Record any dates and times of incidents or observations and any contact with the child's parents/carers, making sure they are factual and do not include personal opinions or assumptions, unless they can be supported by facts.

- Record any explanation for the injuries or behaviour given by the child and/or parent/carer.

- Record who the child has come into contact with since the disclosure or injury (if known).

- Ensure that records containing information on individual children are stored in a secure place on the premises. In the case of group care facilities (for example, nurseries, pre-schools, etc.) records should be kept in a locked place and arrangements made for designated persons to gain access to them. It will not be sufficient for keys to locked storage to be held by only one member of staff.

- My record of the disclosure or injury in the Accident/Incident Record should be cross-referenced to all other records or files that are held about the individual child concerned.

Seeking advice and reporting to the local authority

I am aware that I can seek advice and can take action by reporting suspected abuse/making a child protection referral. I must make a referral to Children's Social Care Services by telephone, where a social worker trained in child protection will support me. The social worker will check whether the family is known to social care services already and will discuss the case with a senior officer.

Enquiries will often begin by asking other people in contact with the child, such as teachers, health visitors or doctors, if they have any concerns for the child. In most cases there will be a discussion between the social worker and the parents and child. Sometimes it soon becomes clear that there is nothing to worry about, but if concern remains about the welfare of the child, the formal Child Protection Enquiry procedures will begin immediately. Because of the confidential nature of this work, I may not be kept informed as the enquiry continues, but my alertness as the childminder will have been the important first step in protecting the child.

- A 'referral' is simply a report of a concern or a request for a service to the local authority Children's Social Care Team by a member of the public, a person who has contact with children in a professional capacity or a relative of the child.
- When making a referral, I would need to be aware that the local authority Children's Social Care Team may already be involved with the family.
- Before making a referral, I will normally be expected to have spoken to the parents/carers about my intention to refer to the local authority Children's Social Care Team, unless – following prior discussions with a social care professional and/or my assistant it is believed that this will place the child at risk of significant harm.
- Whether or not I have sought advice beforehand from a social care professional, making a referral to the local authority Children's Social Care Team will involve providing the following information:

    o The child's name, address, date of birth, parents'/carers' names, GP's name.
    o My (the referring person's) details, for example, position in the setting, address, etc.
    o What the concerns are. How and why they have arisen?; What appear to be the needs of the child?
    o The parents'/carers' reaction to the concerns that have been expressed (if parents/carers are aware of the concerns).
    o Any recent changes in the child's behaviour or presentation.
    o Whether there are any other children in the household (if known).
    o Whether there are any other agencies currently involved with the family (if known).
    o Whether there have been any previous concerns about this child or other children in the household.
    o Whether the child has any disabilities or special needs.

Also:

- Whether any immediate action is necessary to protect the child.
- Clarify who knows about this referral.
- Clarify which information I, as the referrer, am being reported directly and information that has been obtained from a third party. I can speak to my mentor, Early Years Foundation Stage Adviser (EYFSA), Childcare and Playwork Adviser (CAPA) or Childminding Support and Development Officer (CSDO) for advice. This can be useful if I am unsure, but it is not a substitute for a referral and it is essential that it does not delay the reporting process. In the event that I seek advice in this way, my adviser will contact me the next day to check if a referral has been made, and in some cases make a third party referral. The need for a third party referral could signal that you have not acted in accordance with your setting's child protection policies and procedures and may require further investigation.

Communicating with parents and carers

- Every parent/carer should be made aware of my (the childcare provider's) Child Protection Policy. Parents/carers must be informed that I (the childcare provider) have a duty to report suspected child abuse or neglect. This information is included in safeguarding policies and can be included on the setting's registration form.

- If my concerns are that the child may have been deliberately harmed or sexually abused, or if I feel that the child may be at greater risk of harm by discussing with the parents, then I should contact the local authority Children's Social Care Team immediately, without informing the parents that I am doing so (as they may be implicated in the abuse).

- Any injury visible on a child (accidental or non-accidental) is recorded as soon as the child arrives in my setting. Parents should be encouraged to tell me about injuries that have happened outside the childcare setting. If an injury is clearly visible on a child, it is appropriate to ask the parents/carers about the injury, which may be accidental. I do not have to be afraid to ask open questions or make observations, such as, "What happened?" or, "I noticed when she got changed that X had a bruise on her leg." Similarly, changes in a child's behaviour causing me concern need to be discussed with the parents and carers using open questions such as, "Has anything happened at home as I've noticed that X seems very unruly and not his normal self?"

- If I am concerned about signs of neglect in a child or a damaging emotional relationship observed over a period of time, I will normally have discussed these concerns with the parent. If there is no change and I remain concerned about the welfare of the child I should then tell the parent/carer that I am contacting the local authority. (It might be helpful to remind the parents/carers of my duty to report concerns in line with my Safeguarding Policy, which the parents/carers will have seen.)

The above explains the procedures that need to be followed by lone workers in home-based settings when harm or abuse are suspected or alleged, either against them or third parties.

LEARNING OUTCOME 7

UNDERSTANDING THE PRINCIPLES OF SUPPORTING POSITIVE BEHAVIOUR IN HOME-BASED CHILDCARE SETTINGS

7.1 Describing typical behaviours exhibited by children linked to their stage of development and key events in their lives.

This is important in order to understand 'why children are different but develop at same sequence', yet there are strengths and weaknesses that are seen in each child. For instance, Child A may have more physical abilities and Child B may have more communication abilities.

Children do not develop at the same rate as one another. Every child has a different rate of development. One child may walk at 9 months and another at 10 or so. This may bear no underlying issues, for many times such children catch up eventually. However, there is also a need to know, as from my experience, if a child has had difficulties. There are two factors at birth that may impact on the difference between the sequence of development and rate of development, which are important.

Prenatal

A baby who has gone full-term pregnancy is born between 38 and 40 weeks. A premature baby is born between 24 and 37 or earlier. This baby may well be underdeveloped. A premature baby is usually small and weigh less than average. It is not unusual for them to have developmental delays and difficulties. There may be feeding problems, high risk of infections and breathing problems.

Postnatal

The lack of oxygen at birth is one of the problems identified by professionals as a cause for delayed development. I have read upon this subject as my own child suffered during the birthing process with her head being locked in the birth canal. My child in later years has been diagnosed with learning difficulties and autism.

Among the many problems that can result from a complicated birthing process are, e.g. cerebral palsy and severe learning difficulties. However, some of the factors that may affect a child's development include diet, food allergies, health problems, accidents, culture, environment, bereavement, separation/divorce of parents, lack of stimulation and appropriate toys, poverty or learning difficulties.

Areas of development

These are the main areas of development:

1.   physical development;
2.   social development;
3.   intellectual development;
4.   language development.

As there will be differences in the rate of progress of children I have chosen to answer this question giving the example of age range 0-12 years old. Therefore, the following is the guide of rate at which they might develop for the following age ranges. In my setting I have dealt with babies of the age range 0 to children of 12 years. I have also been looking after my own children. Therefore I have established knowledge of personal experience and also read upon children up to age 19. However, for this question I cover the age range 0-12.

Age 0 to 3 years

1.   Physical development: Babies turn their head towards sounds and movements. They like to watch the face of an adult at feeding time. They start sitting with support and gradually sit alone. They raise their hand and aspect to be lifted. They try to walk alone. They try to hold a pencil and try to write.

2.   Social development: In the initial months they will recognise their mother's face and voice. They enjoy playing with others and game tricks like peek-a-boo. They will please adults and perform for the audience. They develop a sense of identity. Some want to do things themselves such as hold a cup/feeding bottle.

3.   Intellectual development: They begin to realise that others are separate beings from themselves. They imitate others and try out different ways of behaving in play. They will become more confident but still they need adult support at all levels.

4.   Language development: Initially they make a variety of happy sounds. As they grow they will make four to five different sounds and turn their head towards sources of sounds. Then they improve from using single words to complex words. By the age of two they will use 30 to 150 words. After that they put words together into sentences. Therefore, the difference between the sequence of development and the rate of development is different yet important.

Age 3 years

In my setting, at 3 years I find that children are entering the time of peak pretend play, and like to use replica objects as the actors in themes they sequence. A doll, for example, might be prepared to attend a birthday party with her doll friends, and they will drive in a toy car, eat food, and play chase or dance at the party. In my setting I find that realistic props, like a realistic toy telephone, enhance pretend play at this age, but these children also start to use objects that are unlike the real item, so they might use a shoe to represent a pillow. They show greater interest in structured games. Gender preferences also become more evident. Girls typically choose dolls, household props, dress-up activities, and art materials, while boys tend to play more with blocks and small vehicle toys, and will engage in more aggressive or rough-and-tumble play. In my setting and through observation I have experienced that at 3 years children can use one foot, hop, climb and slide on play structures with ease, kick or catch a large ball thrown from a short distance, and throw and aim at short distances. For example, they can now put a ball in a basket or target from 4 to 5 feet away. They now have the fine motor skills to take on the challenge of more complex construction play, piecing together smaller puzzle pieces, cutting, pasting, and other art activities. Children at this age are still interested in different ways of manipulating a given art medium and learning about its properties, rather than creating a finished product. They start using lines to represent boundaries; this fosters the ability to draw people. Therefore, the difference between the sequence of development and the rate of development is different yet important.

4 to 5 years

I have experienced in my setting that at age 4 children are able to do drama and pretend play is at its zenith. These children like to invent complex and dramatic make-believe scenarios. They can build upon each other's play themes, create and coordinate several roles in an elaborate scenario, and better understand storylines. Many of these children still have difficulty understanding the differences between fantasy and reality. For example, children of this age may believe that monsters are real. They enjoy stepping into roles of power, like a parent, doctor, policeman, lion, or superhero, which helps them to better understand these roles, to make them less scary, or to fulfil wishes and express a broad range of emotions. As their cognitive and fine-motor skills improve, they begin to desire objects with more realistic detail, yet they still are not very concerned about mirroring reality.

These children further master gross- and fine-motor skills. They enjoy frequent trips outside to run, climb, hop, skip, and chase. They are learning to ride small bicycles, first with and then without training wheels. They are much more able to cut with scissors, paste, trace, draw, colour, and string beads than 3-year olds. They also have enough dexterity and co-ordination to start using a computer keyboard. Therefore, the difference between the sequence of development and the rate of development is different yet important.

6 to 8 years

Through observation and working with children in my setting I have seen that at 6 to 8 years of age these children continue their interest in physical play outdoors, seeking to master more specialised physical skills. They are much stronger, have greater endurance, and are ready for more challenges. Their play includes more rough-and-tumble or risk-taking behaviours. They focus more on playing their games and activities by spontaneous or set rules, either of which can be complex. Common games outside include hide and seek, tag, and sports of all kinds. They often want to focus on and develop specific skills, and are adept at a variety of activities requiring great dexterity, such as complex hand games, jacks, snapping fingers, tying a bow, constructing models, operating hand puppets, needlepoint, sewing, weaving, and braiding. They can make small, controlled marks or movements while drawing or writing. They pay much more attention to detail, which facilitates a desire for collecting. At this stage they start using logic more often to solve problems, organise, or choose from a variety of alternatives. Their appreciation for simple jokes and riddles grows during this period. Licenced characters based on action superhero themes or friendship themes are very popular early on with this age group. Therefore, the difference between the sequence of development and the rate of development is different yet important.

9 to 12 years

In my setting children at age range 9 to 12 develop skills. Children during this period continue to develop their skills at many of the sports, games, and activities from their early primary/elementary years. However, some games become predictable and boring. Therefore, they are looking for a new range of activities to challenge their more advanced motor skills and thinking. Instead of finished products, they often prefer raw materials for creating their own unique products. These children enjoy a variety of activities at a more complex, exacting level of performance, such as woodworking, manipulating marionettes, making pottery, staging plays, advanced science projects, and generating computer graphics. They are beginning a stage where they seek to clarify and express more complex concepts, moving from the concrete to the abstract and applying general principles to the particular. Therefore, the difference between the sequence of development and the rate of development is different yet important.

The above is the description of typical behaviours exhibited by children linked to their stage of development and key events in their lives.

7.2 Explaining how ground rules for behaviour and expectations are developed and implemented.

In my setting, ground rules for behaviour and expectations are developed and implemented to promote children's and young people's positive behaviour. In order to do this I use the policies and procedures of the setting relevant to promoting children's and young people's positive behaviour covering a range of six sectors as follows:

- Behaviour Policy;
- Code of Conduct;
- Rewards and sanctions;
- Dealing with conflict and inappropriate behaviour;
- Anti-bullying;
- Attendance.

Behaviour Policy

A guideline to myself and my assistant is managed. It is important that this policy is constantly being applied to ensure the full safety of the pupils. This is why myself and my assistant must be familiar with this policy.

Code of Conduct

A set of rules/guidelines for the pupils so they understand how they should behave and what is expected of them. It is important that the children are reminded of the code of conduct so that it becomes their routine and they fully understand it.

It is essential that positive behaviour is always promoted, praised and used, as children notice when adults' behaviour is out of character. If positive and professional behaviour is continually used it is more likely that the pupils will also behave in that way.

Rewards and sanctions

Providing a childcare environment that is safe and stimulating for the children in our care. In order to ensure that this is so, there is a policy with set procedures to create a calm, secure and happy working environment for all. There are, however, occasions when individual children exhibit behaviour that is unacceptable. As part of the Discipline Policy of rewards and sanctions, all staff use behaviour modification strategies to change an individual child's behaviour.

By using a positive system of rewards we reinforce good behaviour. We believe that setting high standards and expectations, and focusing on positive achievements is beneficial to the development of good behaviour in children. All members of the childcare setting should respect one another. The setting expects children to be well-behaved, well-mannered and attentive. Children should walk (not run) within the setting. All children should respect their own and other people's property and take care of books and equipment. All children should show regard for others. If a child has a grievance against another child, it should be reported to me or my assistant, who will take appropriate action.

Children should wear the correct appropriate clothing (if they were in a school, a school uniform). Jewellery and (trainers in school) would not be worn. Children should not bring sharp or dangerous instruments to the setting. Foul or abusive language should never be used. Chewing gum is banned. Mobile phones are not allowed.

Physical violence is never acceptable, neither is retaliation. Repeated or serious incidents will lead to a managed move, which means the student will be transferred to another school. Although good behaviour is encouraged in schools, children will still behave inappropriately at times. Consequences for bad behaviour include:

- Name on the board (sad face).
- Miss time out from golden time, break or lunch play.
- Being sent to the head of year/deputy head.
- Being sent to the head teacher and a meeting arranged with parents.

In the event of continuous bad behaviour, the student is put on report. These reports are filled in by the teacher in every lesson on the day, saying whether the student has behaved in class, the student can be on report for a week or longer depending on the response of the student producing good behaviour.

My response to inappropriate behaviour on a daily basis within the setting

In the event of inappropriate behaviour, such as continuous disruption to a lesson, I would ask the student to come outside of the classroom where I would speak to the student in a stern but positive voice, reminding them of the consequences of their behaviour, and in some cases I would take them to their team leader, if the student wasn't responding.

Good behaviour

When promoting positive behaviour in schools there are policies and procedures that all staff need to be aware of. The main policies relating to behaviour will be the behaviour policies but other policies will also have an impact, for example the health and safety policies, child protection policies and anti-bullying policies. All adults in school are expected to act as good role models and to behave in a consistent manner. We make sure that good behaviour is recognised and praised as well as praising children for good work, effort and achievement.

Recognitions for good behaviour can be any of the following:

A smile and a compliment and verbal praise, phone calls home to parents to give praise about how well their child has done. Post cards can be sent home relating to how well their child is doing. Vivo can be given. Children can save these up and buy things from our vivo shop like pens, pencils, chocolate, etc. When they save a lot of vivo then can then buy more expensive item like iPods, mobile top-ups and a whole range of different things. Certificates are awarded for 'Student of the Week' and also for students who have achieved awards for things like sport, performing arts and in all other aspects of school work.

Staff

It is important for me and my assistant to communicate with each other to evaluate children's progress, emotionally and physically, and set fair boundaries for students who don't get it right. I and my assistant work together to ensure fair rules are set to ensure the learning environment isn't disrupted, minimising loss of quality learning. All children have the right to be educated and to be treated equally in a setting. There are set boundaries within a setting that have to be followed to promote a safe and good learning environment. If these rules are not met there are consequences. Detentions can be set for students, or they could lose their breaks to make up for time lost. Children and young people have boundaries in their home environment, which are there for a reason to protect them and keep them safe – the same apply in their learning environment.

More examples of ground rules would be:

Respect each member of the class when they are talking, always put your hand up if you want to speak, not just shouting out. Ground rules set the boundaries within which the students must work. They enable everyone to have an equal opportunity to carry out their study whilst in the classroom. An ideal way to do this with older children would be to put the children into two groups and ask them to discuss in a team, and write down things they think a classroom's rules should be, then each group should read out their ideas. This enables a neutral ground for discussion, giving the students a feeling of teamwork and achievement. When reviewing the lists you have to have a fair and balanced view to all points identified; your objective is to do much more than lay down a few rules. In negotiating with the older children you give them a sense of worth, this helps you gain their trust. Any rules agreed upon within the group are more likely to be adhered to by the students; if broken, peer pressure will hopefully prevail and the student in question will respond. This is much more constructive than having their childminder point the finger of authority, which may then lead to a negative response.

The above is an explanation of how ground rules for behaviour and expectations are developed and implemented as part of my understanding the principles supporting positive behaviour in home-based childcare settings.

CHAPTER 10

ACTIVITIES

In my setting I have used what I do to tackle the requirements of:

ACTIVITIES CONTEXT AND PRINCIPLES OF EARLY YEARS PROVISION

UNIT AIM: To create a play plan or activity plan. To familiarise learners with the requirements and principles of the early years framework within which they work. The unit also requires skills and knowledge relating to the implementation of the relevant framework.

My plan for activities: What we are doing today, and areas I have in my home for different areas of development: The areas of development are the age groups.

Introduction

In my setting I find that children of different ages have different needs. The children's needs are based on each child's stage of growth and development. I always find that two children of the same age can be similar in some ways but different in other ways. I always try to understand the unique characteristics of each child. This helps children to feel good about themselves. This also helps me to plan activities that are developmentally appropriate for each child. I am very sensitive to inclusion and the health and safety observance whilst planning play activity. If any children have learning or physical disabilities I would ensure that there is play that they can engage in. To use appropriate activities helps children learn and are lots of fun. The following would be my plan according to the age/stage of children.

Activities for infants

- I would hold the infant(s), rock and sing to young babies.
- I explain what I am doing throughout the day when I change or feed them.
- I put bright toys near babies.
- I take them outside on nice days.
- I give babies toys they can move and make noise with (like a rattle).
- I play different kinds of music on the CD/DVD/radio (I keep the volume low).
- I give them soft toys (like a stuffed animal/bear or a clean sock) to hold and feel.
- I read aloud story books that have colourful pictures.
- I am aware and always remember that infants put everything in their mouths. I sanitise and wash toys if they become dirty and I make sure they cannot be swallowed.
- I have a large, clean space in the rear activity room of my setting, well-lit with natural light from windows and French-windows for babies to crawl. I put in it bright toys near babies so they can reach out or move toward them.

Activities for toddlers

In my setting I am aware that toddlers like to put things inside of other things and dump them out. I will cut a hole in the middle of the lid of a clean coffee can or plastic margarine tub. I make sure there are no sharp edges to cut the toddler. I let the toddlers put clothes pegs, thread spools, and other safe objects through the hole.

I will make play dough. Mix 3 cups of flour, 1 cup of salt, 3 tablespoons of oil, and 1 cup of water together. Add food colouring for colour. I will let the toddlers use jar lids, clothes pegs, and lollipop sticks to cut and shape the play dough.

I know that children love to play with water. I will fill big buckets or tubs with water. I will give the children soap chips, measuring spoons and cups, plastic bottles, butter tubs, and sponges to play with in the water. I will put towels or newspapers on the floor so the children will not slip on the wet floor.

In my setting I find that toddlers like goop. I can mix corn-starch and water together. I let toddlers play with it in a bucket or in bowls with cups and spoons. I would make the goop thick or thin. I usually ask at the local supermarket for a free large cardboard box. I can cut doors and windows in the box to make a playhouse. Toddlers can draw on it with crayons or paint it with water and big brushes.

I find that toddlers like to draw with short, fat, unwrapped crayons. I give them paper bags (I can tear them open to make large sheets of brown paper) or large pieces of heavy paper to draw on. To help them draw, I tape the paper down so it does not move.

I know that toddlers also like to play house with dolls and housekeeping props such as plastic dishes and spoons. I have these available.

I know that most toddlers are just learning how to walk and run. I go for lots of walks but make sure that I hold onto the toddler's hand to avoid falling over.

I would let toddlers tear old wrapping paper. Then have them paste the pieces to make a collage.

I can allow toddlers to use some swings and low slides at the outside play area. I do not leave them unattended on any piece of playground equipment. They are prone to accidents.

I have toddlers finger paint with shaving henna or cream mixed with food colouring.

Health and safety warning: I always warn my assistant that children need supervision at all times. It only takes a small amount of water to turn a fun activity into a tragedy. I and my assistant must be careful to never let the children out of our sight, not even for one moment. I always remember, that I must be responsible and attentive. I do not allow for any distractions (telephone, doorbell, other children, etc.). If I cannot give the child my undivided attention it may be best not to do any water-based activities.

I have a large, clean space in the rear activity room of my setting, well-lit with natural light from windows and French-windows for water-based activities. The floor is laminated and can be cleaned easily, only when the weather is good, e.g. in summer would I take the water play outside. I have a pump-up water pool, which provides a good water play resource and is movable to where I need it.

Activities for preschool children

Any childcare/play worker should be aware that preschool children like to jump, ride tricycles, play ball, use crayons, and do puzzles. I have a trampoline, and lots of puzzle games.

I let children play with sand in buckets. I give them scoops, muffin tins, funnels, rolling pins, and salt shakers to use (check with the parents first). I find that almost any containers and utensils are fun to play with in the sand.

I make soap bubbles. Adding ½ cup of liquid dish soap to 2 quarters of water. I have the children blow bubbles with small plastic containers (frozen juice) open at both ends. They can also use straws or green plastic berry baskets. I also support and let the children play-wash dishes.

I find that preschoolers like to make things with blocks and plastic building pieces. I always check to make sure wood blocks are smooth and free of splinters.

I poke holes in the bottoms of plastic margarine tubs. I have the children fill them with water and watch it dribble out.

When I allow the children to play with water and sand, I also give them toys like egg beaters, watering cans, and squeeze toys or bottles.

I have some tricycles and bicycles for children, which I would let them ride under supervision. Some are just learning to balance on a tricycle or a bicycle with supports.

I know that preschoolers like to pretend. They learn how to share, and it helps their imaginations grow. I set up a corner of a room like an ice cream store. I use a table, clean ice cream containers, ice cream scoops, and cones made from paper. I can also make a pretend beach. I would provide bathing suits, towels, sunglasses, a radio, and beach toys. Or I can make a supermarket, by gathering empty food boxes and containers, I have a wad of play money, and toy shopping carts. I also encourage children to think and I ask them so I can also get ideas from the children for pretend play.

Activities for school-aged children

In my setting I am aware that school-age children like many of the same activities that toddlers and preschoolers like. These activities include playing with water, cooking, and dancing. So, I make activities more fun for older children by adding more toys and by letting them do more things by themselves (supervised by me and my assistant).

I know that most school-aged children are very active. Older school-aged children like competitive games like football or basketball. Some school-aged children like to play alone. I can take them to a nearby play park for a ball kick about and free runs, which are supervised.

I am sensitive to the likes of children. The girls tend to like to play with girls and boys tend to like to play with boys.

I help the children make water wave jars. I provide these sorts of items: In a jar, mixing one part water with food colouring to two parts oil. Tightly screw on the lid. Hold the jar sideways. The children rock it back and forth to make waves.

Activities for all ages

I would take a trip to the playground, park, or basketball court. I help the children to do errands together, or plan field trips to the library, bank or newspaper office. I am situated in an area where there is a community centre, ski village, and a sports academy. I use all these to enrich the children's activities.

I know that music is fun for everyone. I can make and play instruments with preschoolers and elementary school-aged children. We make pretend guitars, etc. For example, I can help the children to make shakers. We would gather some cans with plastic lids, fill the cans with buttons, bells, and beads, glue on the lids. I would have the children decorate the cans. We can make drums from old coffee cans with plastic lids. To make a shoe box guitar, I cut a hole in a shoe box lid, then tape the lid on the shoe box. Stretch three or four rubber bands across the hole on the lid. The children can pluck the rubber bands. I and my assistant then have the children play their instruments for the younger children and infants.

TV watching: In a setting it is important that the child carer always ask the parents if the child is to watch TV, how long s/he can watch and what shows s/he can watch. I would only use the TV as a learning aid. Children will learn the most from TV if I and my assistant talk about the shows with them. I do not use TV for adult entertainment while children are in my care.

CHAPTER 11

DEVELOPMENT OF POLICIES AND PROCEDURES

INTRODUCING DEVELOPMENT OF POLICIES AND PROCEDURES

In chapter 3 a list of policies was provided. You will require the policies and procedures, which can be handy for those who wish to set-up a new childcare provision. There is virtually a policy for everything, ranging from skipping rope to sun cream, etc. Do not take anything for granted, ask for help and support from your local authority children's department to ensure you are up-to-date with policies. Here is a glimpse of how I would do it.

I use the following format in my setting to introduce my policies to my customers and comply with local and national legislation:

Equal Opportunities, Admission Policy and Codes of Practice.

INTRODUCTION TO POLICIES

The commitment to the profession of childcare is the driver in development of policies and procedures. Whatever you do is guided by that commitment, and you will therefore ensure that you always seek to do the right thing.

I am committed in the pursuit of childcare excellence to equality of opportunity and to a pro-active and inclusive approach to equality, which supports and encourages all under-represented groups, promotes an inclusive culture, and values diversity. My setting is therefore committed to a policy and practice, which requires that, for children, admission to the childcare service will be determined only by personal merit and by availability of space. For staff, entry into employment within my setting will be determined only by personal qualifications of merit and by the application of criteria that are related to the duties and conditions of each particular post and the needs of the children in line with legislation guidelines.

Therefore in my setting, subject to UK statutory provisions, no applicant for admission as a childcare customer, or for a staff appointment, will be treated less favourably than another on the grounds of sex (including gender reassignment), marital or parental status, race, ethnic or national origin, colour, disability, sexual orientation, religion, or age. If any parent whose child is admitted for childcare services considers that s/he is suffering from unequal treatment on any of the above grounds in his/her admission, s/he may make a complaint, which will be dealt with through the agreed procedures for complaints or grievances or the procedures for dealing with bullying and harassment, as appropriate.

My childcare setting will take active steps to promote good practice. In particular it/I will:

- be promoting equality of opportunity;
- be promoting good relations between people of different racial groups, between children, parents (women and men) and between disabled and non-disabled people;
- be having due regard to the need to eliminate discrimination on grounds of colour, race, sex, disability, and all other grounds set out in the statement on equal opportunities;
- be subjecting my policies to continuous assessment in order to examine how they affect all

under-represented groups, especially ethnic minority students and staff, women, and disabled students and staff, and to identify whether its policies help to achieve equality of opportunity for all these groups, or whether they have an adverse impact;

- be monitoring the recruitment and progress of all children/students in my care and staff, paying particular attention to the recruitment and progress of ethnic minority students and staff, women, and disabled students and staff;

- be promoting an inclusive culture, good practice in teaching, learning, and assessment, and good management practice, through the development of codes of best practice, policies, and training;

- be taking positive action wherever possible to support this policy and its aims;

- be publishing this policy widely amongst staff and students, together with policy assessments and results of monitoring.

My childcare setting in the UK will meet all statutory obligations under relevant legislation and, where appropriate, anticipate future legal requirements signalled under EU Directives.

My childcare setting policy statements in the UK are guided by:

- Equal Pay Act (1970);
- Sex Discrimination Act (1975);
- Race Relations Act (1976);
- Disability Discrimination Act (1995);
- Special Educational Needs and Disability Act (2001);
- Human Rights Act (1998);
- Race Relations (Amendment) Act (2000);
- EU Equal Treatment Framework Directive (2000/78);
- Safeguarding Children.

Additionally, I am guided by the Codes of Practice issued by the Equal Opportunities Commission and the Commission for Racial Equality, together with the Codes of Practice on Disability and Age Diversity. These codes are not legally binding (though they are admissible as evidence in employment tribunals) and my childcare setting supports them fully.

I am vigilant that the policy will be amended as appropriate to meet the demands of future legislation.

Further guidance will be issued on the general duty under the Race Relations (Amendment) Act (RR(A)A) to:

- ensure elimination of racial discrimination;

- ensure promoting equality of opportunity and good race relations and on the specific duties under the RR(A)A to:

  o assess the impact of policies on ethnic minority students and staff;

  o monitor the recruitment and progress of ethnic minority students and staff;

  o set out arrangements for publishing the results of impact assessments and monitoring.

Policies can be reviewed and many times they change to suit the needs of the setting, the parents' and children's safety or public/society. To get sample policies or to ensure updated policies in the UK, any setting should secure membership to such agencies as Out of School Network, or Pre-school and Learning Alliance.

CHAPTER 12

INFORMING PARENTS AND PROMOTING YOUR CHILDCARE SETTING

ONCE YOU HAVE SET UP A CHILDCARE PROVISION YOU WLL NEED A WEBSITE AND/OR A HANDBOOK FOR PARENTS INFORMATION. YOU MAY NEED TO VISIT OTHER PROVIDERS TO SEE WHAT HANDBOOKS THEY HAVE. THIS IS A SAMPLE.

MY CHILDCARE SETTING SAMPLE WEBSITE INFORMATION OR HANDBOOK:

Information for Parents - Handbook

ADDRESS OF:

MY CHILDCARE SETTING
888 BLOGGY STREET
BLOGGY CITY
B5 88DD

Tel: 08888888888
E-mail: mychildcare@gmail.com
www.mychildcaresettings.co.uk

WHO I AM/WE ARE?

My childcare setting is a newly established crèche based in .... area of the City of........................... The crèche is based in excellent premises and safe surroundings on a main road. The provision is accessible by car or public transport.

MY/OUR AIM

My childcare setting's aim is to provide a flexible childcare service that meets the needs of the local community in the area. The service we provide is flexible and of a quality standard that focuses on children's individual needs whilst under our care.

MY/OUR VISION

My childcare setting's vision is to improve outcomes for children and families, develop a thriving childcare setting that meets the needs of children, families and the communities we work with in the area.

CHILDCARE PROGRAMMES PROVIDED

My childcare setting provides the following programmes and activities:

- Recreational activities;
- Crèche – our provision are usually for 2 hours session;

- Subject support in Literacy and Numeracy;
- Outings and trips;
- Special needs support for children with additional needs;
- Respite for parents and respite for children who are siblings;
- Encourage and support Parent and Toddlers Group.

QUALITY CHILDCARE MATTERS

It is well known that a growing number of families need supplementary childcare – that is, care provided by someone other than a parent. The value of good childcare is well documented. Early learning experiences that help build resilience, social skills, and the ability to keep learning have social and economic benefits for everyone – children, parents, employers and society as a whole – both now and in the future.

OPENING TIMES

Opening Days: Monday – Friday
Opening Hours: 0800 - 1800

Closed: Bank Holidays

AGES OF CHILDREN

We provide quality childcare for children aged 6 months to 5 years. On admission we will need to have a copy of your child's birth certificate as proof of age and their red book must be seen as proof of immunisation.

THE STAFF TEAM QUALIFICATIONS INCLUDE:

- NVQ Level 3 in Children's Care, Learning and Development.
- All staff members have safeguarding and emergency first aid certificates.
- We have staff members currently working towards NVQ Levels 2 and 3 in Childcare.

OUR TEAM

My childcare setting has a team who are qualified in delivering childcare services. Our team are continuously encouraged to undertake ongoing training to ensure we continue to deliver the highest standards of childcare.

STAFFING RATIOS

The EYFS revised in 2012 provides a clear guideline. (Although politically, the government in the UK during 2013 has been debating to increase ratios so that one carer can look after 5 children. This has been an issue of contention. One can imagine where three babies are crying and demanding attention at the same time what the individual carer would have to do. However those plans were shelved.)

My staff ratios are as follows:

1:3 – children aged 0 to 2 years old
1:4 – children aged 2 years old
1:8 – children 3-5 years old